THE GRAND OLD MAN

OR

The Life and Public Services of The Right Honorable William
Ewart Gladstone Four Times Prime Minister of England

Richard B. Cook, D. D.

1st WORLD
LIBRARY
Literary Society

The Grand Old Man

Richard B. Cook

© 1st World Library, 2006
PO Box 2211
Fairfield, IA 52556
www.1stworldlibrary.com
First Edition

LCCN: 2006938103

Softcover ISBN: 978-1-4218-3403-0
Hardcover ISBN: 978-1-4218-3303-3
eBook ISBN: 978-1-4218-3503-7

Purchase *"The Grand Old Man"*
as a traditional bound book at:
www.1stWorldLibrary.com/purchase.asp?ISBN=978-1-4218-3403-0

1st World Library is a literary, educational organization
dedicated to:

- Creating a free internet library of downloadable ebooks

- Hosting writing competitions and offering book
  publishing scholarships.

Interested in more 1st World Library books?
contact: literacy@1stworldlibrary.com
Check us out at: www.1stworldlibrary.com

1st World Library Literary Society

Giving Back to the World

"If you want to work on the core problem, it's early school literacy."

- James Barksdale, former CEO of Netscape

"No skill is more crucial to the future of a child, or to a democratic and prosperous society, than literacy."

- Los Angeles Times

Literacy... means far more than learning how to read and write... The aim is to transmit... knowledge and promote social participation."

- UNESCO

"Literacy is not a luxury, it is a right and a responsibility. If our world is to meet the challenges of the twenty-first century we must harness the energy and creativity of all our citizens."

- President Bill Clinton

"Parents should be encouraged to read to their children, and teachers should be equipped with all available techniques for teaching literacy, so the varying needs and capacities of individual kids can be taken into account."

- Hugh Mackay

PREFACE

William E. Gladstone was cosmopolitan. The Premier of the British Empire is ever a prominent personage, but he has stood above them all. For more than half a century he has been the active advocate of liberty, morality and religion, and of movements that had for their object the prosperity, advancement and happiness of men. In all this he has been upright, disinterested and conscientious in word and deed. He has proved himself to be the world's champion of human rights. For these reasons he has endeared himself to all men wherever civilization has advanced to enlighten and to elevate in this wide world.

With the closing of the 19th century the world is approaching a crisis in which every nation is involved. For a time the map of the world might as well be rolled up. Great questions that have agitated one or more nations have convulsed the whole earth because steam and electricity have annihilated time and space. Questions that have sprung up between England and Africa, France and Prussia, China and Japan, Russia and China, Turkey and Armenia, Greece and Turkey, Spain and America have proved international and have moved all nations. The daily proceedings of Congress at Washington are discussed in Japan.

In these times of turning and overturning, of discontent and unrest, of greed and war, when the needs of the nations most demand men of world-wide renown, of great experience in government and diplomacy, and of firm hold upon the confidence of the people; such men as, for example, Gladstone, Salisbury, Bismark, Crispi and Li Hung Chang, who have led the mighty advance of civilization, are passing away. Upon younger men falls the heavy burden of the world, and the solution of the mighty problems of this climax of the most momentous of all centuries.

However, the Record of these illustrious lives remains to us for guidance and inspiration. History is the biography of great men. The lamp of history is the beacon light of many lives. The biography of William E. Gladstone is the history, not only of the English Parliament, but of the progress of civilization in the earth for the whole period of his public life. With the life of Mr. Gladstone in his hand, the student of history or the young statesman has a light to guide him and to help him solve those intricate problems now perplexing the nations, and upon the right solution of which depends Christian civilization—the liberties, progress, prosperity and happiness of the human race.

Hence, the life and public services of the Grand Old Man cannot fail to be of intense interest to all, particularly to the English, because he has repeatedly occupied the highest position under the sovereign of England, to the Irish whether Protestant or Catholic, north or south, because of his advocacy of (Reforms) for Ireland; to the Scotch because of his Scottish descent; to the German because he reminds them of their own great chancellor, the Unifier of Germany, Prince Bismarck; and to the American because he was ever the champion of freedom; and as there has been erected in Westminster Abbey a tablet to the memory of Lord Howe, so will the American people enshrine in their hearts, among the greatest of the great, the memory of William Ewart Gladstone.

"In youth a student and in eld a sage;
Lover of freedom; of mankind the friend;
Noble in aim from childhood to the end;
Great is thy mark upon historic page."

CONTENTS

"In thought, word and deed,
How throughout all thy warfare thou wast pure,
I find it easy to believe."

—ROBERT BROWNING

INTRODUCTORY

There are few, even among those who differed from him, who would deny to Mr. Gladstone the title of a great statesman: and in order to appreciate his wonderful career, it is necessary to realize the condition of the world of thought, manners and works at the time when he entered public life.

In medicine there was no chloroform; in art the sun had not been enlisted in portraiture; railways were just struggling into existence; the electric telegraph was unknown; gas was an unfashionable light; postage was dear, and newspapers were taxed.

In literature, Scott had just died; Carlyle was awaiting the publication of his first characteristic book; Tennyson was regarded as worthy of hope because of his juvenile poems; Macaulay was simply a brilliant young man who had written some stirring verse and splendid prose; the Brontës were schoolgirls; Thackeray was dreaming of becoming an artist; Dickens had not written a line of fiction; Browning and George Eliot were yet to come.

In theology, Newman was just emerging from evangelicalism; Pusey was an Oxford tutor; Samuel Wilberforce a village curate; Henry Manning a young graduate; and Darwin was commencing that series of investigations which revolutionized the popular conception of created things.

Princess, afterwards Queen Victoria, was a girl of thirteen;

Cobden a young calico printer; Bright a younger cotton spinner; Palmerston was regarded as a man-about-town, and Disraeli as a brilliant and eccentric novelist with parliamentary ambition. The future Marquis of Salisbury and Prime Minister of Great Britain was an infant scarcely out of arms; Lord Rosebery, (Mr. Gladstone's successor in the Liberal Premiership), Lord Spencer, Lord Herschell, Mr. John Morley, Mr. Campbell-Bannerman, Mr. Asquith, Mr. Brice, Mr. Acland and Mr. Arnold Morley, or more than half the members of his latest cabinet remained to be born; as did also the Duke of Devonshire, Mr. Balfour and Mr. Chamberlain, among those who were his keenest opponents toward the end of his public career.

At last the end of Mr. Gladstone's public life arrived, but it had been extended to an age greater than that at which any English statesman had ever conducted the government of his country.

Of the significance of the life of this great man, it would be superfluous to speak. The story will signally fail of its purpose if it does not carry its own moral with it. We can best conclude these introductory remarks by applying to the subject of the following pages, some words which he applied a generation ago to others:

In the sphere of common experience we see some human beings live and die, and furnish by their life no special lessons visible to man, but only that general teaching in elementary and simple forms which is derivable from every particle of human histories. Others there have been, who, from the times when their young lives first, as it were, peeped over the horizon, seemed at once to—

"Flame in the forehead of the evening sky,"
—Whose lengthening years have been but one growing splendor, and who at last—
"—Leave a lofty name,
A light, a landmark on the cliffs of fame."

Richard B. Cook

CHAPTER I

ANCESTRY AND BIRTH

All history, says Emerson, "resolves itself into the biographies of a few stout and earnest persons." These remarks find exemplification in the life of William Ewart Gladstone, of whom they are pre-eminently true. His recorded life, from the early period of his graduation to his fourth premiership, would embrace in every important respect not only the history of the British Empire, but very largely the international events of every nation of the world for more than half a century.

William Ewart Gladstone, M.P., D.C.L., statesman, orator and scholar, was born December 27, 1809, in Liverpool, England. The house in which he was born, number 62 Rodney Street, a commodious and imposing "double-fronted" dwelling of red brick, is still standing. In the neighborhood of the Rodney Street house, and a few years before or after the birth of William E. Gladstone, a number of distinguished persons were born, among them William Roscoe, the writer and philanthropist, John Gibson, the sculptor, Doctor Bickersteth, the late Bishop of Ripon, Mrs. Hemans, the poetess, and Doctor James Martineau, Professor of Mental and Moral Philosophy in Manchester New College, and the brother of Harriet Martineau, the authoress.

The Gladstone family, or Gledstanes, which was the original family name, was of Scottish origin. The derivation of the name is obvious enough to any one familiar with the ancestral home. A *gled* is a hawk, and that fierce and beautiful bird would have found its natural refuge among the *stanes*, or rocks, of the craggy moorlands which surround the "fortalice of gledstanes." As far back as 1296 Herbert de Gledstane figures in the Ragman Roll as one of the lairds who swore fealty to Edward I. His descendants for generations held knightly rank, and bore their part in the adventurous life of the Border. The chief stock was settled at Liberton, in the upper part of Clydesdale. It was a family of Scottish lairds, holding large estates in the sixteenth century. The estate dwindled, and in the beginning of the seventeenth century passed out of their hands, except the adjacent property of Authurshiel, which remained in their possession for a hundred years longer. A younger branch of the family—the son of the last of the Gledstanes of Arthurshiel—after many generations, came to dwell at Biggar, in Lanarkshire, where he conducted the business of a "maltster," or grain merchant.

Here, and at about this time, the name was changed to Gladstones, and a grandson of the maltster of Biggar, Thomas Gladstones, settled in Leith and there became a "corn-merchant." He was born at Mid Toftcombs, in 1732, and married Helen Neilson, of Springfield. His aptitude for business was so great that he was enabled to make ample provision for a large family of sixteen children. His son, John Gladstone, was the father of William E. Gladstone, the subject of our sketch.

Some have ascribed to Mr. Gladstone an illustrious, even a royal ancestry, through his father's marriage. He met and married a lovely, cultured and pious woman of Dingwall, in Orkney, the daughter of Andrew Robertson, Provost of Dingwall, named Ann Robertson, whom the unimpeachable Sir Bernard Burke supplied with a pedigree from Henry III, king of England, and Robert Bruce, of Bannockburn, king of Scotland, so that it is royal English and Scottish blood that runs in the veins of Mr. Gladstone.

"This alleged illustrious pedigree," says E.B. Smith, in his elaborate work on William E. Gladstone, "is thus traced: Lady Jane Beaufort, who was a descendant of Henry III, married James I, of Scotland, who was a descendant of Bruce. From this alliance it is said that the steps can be followed clearly down to the father of Miss Robertson. A Scottish writer upon genealogy, also referring to this matter, states that Mr. Gladstone is descended on the mother's side from the ancient Mackenzie of Kintail, through whom is introduced the blood of the Bruce, of the ancient Kings of Man, and of the Lords of the Isles and Earls of Ross; also from the Munros of Fowlis, and the Robertsons of Strowan and Athole. What was of more consequence to the Gladstones of recent generations, however, than royal blood, was the fact that by their energy and honorable enterprise they carved their own fortunes, and rose to positions of public esteem and eminence." It has been their pride that they sprang from the ranks of the middle classes, from which have come so many of the great men of England eminent in political and military life.

In an address delivered at the Liverpool Collegiate Institute, December 21, 1872, Sir John Gladstone said; "I know not why the commerce of England should not have its old families rejoicing to be connected with commerce from generation to generation. It has been so in other countries; I trust it may be so in this country. I think it is a subject of sorrow, and almost of scandal, when those families who have either acquired or recovered wealth and station through commerce, turn their backs upon it and seem to be ashamed of it. It certainly is not so with my brother or with me. His sons are treading in his steps, and one of my sons, I rejoice to say, is treading in the steps of my father and my brother."

George W.E. Russell, in his admirable biography of Mr. William E. Gladstone, says, "Sir John Gladstone was a pure Scotchman, a lowlander by birth and descent. Provost Robertson belonged to the Clan Donachie, and by this marriage the robust and business-like qualities of the Lowlander were blended with the poetic imagination, the sensibility and fire of the Gael."

An interesting story is told, showing how Sir John Gladstone, the father of William E. Gladstone, came to live in Liverpool, and enter upon his great business career, and where he became a merchant prince. Born at Leith in 1763, he in due time entered his father's business, where he served until he was twenty-one years old. At that time his father sent him to Liverpool to dispose of a cargo of grain, belonging to him, which had arrived at that port. His demeanor and business qualities so impressed Mr. Corrie, a grain merchant of that place, that he urged his father to let him settle there. Consent was obtained and young Gladstone entered the house of Corrie & Company as a clerk. His tact and shrewdness were soon manifest, and he was eventually taken into the firm as a partner, and the name of the house became Corrie, Gladstone & Bradshaw.

John Gladstone on one occasion proved the temporary preserver of the firm of which he had become a member. He was sent to America to buy grain for the firm, in a time of great scarcity in Europe, owing to the failure of the crops, but he found the condition of things the same in America. There was no grain to be had. While in great perplexity as to what to do he received advices from Liverpool that twenty-four vessels had been dispatched for the grain he was expected to purchase, to bring it to Europe. The prospect was that these vessels would have to return to Europe empty as they had come, and the house of Corrie & Company be involved thereby in ruin. It was then that John Gladstone rose to the emergency of the occasion, and by his enterprise and energy saved himself and partners from financial failure, to the great surprise and admiration of the merchants of Liverpool. It was in this way: He made a thorough examination of the American markets for articles of commerce that could be sold in Europe to advantage, and filling his vessels with them sent them home. This sagacious movement not only saved his house, but gave him a name and place among the foremost merchants of his day. His name was also a synonym for push and integrity, not only on the Liverpool exchange, but in London and throughout all England. The business of the firm became very great and the wealth of its members very large.

During the war with Napoleon, on the continent, and the war of 1812 with the United States, the commerce of England, as mistress of the seas, was injured, and the Gladstone firm suffered greatly and was among the first to seek peace, for its own sake and in the interests of trade. In one year the commerce of Liverpool declined to the amount of 140,000 tons, which was about one-fourth of the entire trade, and there was a decrease of more than $100,000 in the dock-dues of that port. John Gladstone was among those who successfully petitioned the British government for a change of its suicidal policy towards the American States.

After sixteen years of successful operations, during a part of which time it had been government agent, the firm was dissolved and its business was continued by John Gladstone. His six brothers having followed him from Leith to Liverpool, he took into partnership with him his brother Robert. Their business became very extensive, having a large trade with Russia, and as sugar importers and West India merchants. John Gladstone was the chairman of the West India Association and took an active part in the improvement and enlargement of the docks of Liverpool. In 1814, when the monopoly of the East India Company was broken and the trade of India and China thrown open to competition, the firm of John Gladstone & Company was the first to send a private vessel to Calcutta.

John Gladstone was a public-spirited man and took great interest in the welfare of his adopted city. He was ever ready to labor for its prosperity, and consequently endeared himself to the people of all classes and conditions, and of every shade of political opinion.

The high estimation in which he was held by the citizens of Liverpool was especially manifest October 18, 1824, when they presented him with a testimonial, consisting of a magnificent service of plate, of twenty-eight pieces, and bearing the following inscription: "*To John Gladstone, Esq., M.P., this service of plate was presented MDCCCXXIV, by his fellow townsmen and friends, to mark their high sense of his successful exertions for the promotion of trade and commerce, and in acknowledgment of his most important services rendered to the town of Liverpool.*"

John Gladstone, though devoted to commerce, had time for literary pursuits. He wrote a pamphlet, "On the Present State of Slavery in the British West Indies and in the United States of America; and on the Importation of Sugar from British Settlements in India." He also published, in 1830, another pamphlet, containing a statement of facts connected with the same general subject, "in a letter addressed to Sir Robert Peel." In 1846 he published a pamphlet, entitled "Plain facts intimately connected with the intended Repeal of the Corn Laws; or Probable Effects on the Public Revenue and the Prosperity of the Country."

From the subject discussed it can be readily and truly imagined that John Gladstone had given thought to political subjects. He was in favor of a qualified reform which, while affording a greater enfranchisement of the people, looked also to the interests of all. Having an opinion, and not being afraid to express it, he was frequently called upon to address public meetings. The matters discussed by him were, however, rather national than municipal, rather humane than partisan. He was a strong advocate for certain reforms at home in 1818, and in 1823 on the seas, and for Greek independence in 1824. "On the 14th of February, 1824, a public meeting was held in Liverpool Town Hall, 'for the purpose of considering the best means of assisting the Greeks in their present important struggle for independence.' Mr. Gladstone spoke impressively in favor of the cause which had already evoked great enthusiasm amongst the people, and enlisted the sympathies and support of Lord Byron and other distinguished friends of freedom."

It was in 1818 that he addressed a meeting called "to consider the propriety of petitioning Parliament to take into consideration the progressive and alarming increase in the crimes of forging and uttering forged Bank of England notes." The penalties for these crimes were already heavy, but their infliction did not deter men from committing them, and these crimes increased at an enormous rate. Resolutions were passed at the Liverpool meeting, recommending the revision and amendment of existing laws.

Then again, so late as the year 1823, the navigation between Liverpool and Dublin was in a lamentable condition, and human life was recklessly imperiled, and no one seemed willing to interfere and to interest himself in the interests of humanity. It was then that he again came to the front to advocate a just cause. To illustrate the dangers to vessels and passengers, the case of the sloop *Alert* may be cited. It was wrecked off the Welsh coast, with between 100 and 140 persons on board, of whom only seventeen were saved. For the safety and rescue of all those souls on board this packet-boat there was only one small shallop, twelve feet long. Mr. Gladstone was impressed with the terrible nature of the existing evil, and obtained an amendment to the Steamboat Act, requiring imperatively that every passenger vessel should be provided with boats sufficient for every passenger it was licensed to carry. By this wise and humane provision thousands of lives were doubtless saved that would otherwise have been lost—the victims of reckless seamanship and commercial greed.

John Gladstone, either through the influence of Mr. Canning, or from having imbibed some political taste, sat in the House of Commons nine years, representing Lancaster in 1819, Woodstock from 1821 to 1826, and Berwick in 1827; but he never would consent to sit in Parliament for the city of Liverpool, for he thought that so large and important a constituency required peculiar representation such as he was unqualified to give.

He was the warm supporter and intimate friend of the celebrated Canning. At first he was a Whig, but finally came to support Mr. Canning, and became a Liberal Conservative. In 1812 he presided over a meeting at Liverpool, which was called to invite Mr. Canning to represent the borough in Parliament. After the election the successful candidates were claimed and carried in procession through the streets. The procession finally halted at Mr. Gladstone's house, in Rodney Street, from the balcony of which Mr. Canning addressed the populace. His election laid the foundation of a deep and lasting friendship between Mr. Canning and Mr. Gladstone. "At this time the son of the latter was but three years of age. Shortly afterwards—that is, as soon as he was able to understand anything of public men, and public movements and events"—says G.B. Smith, "the name of Canning began to exercise that strange fascination over the mind of William Ewart Gladstone which has never wholly passed away," and Mr. Gladstone himself acknowledged that he was brought up "under the shadow of the great name of Canning."

John Gladstone presided at a farewell dinner given by the Liverpool Canning Club, in August, 1822, in honor of Mr. Canning, who had been Governor-General of India. But Mr. Canning, instead of going to India, entered the British Cabinet, and in 1827 became Prime Minister, and John Gladstone moved a congratulatory address to the king upon the formation of the Canning Ministry.

In 1845 John Gladstone was created a baronet by Sir Robert Peel, but he lived to enjoy his deserved honors but a short time, for he died in 1851, at the advanced age of eighty-eight. His motto had ever been, "Diligent in business." His enormous wealth enabled him to provide handsomely for his family, not only after death, but during his lifetime.

At the time of his father's death, William E. Gladstone was still an adherent of the Tory party, yet his steps indicated that he was advancing towards Liberalism; and he had already reached distinction as a statesman, both in Parliament and in the Cabinet, while as yet he was but 42 years old, which was about half of his age when called for the fourth time to be Prime

Richard B. Cook

Minister of England.

Sir John Gladstone and his wife had six children—four sons, Thomas Gladstone, afterwards baronet; John Gladstone, who became a captain, and died in 1863; Robert Gladstone, brought up a merchant, who died in 1875, and two daughters, Annie McKenzie Gladstone, who died years ago, and Helen Jane Gladstone. William E. Gladstone was the fourth son. The following is from the pen of the son, who says of his aged father, Sir John Gladstone: "His eye was not dim, nor his natural force abated; he was full of bodily and mental vigor; whatsoever his hand found to do he did it with his might; he could not understand or tolerate those who, perceiving an object to be good, did not at once and actively pursue it; and with all this energy he gained a corresponding warmth, and, so to speak, eagerness of affection, a keen appreciation of humor, in which he found a rest, and an indescribable frankness and simplicity of character, which, crowning his other qualities, made him, I think, and I strive to think impartially, nearly or quite the most interesting old man I ever knew."

Personally, Sir John Gladstone was a man of much intelligence and of sterling principle, of high moral and religious character, and his house consequently was a model home. "His house was by all accounts a home pre-eminently calculated to mould the thoughts and direct the course of an intelligent and receptive nature. There was a father's masterful will and keen perception, the sweetness and piety of the mother, wealth with all its substantial advantages and few of its mischiefs, a strong sense of the value of money, a rigid avoidance of extravagance and excesses; everywhere a strenuous purpose in life, constant employment, and concentrated ambition."

Mrs. John Gladstone, the wife and mother, is described by one who knew her intimately as "a lady of very great accomplishments; of fascinating manners, of commanding presence and high intellect; one to grace any home and endear any heart."

The following picture of the everyday life of the family is

interesting and instructive, on account of Sir John Gladstone, as well as on that of his more distinguished son, and is from the pen of an eye-witness: "Nothing was ever taken for granted between him and his sons. A succession of arguments on great topics and small topics alike—arguments conducted with perfect good humor, but also with the most implicable logic—formed the staple of the family conversation. The children and their parents argued upon everything. They would debate as to whether a window should be opened, and whether it was likely to be fair or wet the next day. It was all perfectly good-humored, but curious to a stranger, because of the evident care which all the disputants took to advance no proposition, even as to the prospect of rain, rashly."

In such a home as this was William E. Gladstone in training as the great Parliamentary debater and leader, and for the highest office under the British crown. This reminds us of a story of Burke. The king one day, unexpectedly entering the office of his minister, found the elder Burke sitting at his desk, with his eyes fixed upon his young son, who was standing on his father's desk in the attitude of speaking. "What are you doing?" asked the astonished king. "I am making the greatest minister England ever saw," was the reply. And so in fact, and yet all unconsciously, was Sir John doing for his son, William.

William E. Gladstone "was born," says his biographer, G.W.E. Russell, "at a critical moment in the fortunes of England and of Europe. Abroad the greatest genius that the world has ever seen was wading through slaughter to a universal throne, and no effectual resistance had as yet been offered to a progress which menaced the liberty of Europe and the existence of its States. At home, a crazy king and a profligate heir-apparent presided over a social system in which all civil evils were harmoniously combined. A despotic administration was supported by a parliamentary representation as corrupt as illusory; a church, in which spiritual religion was all but extinct, had sold herself as a bondslave to the governing classes. Rank and wealth and territorial ascendency were divorced from public duty, and even learning had become the handmaid of tyranny.

Richard B. Cook

The sacred name of justice was prostituted to sanction a system of legal murder. Commercial enterprise was paralyzed by prohibitive legislation; public credit was shaken to its base; the prime necessaries of life were ruinously dear. The pangs of poverty were aggravated by the concurrent evils of war and famine, and the common people, fast bound in misery and iron, were powerless to make their sufferings known or to seek redress, except by the desperate methods of conspiracy and insurrection. None of the elements of revolution were wanting, and the fates seemed to be hurrying England to the brink of a civil catastrophe.

"The general sense of insecurity and apprehension, inseparable from such a condition of affairs, produced its effect upon even the robust minds. Sir John Gladstone was not a likely victim of panic, but he was a man with a large stake in the country, the more precious because acquired by his own exertion; he believed that the safeguards of property and order were imperilled by foreign arms and domestic sedition; and he had seen with indignation and disgust the excesses of a factious Whiggery, which was not ashamed to exult in the triumph of the French over the English Government. Under the pressure of these influences Sir John Gladstone gradually separated himself from the Whigs, with whom in earlier life he had acted, and became the close ally of Canning, whose return for Liverpool he actually promoted."

With such surroundings it is not to be wondered at that William E. Gladstone entered political life a Tory, contending against the principles he afterwards espoused. His original bent, however, was not towards politics, but the church; and it was only at the earnest desire of his father that he ultimately decided to enter Parliament, and serve his country in the Legislature.

His subsequent life proved the wisdom of the choice. In the Legislature of his country was begun, carried on and consummated grandly, one of the most remarkable careers in the annals of history for versatility, brilliancy, solidity and long continuance. Rarely has there been exhibited so complete a combination of qualities in statesmanship. His intellectual endowments were almost without a parallel, and his achievements without a precedent. In him seemed to be centered a rich collection of the highest gifts of genius, great learning and readiness in debate and discourse in the House of Commons, and extraordinary wisdom in the administration of the affairs of the nation. His financial talent, his business aptitude, his classical attainments, and above all his moral fervor, and religious spirit were conspicuous. Some men would have been contented with political power, or classical learning, or literary distinction, but he excelled in all these—not only as a statesman, but as a man of letters and a classical scholar. Neither has held him exclusively as its own—he belongs to all, or rather they belong to him—for he explored and conquered them. His literary productions equal in merit his papers of State, while his knowledge of the classics would do credit to any scholar.

He possessed the unusual quality of throwing the light of his own mind on the greatest questions of national and international importance, of bringing them down to the understanding and appreciation of the masses of the people, of infusing, by his earnestness, the fire of his own soul in the people, and of arousing in them the greatest enthusiasm.

In the biography of this wonderful person we propose to set before the reader the man himself—his words and his deeds. This method enables him to speak for himself, and thus the reader may study him and know him, and because thereof be lifted into a higher plane of nobler and better being. The acts and utterances of such a character are his best biography, and especially for one differing so largely from all other men as to have none to be compared with him.

In this record we simply spread before the reader his private life and public services, connected together through many startling changes, from home to school, from university to Parliament, from Tory follower to Liberal leader, from the

Richard B. Cook

early start in his political course to the grand consummation of the statesman's success in his attainment to the fourth Premiership of this Grand Old Man, and the glorious end of an eventful life.

We could not do better, in closing this chapter, than to reproduce a part of the character sketch of William E. Gladstone, from the pen of William T. Stead, and published in the "Review of Reviews:"

"So much has been written about Mr. Gladstone that it was with some sinking of heart I ventured to select him as a subject for my next character sketch. But I took heart of grace when I remembered that the object of these sketches is to describe their subject as he appears to himself at his best, and his countrymen. There are plenty of other people ready to fill in the shadows. This paper claims in no way to be a critical estimate or a judicial summing up of the merits and demerits of the most remarkable of all living Englishmen. It is merely an attempt to catch, as it were, the outline of the heroic figure which has dominated English politics for the lifetime of this generation, and thereby to explain something of the fascination which his personality has exercised and still exercises over the men and women of his time. If his enemies, and they are many, say that I have idealized a wily old opportunist out of all recognition, I answer that to the majority of his fellow-subjects my portrait is not overdrawn. The real Gladstone may be other than this, but this is probably more like the Gladstone for whom the electors believe they are voting, than a picture of Gladstone, 'warts and all,' would be. And when I am abused, as I know I shall be, for printing such a sketch, I shall reply that there is at least one thing to be said in its favor. To those who know him best, in his own household, and to those who only know him as a great name in history, my sketch will only appear faulty because it does not do full justice to the character and genius of this extraordinary man."

Mr. Gladstone appeals to the men of to-day from the vantage point of extreme old age. Age is so frequently dotage, that when a veteran appears who preserves the heart of a boy and the happy audacity of youth, under the 'lyart haffets wearing thin and bare' of aged manhood, it seems as if there is something supernatural about it, and all men feel the fascination and the charm. Mr. Gladstone, as he gleefully remarked the other day, has broken the record. He has outlived Lord Palmerston, who died when eighty-one, and Thiers, who only lived to be eighty. The blind old Dandolo in Byron's familiar verse—

The octogenarian chief, Byzantium's conquering foe,

had not more energy than the Liberal leader, who, now in his eighty-third year, has more nerve and spring and go than any of his lieutenants, not excluding the youngest recruit. There is something imposing and even sublime in the long procession of years which bridge as with eighty-two arches the abyss of past time, and carry us back to the days of Canning, and of Castlereagh, of Napoleon, and of Wellington. His parliamentary career extends over sixty years—the lifetime of two generations. He is the custodian of all the traditions, the hero of the experience of successive administrations, from a time dating back longer than most of his colleagues can remember. For nearly forty years he has had a leading part in making or unmaking of Cabinets; he has served his Queen and his country in almost every capacity in office and in opposition, and yet to-day, despite his prolonged sojourn in the malaria of political wire-pulling, his heart seems to be as the heart of a little child. If some who remember 'the old Parliamentary hand' should whisper that innocence of the dove is sometimes compatible with the wisdom of the serpent, I make no dissent. It is easy to be a dove, and to be as silly as a dove. It is easy to be as wise as a serpent, and as wicked, let us say, as Mr. Governor Hill or Lord Beaconsfield. But it is the combination that is difficult, and in Mr. Gladstone the combination is almost ideally complete.

"Mr. Gladstone is old enough to be the grandfather of the younger race of politicians, but still his courage, his faith, his versatility, put the youngest of them to shame. It is this ebullience of youthful energy, this inexhaustible vitality, which is the admiration and despair of his contemporaries. Surely when a schoolboy at Eton he must somewhere have discovered the elixir of life, or have been bathed by some beneficent fairy in the well of perpetual youth. Gladly would many a man of fifty exchange physique with this hale and hearty octogenarian. Only in one respect does he show any trace of advancing years. His hearing is not quite so good as it was, but still it is far better than that of Cardinal Manning, who became very deaf in his closing years. Otherwise Mr. Gladstone is hale and hearty. His eye is not dim, neither is his natural force abated. A splendid physical frame, carefully preserved, gives every promise of a continuance of his green old age."

"His political opponents, who began this Parliament by confidently calculating upon his death before the dissolution, are now beginning to admit that it is by no means improbable that Mr. Gladstone may survive the century. Nor was it quite so fantastic as it appears at first sight, when an ingenious disciple told him the other day that by the fitness of things he ought to live for twenty years yet. 'For,' said this political arithmetician, 'you have been twenty-six years a Tory, twenty-six years a Whig Liberal, and you have been only six years a Radical Home Ruler. To make the balance even you have twenty years still to serve.'"

"Sir Provo Wallis, the Admiral of the Fleet, who died the other day at the age of one hundred, had not a better constitution than Mr. Gladstone, nor had it been more carefully preserved in the rough and tumble of our naval war. If the man who smelt powder in the famous fight between the Chesapeake and the Shannon lived to read the reports of the preparations for the exhibition at Chicago, it is not so incredible that Mr. Gladstone may at least be in the foretop of the State at the dawn of the twentieth century."

"The thought is enough to turn the Tories green with sickening despair, that the chances of his life, from a life insurance office point of view, are probably much better than Lord Salisbury's. But that is one of the attributes of Mr. Gladstone which endear him so much to his party. He is always making his enemies sick with despairing jealousy. He is the great political evergreen, who seems, even in his political life, to have borrowed something of immortality from the fame which he has won. He has long been the Grand Old Man. If he lives much longer he bids fair to be known as the immortal old man in more senses than one."

CHAPTER II

AT ETON AND OXFORD

There is very little recorded of the boyhood of some great men, and this is true of the childhood of William E. Gladstone, until he leaves the parental home for school, which he does in 1821, at the early age of eleven. He was fortunate in his parentage, but no less so in his early associations, both in and out of school. We refer particularly to his private preceptors, two of whom, the venerable Archdeacon Jones and the Rev. William Rawson, first Vicar of Seaforth, a watering-place near Liverpool, were both men of high character and great ability. Mr. Gladstone always highly esteemed Mr. Rawson, his earliest preceptor, and visited him on his death-bed. Dr. Turner, afterwards Bishop of Calcutta, was for two years young Gladstone's private tutor, beginning his instruction when his pupil left Eton in 1827.

Besides these associations of his early life there were Canning, a frequent visitor, as has been mentioned, at his father's house, and Hannah More—"Holy Hannah," as Horace Walpole called her. She singled out "Billy" Gladstone for her especial pet out of the group of eleven children in whom her warm heart delighted, and it has been asked wonderingly if Miss More could preternaturally have lengthened her days until William E. Gladstone's present glory, whether she would have gone on dubbing him "Billy" in undignified brevity until the end.

William E. Gladstone, when very young, gave such evidence of uncommon intellectual ability and promise of future greatness that his father resolved upon educating him in the best schools of England. There are four or five great schools in England in which the English youth are prepared in four or five years for Cambridge or Oxford. "Eton, the largest and the most celebrated of the public schools of England, ranks as the second in point of antiquity, Winchester alone being older." After the preparation at home, under private teachers, to which we have referred, William E. Gladstone was sent to Eton, in September, 1821. His biographer, George W.E. Russell, writes, "From a provincial town, from mercantile surroundings, from an atmosphere of money-making, from a strictly regulated life, the impressible boy was transplanted, at the age of eleven, to the shadow of Windsor and the banks of the Thames, to an institution which belongs to history, to scenes haunted by the memory of the most illustrious Englishmen, to a free and independent existence among companions who were the very flower of English boyhood. A transition so violent and yet so delightful was bound to produce an impression which lapse of time was powerless to efface, and no one who knows the man and the school can wonder that for seventy years Mr. Gladstone has been the most enthusiastic of Etonians."

Eton of to-day is not in all respects the Eton of three-quarters of a century ago, and yet in some particulars it is as it was when young "Billy" Gladstone studied within its walls. The system of education and discipline pursued has undergone some modifications in recent years—notably during the provostship of the Rev. Francis Hodgson; but radical defects are still alleged against it. It is not remarkable, however, that every Eton boy becomes deeply attached to the school, notwithstanding the apprenticeship to hardships he may have been compelled to undergo.

The "hardships" there must have been particularly great when young Gladstone entered Eton, at the close of the summer holidays of 1821. The school was under the head-mastership of "the terrific Dr. Keate." He was not the man to spare even

Richard B. Cook

the scholar who, upon the emphatic testimony of Sir Roderick Murchison, was "the prettiest boy that ever went to Eton," and who was as studious and well-behaved as he was good-looking.

The town of Eton, in which the school is located, about 22 miles from London, in Berkshire, is beautifully situated on the banks of the river Thames, opposite Windsor Castle, the residence of the Queen of England.

Eton College is one of the most famous and best endowed educational institutions of learning in England. It was founded in 1440 by Henry VI. The king was very solicitous that the work should be of a durable kind, and he provided for free scholarships. Eton of Mr. Gladstone's day, according to a critic, was divided into two schools—the upper and the lower. It also had two kinds of scholars, namely, seventy called king's scholars or "collegers," who are maintained gratuitously, sleep in the college, and wear a peculiar dress; and another class—the majority—called "oppidans," who live in the town. Between these two classes of students there prevails perpetual hostility. At Cambridge, there was founded, in connection with Eton, what is called King's College, to receive as fellows students from Eton, and to give them gratuitously an education. The ground on which students of Eton were promoted to King's College and these fellowships was, strangely to say, upon that of seniority, or long residence, and not of merit. Because there was no competition, scholars who were deficient in education at Eton were promoted to Cambridge, where they had no incentive to work, being exempt from the ordinary university examination.

At Eton "no instruction was given in any branch of mathematical, physical, metaphysical or moral science, nor in the evidences of Christianity. The only subjects which it professed to impart a knowledge of were the Greek and Latin languages; as much divinity as can be gained from construing the Greek Testament, and reading a portion of Tomline on the Thirty-nine Articles, and a little ancient and modern geography." So much for the instruction imparted. As regards the hours of tuition, there seems to have been fault there, in that they were too few and insufficient, there being in all only eleven hours a week study. Then as to the manner of study, no time was given the scholar to study the style of an author; he was "hurried from Herodotus to Thucydides, from Thucydides to Xenophon, from Xenophon to Lucian, without being habituated to the style of any one author—without gaining an interest in the history, or even catching the thread of the narrative; and when the whole book is finished he has probably collected only a few vague ideas about Darius crying over a great army, Abydos and Nicias and Demosthenes being routed with a great army near Syracuse, mixed up with a recollection of the death of Cyrus and Socrates, some moral precept from Socrates, and some jokes against false philosophers and heathen gods." Hence the Eton student who goes to Cambridge finds he has done but a little desultory reading, and that he must begin again. It was charged that the system of education at Eton failed in every point. The moral discipline of the school was also called in question. The number of scholars was so great that the proper control of them seemed impossible under the management. Great laxity prevailed among the larger boys, while the younger and weaker students were exposed to the tyranny of the older and stronger ones without hope of redress. The result was that the system of "fagging," or the acting of some boys as drudges for the others, flourished. "The right" of fagging depended upon the place in the school; all boys in the sixth and fifth forms had the power of ordering—all below the latter form being bound to obey. This system of fagging has a very injurious effect upon most of the boys; "it finds them slaves and leaves them despots. A boy who has suffered himself, insensibly learns to see no harm in making others suffer in turn. The whole thing is wrong in principle, and engenders passions which should be stifled and not encouraged." Why free and enlightened England should tolerate, even then, such barbarous slavery cannot be understood and yet there are outrageous customs prevailing among college students of our day in every civilized land that should be suppressed.

Flogging was in vogue, too, at Eton, with all its degrading and

Richard B. Cook

demoralizing effects, and was performed by the Head-Master himself. In 1820, the year before Mr. Gladstone entered Eton, there were 280 upper students and 319 lower, a total of 612, and none were exempt.

Some curious stories are told of flogging, which has ever existed at Eton, and from which even the largest boys were not exempt. Mr. Lewis relates how a young man of twenty, just upon the point of leaving school, and engaged to be married to a lady at Windsor, was well and soundly whipped by Dr. Goodford, for arriving one evening at his tutor's house after the specified time. And it is related that Arthur Wellesley, afterwards the Iron Duke of Wellington, was flogged at Eton for having been "barred out." At the same time there were eighty boys who were whipped.

And the Eton of twenty years later was very little improved over its condition in Mr. Gladstone's time there, or in 1845. John D. Lewis, speaking of this period, says that after the boys reached the fifth form, then began "some of the greatest anomalies and absurdities of the then Etonian system." The student was now safe from the ordeal of examinations, and that the higher classes, including ten senior collegers and ten senior oppidans, contained some of the very worst scholars. "A boy's place on the general roll was no more a criterion of his acquirements and his industry than would be the 'year' of a young man at Oxford or Cambridge." The collegers, however, were required to pass some kind of examination, in accordance with which their place on the list for the King's college was fixed. But the evils regarding the hours of study and the nature of the studies were as bad. "The regular holidays and Saints' days, two whole holidays in a week, and two half-holidays, were a matter of common occurrence."

Lord Morley, in his examination before the Commission on Public Schools, was asked whether a boy would be looked down upon at Eton for being industrious in his studies, replied, "Not if he could do something else well." And this seems to be the spirit of the Eton boy with whom a lack of scholarship is more than made up by skill in river or field sports.

This is true to-day; for a recent writer in the *Forum,* upon "The Training of Boys at Eton," says: "Athletic prominence is in English public schools almost synonymous with social prominence; many a boy whose capacity and character commanded both respect and liking at the universities and in after life, is almost a nobody at a public school, because he has no special athletic gifts.... Great athletic capacity may co-exist with low moral and intellectual character."

There were few inducements to study and to excel in scholarship, and plenty to idleness and neglect, hence he who did so must study in hours and out of hours, in season and out of season. The curriculum is still strictly classical, but French, German and mathematics are taught. The collegers of recent years have done very fair work and carried off many distinctions at Cambridge. With all these odds against them, and these difficulties to surmount, yet there were Eton boys whose attainments were deep and solid, and who became famous men, and one of these was William E. Gladstone.

When young Gladstone entered Eton his brothers, Thomas and Robertson Gladstone, were already there, and the three boys boarded at Mrs. Shurey's, whose house "at the south end of the broad walk in front of the schools and facing the chapel," was rather nearer the famous "Christopher Inn" than would be thought desirable nowadays. On the wall opposite the house the name of "Gladstone" is carved. Thomas Gladstone was in the fifth form, and William was placed in the middle remove of the fourth form, and became his eldest brother's "fag." This doubtlessly saved him much annoyance and suffering, and allowed him better to pursue the studious bent of his indications.

William E. Gladstone was what Etonians called a "sap"—in other words, a student faithful in the discharge of every duty devolving upon him at school—one who studied his lessons and was prepared for his recitations in the classroom. This agreeable fact has been immortalized in a famous line in Lord Lytton's "New Timon." He worked hard at his classical studies, as required by the rules of the school, and applied himself diligently to the study of mathematics during the holidays.

It is said that his interest in the work of the school was first aroused by Mr. Hawtrey, who afterwards became Head-Master, who commended some of his Latin verses, and "sent him up for good." This led the young man to associate intellectual work with the ideas of ambition and success. While he did not seem to be especially an apt scholar in the restricted sense for original versification in the classical languages, or for turning English into Greek or Latin, yet he seemed to seize the precise meaning of the authors and to give the sense. "His composition was stiff," but yet, says a classmate, "when there were thrilling passages of Virgil or Homer, or difficult passages in 'Scriptores Graeci' to translate, he or Lord Arthur Hervey was generally called up to edify the class with quotations or translations."

He had no prizes at Eton except what is called being sent up for good, on account of verses, and he was honored on several occasions. Besides he took deep interest in starting a college periodical, and with some of the most intellectual of the students sustained it with his pen. The more studious of Eton boys have on several occasions in the present century been in the habit of establishing periodicals for the purpose of ventilating their opinions. In 1786 Mr. Canning and Mr. Hookham Frere established the *Microcosm*, whose essays and *jeux d'esprit*, while having reference primarily to Eton, demonstrated that the writers were not insensible to what was going on in the great world without. It was for this college paper that Canning wrote his "Essay on the Epic of the Queen of Hearts," which, as a burlesque criticism, has been awarded a high place in English literature. Lord Henry Spencer, Hookham Frere, Capel Lofft, and Mr. Millish, were also contributors to the columns of the *Microcosm*. In the year

1820 W. Mackworth Praed set on foot a manuscript journal, entitled *Apis Matina*. This was in turn succeeded by the *Etonian*, to which Praed contributed some of his most brilliant productions. John Moultrie, Henry Nelson Coleridge, Walter Blunt, and Chauncy Hare Townshend were also among the writers for its papers, who helped to make it of exceptional excellence. Its articles are of no ordinary interest even now.

In the last year of William E. Gladstone's stay at Eton, in 1827, and seven years after Praed's venture, he was largely instrumental in launching the *Eton Miscellany*, professedly edited by Bartholomew Bouverie, and Mr. Gladstone became a most frequent, voluminous and valuable contributor to its pages. He wrote articles of every kind—prologues, epilogues, leaders, historical essays, satirical sketches, classical translations, humorous productions, poetry and prose. And among the principal contributors with him were Sir Francis Doyle, George Selwyn, James Colville, Arthur Hallam, John Haumer and James Milnes-Gaskell. The introduction, written by and signed "William Ewart Gladstone" for this magazine, contained the following interesting and singular passage, which probably fairly sets forth the hopes and fears that beset statesmen in maturer years, as well as Eton boys of only seventeen years of age:

"In my present undertaking there is one gulf in which I fear to sink, and that gulf is Lethe. There is one stream which I dread my inability to stem—it is the tide of Popular Opinion. I have ventured, and no doubt rashly ventured—

Like little wanton boys that swim on bladders,
To try my fortune in a sea of glory,
But far beyond my depth."

At present it is hope alone that buoys me up; for more substantial support I must be indebted to my own exertions, well knowing that in this land of literature merit never wants its reward. That such merit is mine I dare not presume to think; but still there is something within me that bids me hope that I may be able to glide prosperously down the stream of public estimation; or, in the words of Virgil,

'—Celerare viam rumore secundo.'

"I was surprised even to see some works with the names of Shakespeare and Milton on them sharing the common destiny, but on examination I found that those of the latter were some political rhapsodies, which richly deserved their fate; and that the former consisted of some editions of his works which had been burdened with notes and mangled with emendations by his merciless commentators. In other places I perceived authors worked up into frenzy by seeing their own compositions descending like the rest. Often did the infuriated scribes extend their hands, and make a plunge to endeavor to save their beloved offspring, but in vain; I pitied the anguish of their disappointment, but with feelings of the same commiseration as that which one feels for a malefactor on beholding his death, being at the same time fully conscious how well he has deserved it."

Little did this diffident and youthful editor imagine that he was forecasting the future for himself by the aid of youth's most ardent desires, and that he would live to become the Primate of all England and the foremost statesman of his day.

There were two volumes of the *Miscellany*, dated June-July and October-November, respectively, and Mr. Gladstone contributed thirteen articles to the first volume. Among the contributions were an "Ode to the Shade of Watt Tyler," a vigorous rendering of a chorus from the Hucuba of Euripides, and a letter under the name of "Philophantasm," detailing an encounter he had with the poet Virgil, in which the great poet appeared muttering something which did not sound like Latin to an Eton boy, and complaining that he knew he was hated by the Eton boys because he was difficult to learn, and pleading to be as well received henceforth as Horace.

We give a quotation from a poem, consisting of some two

hundred and fifty lines, from his pen, which, appeared also in the *Miscellany*:

"Who foremost now the deadly spear to dart,
And strike the javelin to the Moslem's heart?
Who foremost now to climb the leaguered wall,
The first to triumph, or the first to fall?
Lo, where the Moslems rushing to the fight,
Back bear their squadrons in inglorious flight.
With plumed helmet, and with glittering lance,
'Tis Richard bids his steel-clad bands advance;
'Tis Richard stalks along the blood-dyed plain,
And views unmoved the slaying and the slain;
'Tis Richard bathes his hands in Moslem blood,
And tinges Jordan with the purple flood.
Yet where the timbrels ring, the trumpets sound,
And tramp of horsemen shakes the solid ground,
Though 'mid the deadly charge and rush of fight,
No thought be theirs of terror or of flight,—
Ofttimes a sigh will rise, a tear will flow,
And youthful bosoms melt in silent woe;
For who of iron frame and harder heart
Can bid the mem'ry of his home depart?
Tread the dark desert and the thirsty sand,
Nor give one thought to England's smiling land?
To scenes of bliss, and days of other years—
The Vale of Gladness and the Vale of Tears;
That, passed and vanish'd from their loving sight,
This 'neath their view, and wrapt in shades of night?"

Among other writers who contributed to the first volume of the *Miscellany* were Arthur Henry Hallam and Doyle, also G.A. Selwyn, afterwards Bishop Selwyn, the friend of Mr. Gladstone, and to whom he recently paid the following tribute: "Connected as tutor with families of rank and influence, universally popular from his frank, manly, and engaging character—and scarcely less so from his extraordinary rigor as an athlete—he was attached to Eton, where he resided, with a love surpassing the love of Etonians. In himself he formed a large part of the life of Eton, and Eton formed a large part of his life. To him is due no small share of the beneficial movement in the direction of religious earnestness which marked the Eton of forty years back, and which was not, in my opinion, sensibly affected by any influence extraneous to the place itself. At a moment's notice, upon the call of duty, he tore up the singularly deep roots which his life had struck deep into the soil of England."

Both Mr. Gladstone and the future Bishop of Selwyn contributed humorous letters to "The Postman," the correspondence department of the *Eton Miscellany.*

In the second volume of the *Eton Miscellany* are articles of equal interest to those that appeared in the first. Doyle, Jelf, Selwyn, Shadwell and Arthur Henry Hallam were contributors, the latter having written "The Battle of the Boyne," a parody upon Campbell's "Hohenlinden." But here again Mr. Gladstone was the principal contributor, having contributed to this even more largely than to the first, having written seventeen articles, besides the introductions to the various numbers of the volume. Indeed one would think from his devotion to these literary pursuits during his last year at Eton, that he had very little leisure for those ordinary sports so necessary to Eton boys. He seems to have begun his great literary activity. Among them may be mentioned an "Ode to the Shade of Watt Tyler," mentioned before, which is an example of his humorous style:

"Shade of him whose valiant tongue
On high the song of freedom sung;
Shade of him, whose mighty soul
Would pay no taxes on his poll;
Though, swift as lightning, civic sword
Descended on thy fated head,
The blood of England's boldest poured,
And numbered Tyler with the dead!

"Still may thy spirit flap its wings

At midnight o'er the couch of kings;
And peer and prelate tremble, too,
In dread of mighty interview!
With patriot gesture of command,
With eyes that like thy forges gleam,
Lest Tyler's voice and Tyler's hand
Be heard and seen in nightly dream.

"I hymn the gallant and the good
From Tyler down to Thistlewood,
My muse the trophies grateful sings,
The deeds of Miller and of Ings;
She sings of all who, soon or late,
Have burst Subjection's iron chain,
Have seal'd the bloody despot's fate,
Or cleft a peer or priest in twain.

"Shades, that soft Sedition woo,
Around the haunts of Peterloo!
That hover o'er the meeting-halls,
Where many a voice stentorian bawls!
Still flit the sacred choir around,
With 'Freedom' let the garrets ring,
And vengeance soon in thunder sound
On Church, and constable, and king."

In a paper on "Eloquence," in the same volume, he shows that even then his young mind was impressed by the fame attached to successful oratory in Parliament. Visions of glory and honor open before the enraptured sight of those devoted to oratorical pursuits, and whose ardent and aspiring minds are directed to the House of Commons. Evidently the young writer himself "had visions of parliamentary oratory, and of a successful *debut* in the House of Commons, with perhaps an offer from the Minister, a Secretaryship of State, and even the Premiership itself in the distance." But then there are barriers to pass and ordeals to undergo. "There are roars of coughing, as well as roars of cheering" from the members of the House, "and maiden speeches sometimes act more forcibly on the lungs of hearers than the most violent or most cutting of all the breezes which AEOLUS can boast." But the writer draws comfort from the fact that Lord Morfeth, Edward Geoffrey, Stanley and Lord Castlereagh who were all members of the Eton college debating society were then among the most successful young speakers in Parliament. This sounds more like prophecy than dreams, for within a very few years after writing this article the writer himself had passed the dreaded barrier and endured the ordeal, and had not only made his appearance in the House of Commons, but had been invited to fill an honorable place in the Cabinet of the Ministry then in power.

Another contribution of Mr. Gladstone's to the *Miscellany*, and perhaps the most meritorious of the youthful writer's productions, was entitled, "Ancient and Modern Genius Compared," in which the young Etonian editor ardently and affectionately apostrophized the memory of Canning, his father's great friend and his own ideal man and statesman, who had just then perished untimely and amid universal regret. In this article he first takes the part of the moderns as against the ancients, though he by no means deprecates the genius of the latter, and then eloquently apostrophizes the object of his youthful hero-worship, the immortal Canning, whose death he compares to that of the lamented Pitt. The following are extracts from this production:

"It is for those who revered him in the plenitude of his meridian glory to mourn over him in the darkness of his premature extinction: to mourn over the hopes that are buried in his grave, and the evils that arise from his withdrawing from the scene of life. Surely if eloquence never excelled and seldom equalled—if an expanded mind and judgment whose vigor was paralleled only by its soundness—if brilliant wit—if a glowing imagination—if a warm heart, and an unbending firmness—could have strengthened the frail tenure, and prolonged the momentary duration of human existence, that man had been immortal! But nature could endure no longer. Thus has Providence ordained that inasmuch as the intellect is more brilliant, it shall be more short-lived; as its sphere is more expanded, more swiftly is it summoned away. Lest we should give to man the honor due to God—lest we should exalt the object of our admiration into a divinity for our worship—He who calls the weary and the mourner to eternal rest hath been pleased to remove him from our eyes.

"The degrees of inscrutable wisdom are unknown to us; but if ever there was a man for whose sake it was meet to indulge the kindly though frail feelings of our nature—for whom the tear of sorrow was to us both prompted by affection and dictated by duty—that man was George Canning."

After Hallam, Selwyn and other contributors to the *Miscellany* left Eton, at midsummer, 1827, Mr. Gladstone still remained and became the mainstay of the magazine. "Mr. Gladstone and I remained behind as its main supporters," writes Sir Francis Doyle, "or rather it would be more like the truth if I said that Mr. Gladstone supported the whole burden upon his own shoulders. I was unpunctual and unmethodical, so were his other vassals; and the '*Miscellany*' would have fallen to the ground but for Mr. Gladstone's untiring energy, pertinacity and tact."

Although Mr. Gladstone labored in editorial work upon the *Miscellany*, yet he took time to bestow attention upon his duties in the Eton Society of the College, learnedly called "The Literati," and vulgarly called "Pop," and took a leading part in the debates and in the private business of the Society. The Eton Society of Gladstone's day was a brilliant group of boys. He introduced desirable new members, moved for more readable and instructive newspapers, proposing new rules for better order and more decorous conduct, moving fines on those guilty of disorder or breaches of the rules, and paying a fine imposed upon himself for putting down an illegal question. "In debate he champions the claims of metaphysics against those of mathematics, and defends aristocracy against democracy;" confesses innate feelings of dislike to the French; protests against disarmament of the Highlanders as inexpedient and unjust; deplores the fate of Strafford and the action of the

House of Commons, which he claimed they should be able to "revere as our glory and confide in as our protection." The meetings of the Eton Society were held over Miss Hatton's "sock-shop."

In politics its members were Tory—intensely so, and although current politics were forbidden subjects, yet, political opinions were disclosed in discussions of historical or academical questions. "The execution of Strafford and Charles I, the characters of Oliver Cromwell and Milton, the 'Central Social' of Rousseau, and the events of the French Revolution, laid bare the speakers' political tendencies as effectually as if the conduct of Queen Caroline, the foreign policy of Lord Castlereagh, or the repeal of the Test and Corporation Act had been the subject of debate."

It was October 15, 1825, when Gladstone was elected a member of the Eton Society, and on the 29th of the same month made his maiden speech on the question "Is the education of the poor on the whole beneficial?" It is recorded in the minutes of the meeting that "Mr. Gladstone rose and eloquently addressed the house." He spoke in favor of education; and one who heard him says that his opening words were, "Sir, in this age of increased and increasing civilization." Says an eminent writer, by way of comment upon these words, "It almost oppresses the imagination to picture the shoreless sea of eloquence which rolls between that exordium and the oratory to which we still are listening and hope to listen for years to come."

"The peroration of his speech on the question whether Queen Anne's Ministers, in the last four years of her reign, deserved well of their country, is so characteristic, both in substance and in form," that we reproduce it here from Dr, Russell's work on Gladstone:

"Thus much, sir, I have said, as conceiving myself bound in fairness not to regard the names under which men have hidden their designs so much as the designs themselves. I am well aware that my prejudices and my predilections have long been enlisted on the side of Toryism (cheers) and that in a cause like this I am not likely to be influenced unfairly against men bearing that name and professing to act on the principles which I have always been accustomed to revere. But the good of my country must stand on a higher ground than distinctions like these. In common fairness and in common candor, I feel myself compelled to give my decisive verdict against the conduct of men whose measures I firmly believe to have been hostile to British interests, destructive of British glory, and subversive of the splendid and, I trust, lasting fabric of the British constitution."

The following extracts from the diary of William Cowper, afterwards Lord Mount-Temple, we also reproduce from the same author: "On Saturday, October 27, 1827, the subject for debate was:"

"'Whether the deposition of Richard II was justifiable or not.' Jelf opened; not a good speech. Doyle spoke *extempore*, made several mistakes, which were corrected by Jelf. Gladstone spoke well. The Whigs were regularly floored; only four Whigs to eleven Tories, but they very nearly kept up with them in coughing and 'hear, hears,' Adjourned to Monday after 4."

"Monday, 29.—Gladstone finished his speech, and ended with a great deal of flattery of Doyle, saying that he was sure he would have courage enough to own that he was wrong. It succeeded. Doyle rose amidst reiterated cheers to own that he was convinced by the arguments of the other side. He had determined before to answer them and cut up Gladstone!"

"December 1.—Debate, 'Whether the Peerage Bill of 1719 was calculated to be beneficial or not.' Thanks voted to Doyle and Gladstone; the latter spoke well; will be a great loss to the Society."

There were many boys at Eton—schoolfellows of Mr. Gladstone—who became men of note in after days. Among them the Hallams, Charles Canning, afterwards Lord Canning and Governor-General of India; Walter Hamilton, Bishop of Salisbury; Edward Hamilton, his brother, of Charters; James Hope, afterwards Hope-Scott; James Bruce, afterwards Lord Elgin; James Milnes-Gaskell, M.P. for Wenlock; Henry Denison; Sir Francis Doyle; Alexander Kinglake; George Selwyn, Bishop of New Zealand and of Litchfield; Lord Arthur Hervey, Bishop of Bath and Wells; William Cavendish, Duke of Devonshire; George Cornwallis Lewis; Frederic Tennyson; Gerald Wellesley, Dean of Windsor; Spencer Walpole, Home Secretary; Frederic Rogers, Lord Blachford; James Colvile, Chief Justice at Calcutta, and others.

By universal acknowledgment the most remarkable youth at Eton in that day was Arthur Hallam, "in mind and character not unworthy of the magnificent eulogy of 'In Memoriam.'" He was the most intimate friend of young Gladstone. They always took breakfast together, although they boarded apart in different houses, and during the separation of vacations they were diligent correspondents.

The father of William E. Gladstone, as we have seen, discovered premonitions of future greatness in his son, and we may well ask the question what impression was made by him upon his fellow school-mates at Eton. Arthur Hallam wrote: "Whatever may be our lot, I am confident that *he* is a bud that will bloom with a richer fragrance than almost any whose early promise I have witnessed."

James Milnes-Gaskell says: "Gladstone is no ordinary individual; and perhaps if I were called on to select the individual I am intimate with to whom I should first turn in an emergency, and whom I thought in every way pre-eminently distinguished for high excellence, I think I should turn to Gladstone. If you finally decide in favor of Cambridge, my separation from Gladstone will be a source of great sorrow to me." And the explanation of this latter remark is that the writer's mother wanted him to go to Cambridge, while he wished to go to Oxford, because Gladstone was going there.

Sir Francis Doyle writes: "I may as well remark that my father, a man of great ability, as well as of great experience of life, predicted Gladstone's future eminence from the manner in which he handled this somewhat tiresome business. [The editorial work and management of the *Eton Miscellany*.] 'It is not' he remarked, 'that I think his papers better than yours or Hallam's—that is not my meaning at all; but the force of character he has shown in managing his subordinates, and the combination of ability and power that he has made evident, convince me that such a young man cannot fail to distinguish himself hereafter.'"

The recreations of young Gladstone were not in all respects like his school-mates. He took no part in games, for he had no taste in that direction, and while his companions were at play he was studiously employed in his room. One of the boys afterwards declared, "without challenge or contradiction, that he was never seen to run." Yet he had his diversions and was fond of sculling, and kept a "lock-up," or private boat, for his own use. He liked walking for exercise, and walked fast and far. His chief amusement when not writing, reading or debating, was to ramble among the delights of Windsor with a few intimate friends; and he had only a few whom he admitted to his inner circle. To others beyond he was not known and was not generally popular. Gladstone, Charles Canning, Handley, Bruce, Hodgson, Lord Bruce and Milnes-Gaskell set up a Salt Hill Club. They met every whole holiday or half-holiday, as was convenient, after twelve, "and went up to Salt Hill to bully the fat waiter, eat toasted cheese, and drink egg-wine." It is startling to hear from such an authority as James Milnes-Gaskell that "in all our meetings, as well as at almost every time, Gladstone went by the name of Mr. Tipple."

The strongest testimony is borne to the moral character of young Gladstone while at Eton. By common consent he was pre-eminently God-fearing, orderly and conscientious. Bishop Hamilton, of Salisbury, writes: "At Eton I was a thoroughly idle boy; but I was saved from some worse things by getting to know Gladstone." This is the strong testimony of one school-boy after he has reached maturity and distinction for another. "To have exercised, while still a school-boy, an influence for good upon one of the greatest of contemporary saints, is surely such a distinction as few Prime Ministers ever attain."

Two stories are told of him while at Eton that go to show the moral determination of the boy to do right. On one occasion he turned his glass upside down and refused to drink a coarse toast proposed, according to annual custom, at an election dinner at the "Christopher Inn." This shows the purity of his mind, but there is another illustrating the humane feeling in his heart. He came forth as the champion of some miserable pigs which it was the inhumane custom to torture at Eton Fair on Ash Wednesday, and when he was bantered by his school-fellows for his humanity, he offered to write his reply "in good round hand upon their faces."

At Christmas, 1827, Gladstone left Eton, and after that studied six months under private tutors, Dr. Turner, afterwards Bishop of Calcutta, being one. Of this Mr. Gladstone writes: "I resided with Dr. Turner at Wilmslow (in Cheshire) from January till a few months later. My residence with him was cut off by his appointment to the Bishopric of Calcutta.... My companions were the present (1877) Bishop of Sodor and Man, and Sir C.A. Wood, Deputy-Chairman of the G.W. Railway. We employed our spare time in gymnastics, in turning, and in rambles. I remember paying a visit to Macclesfield. In a silk factory the owner showed us his silk handkerchiefs, and complained much of Mr. Huskisson for having removed the prohibition of the foreign article. The thought passed through my mind at the time: Why make laws to enable people to produce articles of such hideous pattern and indifferent quality as this? Alderly Edge was a favorite place of resort. We dined with Sir John Stanley (at Alderly) on the day when the king's speech was received; and I recollect that he ridiculed (I think very justly) the epithet *untoward*, which was applied in it to the Battle of Navarino."

In 1828, and after two years as a private pupil of Dr. Turner, Mr. Gladstone entered Christ Church College, Oxford and in the following year was nominated to a studentship on the foundation. Although he had no prizes at Oxford of the highest class, unless honors in the schools be so called—and in this respect he achieved a success which falls to the lot of but few students. In the year 1831, when he went up for his final examination, he completed his academical education by attaining the highest honors in the university—graduating double-first-class.

Of the city of Oxford, where Oxford University is situated, Matthew Arnold writes: "Beautiful city! So venerable, so lovely, so unravaged by the fierce intellectual life of our century, so serene! And yet, steeped in sentiment as she lies, spreading her gardens to the moonlight, or whispering from her towers the last enchantments of the Middle Age, who will deny that Oxford, by her ineffable charm, keeps ever calling us near to the true goal of all of us, to the ideal, to perfection—to beauty, in a word, which is only truth seen from another side."

Describing Christ Church College, a writer has said that there is no other College where a man has so great a choice of society, or a man entire freedom in choosing it.

As to the studies required, a greater stress was laid upon a knowledge of the Bible and of the evidences of Christianity than upon classical literature; some proficiency was required also, either in mathematics or the science of reasoning. The system of education accommodated itself to the capacity and wants of the students, but the man of talent was at no loss as to a field for his exertions, or a reward for his industry. The honors of the ministry were all within his reach. In the cultivation of taste and general information Oxford afforded every opportunity, but the modern languages were not taught.

An interesting fact is related of young Gladstone when he entered Oxford, as to his studies at the university. He wrote his father that he disliked mathematics, and that he intended to concentrate his time and attention upon the classics. This was a great blow to his father, who replied that he did not think a man was a man unless he knew mathematics. The dutiful son yielded to his father's wishes, abandoned his own plan, and applied himself with energy and success to the study of mathematics. But for this change of study he might not have become the greatest of Chancellors of the Exchequer.

Gladstone's instructors at Oxford were men of reputation. Rev. Robert Biscoe, whose lectures on Aristotle attracted some of the best men to the university, was his tutor; he attended the lectures of Dr. Burton on Divinity, and of Dr. Pusey on Hebrew, and read classics privately with Bishop Wordsworth. He read steadily but not laboriously. Nothing was ever allowed to interfere with his morning's work. He read for four hours, and then took a walk. Though not averse to company and suppers, yet he always read for two or three hours before bedtime.

Among the undergraduates at Oxford then, who became conspicuous, were Henry Edward Manning, afterwards Cardinal Archbishop; Archibald Campbell Tait, Archbishop of Canterbury; Sidney Herbert, Robert Lowe, Lord Sherbrooke, and Lord Selborne. "The man who *took* me most," says a visitor to Oxford in 1829, "was the youngest Gladstone of Liverpool—I am sure a very superior person."

Gladstone's chosen friends were all steady and industrious men, and many of them were more distinctively religious than is generally found in the life of undergraduates. And his choice of associates in this respect was the subject of criticism on the part of a more secularly minded student who wrote, "Gladstone has mixed himself up with the St. Mary Hall and Oriel set, who are really, for the most part, only fit to live with maiden aunts and keep tame rabbits." And the question, Which was right—Gladstone or the student? may be answered by another, Which one became Prime Minister of England?

"Gladstone's first rooms were in the 'old library,' near the hall;

but for the greater part of his time he occupied the right-hand rooms on the first floor of the first staircase, on the right as the visitor enters Canterbury gate. He was, alike in study and in conduct, a model undergraduate, and the great influence of his character and talents was used with manly resolution against the riotous conduct of the 'Tufts,' whose brutality caused the death of one of their number in 1831. We read this note in the correspondence of a friend: 'I heard from Gladstone yesterday; he says that the number of gentlemen commoners has increased, is increasing, and ought to be diminished.' Every one who has experienced the hubristic qualities of the Tufted race, and its satellites, will cordially sympathize with this sentiment of an orderly and industrious undergraduate. He was conspicuously moderate in the use of wine. His good example in this respect affected not only his contemporaries but also his successors at the university; men who followed him to Oxford ten years later found it still operative, and declare that undergraduates drank less in the forties, because Gladstone had been courageously abstemious in the thirties."

But there were those who better estimated Gladstone's worth and looked approvingly upon his course, as "the blameless schoolboy became the blameless undergraduate; diligent, sober, regular alike in study and devotion, giving his whole energies to the duties of the place, and quietly abiding in the religious faith in which he had been trained. Bishop Charles Wordsworth said that no man of his standing in the university habitually read his Bible more or knew it better. Cardinal Manning described him walking in the university with his 'Bible and Prayer-book tucked under his arm.' ... He quitted Oxford with a religious belief still untinctured by Catholic theology. But the great change was not far distant, and he had already formed some of the friendships which, in their development were destined to effect so profoundly the course of his religious thought."

In reference to the religious and political opinions and influences prevailing at Oxford, it may be remarked that the atmosphere of Oxford was calculated to strengthen Mr.

Gladstone's conservative views, and did have this effect, and as English statesmen had not then learned to put their trust in the people, the cause of reform found few or no friends at the university, and he was among those hostile to it, and was known for his pronounced Tory and High Church opinions.

He belonged to the famous debating society known as the Oxford Union, was a brilliant debater, and in 1831 was its secretary, and later its president. On various occasions he carried, by a majority of one only, a motion that the Wellington Administration was undeserving of the confidence of the country; he defended the results of the Catholic Emancipation; he opposed a motion for the removal of Jewish disabilities, and he persuaded 94 students out of 130 to condemn Earl Grey's Reform Bill as a measure "which threatened not only to change the form of government, but ultimately to break up the very foundation of social order." His last speech at Oxford was in support of his own amendment to a motion for the immediate emancipation of the slaves in the West Indies. On a certain occasion he entertained a party of students from Cambridge, consisting of Sir Francis Doyle, Monckton Milnes, Sunderland, and Arthur H. Hallam, who discussed among them the superiority of Shelley over Byron as a poet. The motion was opposed by one Oxonion, the late Cardinal Manning, but Shelley received 90 votes to 33 for Byron.

One who heard the debate on the Reform Bill says that "it converted Alston, the son of the member in Parliament for Hertford, who immediately on the conclusion of Gladstone's speech walked across from the Whig to the Tory side of the house, amidst loud acclamations." Another who was present writes, "Most of the speakers rose, more or less, above their usual level, but when Mr. Gladstone sat down we all of us felt that an epoch in our lives had occurred. It certainly was the finest speech of his that I ever heard." And Bishop Charles Wordsworth writes his experience of Mr. Gladstone at this time, "made me feel no less sure than of my own existence that Gladstone, our then Christ-Church undergraduate, would one day rise to be Prime Minister of England."

In the spring of 1832 Mr. Gladstone quitted Oxford. In summing up results it may be said, in the language of Mr. Russell: "Among the purely intellectual effects produced on Mr. Gladstone by the discipline of Oxford, it is obvious to reckon an almost excessive exactness in the statement of propositions, a habit of rigorous definition, a microscopic care in the choice of words, and a tendency to analyze every sentiment and every phrase, and to distinguish with intense precaution between statements almost exactly similar. From Aristotle and Bishop Butler and Edmund Burke he learned the value of authority, the sacredness of law, the danger of laying rash and inconsiderate hands upon the ark of State. In the political atmosphere of Oxford he was taught to apply these principles to the civil events of his time, to dread innovation, to respect existing institutions, and to regard the Church and the Throne as inseparably associated by Divine ordinance."

Richard B. Cook

CHAPTER III

EARLY PARLIAMENTARY EXPERIENCES

It is customary for the sons of gentlemen who graduate at Cambridge and Oxford to spend some time in travel on the continent upon the completion of their university studies. The custom was observed in Mr. Gladstone's early days even more than at the present. In accordance then with the prevailing usage he went abroad after graduating at Oxford. In the spring of 1832 he started on his travels and spent nearly the whole of the next six months in Italy, "learning the language, studying the art, and revelling in the natural beauties of that glorious land." In the following September, however, he was suddenly recalled to England to enter upon his first Parliamentary campaign.

At Oxford Toryism prevailed, and was of the old-fashioned type, far removed from the utilitarian conservatism of the present day. Charles I was a saint and a martyr, the claims of rank and birth were admitted with a childlike simplicity, the high functions of government were the birthright of the few, and the people had nothing to do with the laws, except to obey them. Mr. Gladstone was a Tory. The political views he held upon leaving Oxford had much to do with his recall from abroad and his running for a seat in the House of Commons. Of these opinions held by him then, and afterwards repudiated, he, in a speech delivered at the opening of the Palmerston Club, Oxford, in December, 1878, says: "I trace in the education of Oxford of my own time one great defect.

Perhaps it was my own fault; but I must admit that I did not learn, when at Oxford, that which I have learned since, viz., to set a due value on the imperishable and inestimable principles of human liberty. The temper which, I think, too much prevailed in academic circles, was that liberty was regarded with jealousy and fear, which could not be wholly dispensed with, but which was continually to be watched for fear of excess.... I think that the principle of the Conservative party is jealousy of liberty and of the people, only qualified by fear; but I think the policy of the Liberal party is trust in the people, only qualified by prudence. I can only assure you, gentlemen, that now I am in front of extended popular privileges. I have no fear of those enlargements of the Constitution that seem to be approaching. On the contrary, I hail them with desire. I am not in the least degree conscious that I have less reverence for antiquity, for the beautiful, and good, and glorious charges that our ancestors have handed down to us as a patrimony to our race, than I had in other days when I held other political opinions. I have learnt to set the true value upon human liberty, and in whatever I have changed, there, and there only, has been the explanation of the change."

It was Mr. Gladstone's Tory principles that led to an invitation from the Duke of Newcastle, whose son, the Earl of Lincoln, afterwards a member of Lord Aberdeen's Cabinet during the Crimean War, had been his schoolmate at Eton and Oxford, and his intimate friend; to return to England and to contest the representation of Newark in Parliament. In accordance with this summons he hurried home.

Let us review the national situation. It was a time of general alarm and uncertainty, from political unrest, commercial stagnation, and devastating pestilence. "The terrors of the time begat a hundred forms of strange fanaticism; and among men who were not fanatics there was a deep and wide conviction that national judgments were overtaking national sins, and that the only hope of safety for England lay in a return to that practical recognition of religion in the political sphere at the proudest moments of English history. 'The beginning and the end of what is the matter with us in these days,' wrote Carlyle, 'is that we have forgotten God.'"

England was in a condition of great political excitement and expectancy. One of the greatest battles in Parliamentary history had just been fought and won by the people. The Reform Bill, which admitted large classes, hitherto unrepresented, to the right of citizenship, had passed, after a long struggle, during which law and order were defied and riots prevailed in various parts of the kingdom.

The King clearly perceiving that the wish of the people could no longer be disregarded with safety, and heedless of the advice of the aristocracy, gave his assent to the measure. This bill, which became a law June 7, 1832, "transformed the whole of the Electoral arrangements of the United Kingdom." It was demanded that the King be present in the House of Lords to witness the ceremony of the subjugation of his crown and peers, as it was deemed, but the King, feeling he had yielded enough to the popular will, refused. Walpole, in his history, writes: "King and Queen sat sullenly apart in their palace. Peer and country gentleman moodily awaited the ruin of their country and the destruction of their property. Fanaticism still raved at the wickedness of a people; the people, clamoring for work, still succumbed before the mysterious disease which was continually claiming more and more victims. But the nation cared not for the sullenness of the Court, the forebodings of the landed classes, the ravings of the pulpit, or even the mysterious operations of a new plague. The deep gloom that had overshadowed the land had been relieved by one single ray. The victory had been won. The bill had become law."

The first reformed House of Commons, after the passage of the terrible Reform Bill, met and was looked upon by some of the friends of Reform with fond hopes and expectations, and by others, the Tories, with fear and apprehension. The poor looked upon the Reform Bill as a measure for their redemption, and the landed proprietors regarded it as the first sign of departed national greatness. Both classes were disappointed. It neither revived business nor despoiled owners. The result was a surprise to politicians of both parties. The Reformers did not, as was anticipated, carry their extreme measures, and the Tories did not realize the great losses they expected. While the Ministry preserved its power and even obtained some victories in England and Scotland, it sustained serious defeats in Ireland. In England many earnest and popular friends of Reform were defeated in the election, and some counties, among them Bristol, Stamford, Hertford, Norwich and Newark, were pronounced against the Ministry.

The Duke of Newcastle, who was one of the chief potentates of the high Tory party, and had lost his control of Newark in 1831, by the election of a Radical, was determined to regain it. He regarded it as his right to be represented in the House of Commons, or that Newark should elect whom he nominated. And he had propounded the memorable political maxim, "Have I not a right to do what I like with my own?" The Duke wanted a capable candidate to help him regain his ascendency. His son, Lord Lincoln, here came to his aid. He had heard the remarkable speech of his friend, Mr. Gladstone, in the Oxford Union, against the Reform Bill, and had written home regarding him, that "a man had uprisen in Israel." At his suggestion the Duke invited the young graduate of Oxford to run as the Tory candidate for a seat in Parliament from Newark. The wisdom of this selection for the accomplishment of the purpose in view, was fully demonstrated.

His personal appearance at this time may be thus described: He was somewhat robust. His youthful face bore none of those deep furrows which have rendered his countenance so remarkable in maturer years. But there was the same broad intellectual forehead, the massive nose, the same anxious eyes and the earnest enthusiasm of later years. His look was bright and thoughtful and his bearing attractive. He was handsome and possessed a most intelligent and expressive countenance. Says his biographer, Mr. Russell: "William Ewart Gladstone was now twenty-two years old, with a physical constitution of unequalled vigor, the prospect of ample fortune, great and varied knowledge, and a natural tendency to political theorization, and an inexhaustible copiousness and readiness of speech. In person he was striking and attractive, with strongly marked features, a pale complexion, abundance of dark hair and eyes of piercing lustre. People who judged only by his external aspect considered that he was delicate."

Young Gladstone found two opponents contesting with him to represent Newark in Parliament, W.F. Handley and Sergeant Wilde, afterwards Lord Chancellor Truro. The latter was an advanced Liberal and had unsuccessfully contested the borough in 1829 and 1830, and had in consideration of his defeat received from his sympathetic friends a piece of plate inscribed: "By his ardent friends, the Blue electors of the borough, who by their exertions and sufferings in the cause of independence, largely conduced to awaken the attention of the nation to the necessity of Reform in Parliament. Upon this humble token of respect (contributed in the hour of defeat) the Blue electors of Newark inscribe their sense of the splendid ability, unwearied perseverance, and disinterested public spirit displayed by Sergeant Wilde in maintaining the two contests of 1829 and 1830, in order to emancipate the borough from political thraldoms, and restore to its inhabitants the free exercise of their long-lost rights." But Sergeant Wilde was more successful the following year, 1831, when the "Reform fever" was at its height, and defeated the Duke of Newcastle's nominee and became member of the House of Commons for the borough. These facts made the coming election, which followed the passage of the Reform Bill, of unusual interest, to those concerned, and the struggle would be of a close and determined character.

Mr. Gladstone entered upon the contest with his experienced, able and popular antagonist, with much against him, for he was young, unknown and untried; but his youth and personal appearance and manly bearing were in his favor, and these, with his eloquence and ready wit, gained for him many friends. His speeches demonstrated that he lacked neither arguments, nor words wherewith to clothe them. He needed, however, to call into requisition all his abilities, for Sergeant Wilde was a powerful antagonist, and had no thought of being displaced by his youthful opponent, "a political stripling," as he called him, without a desperate struggle. But Mr. Gladstone had behind him the ducal influence and the support of the Red Club, so he entered upon the contest with energy and enthusiasm.

The young Tory's first election address was delivered upon this occasion. It was dated October 9th, 1832, was all such an address should be, and was addressed, "To the worthy and independent electors of the borough of Newark." It began by saying that he was bound in his opinions by no man and no party, but that he deprecated the growing unreasonable and indiscriminating desire for change then so common, but confessed that labor has a right to "receive adequate remuneration." On the question of human slavery, then greatly agitated, he remarked, "We are agreed that both the physical and the moral bondage of the slave are to be abolished. The question is as to the *order*, and the order only; now Scripture attacks the moral evil *before* the corporal one, the corporal one *through* the moral one, and I am content with the order which Scripture has established." He saw insurmountable obstacles against immediate emancipation, one of which was that the negro would exchange the evil now affecting him for greater ones—for a relapse into deeper debasement, if not for bloodshed and internal war.

He therefore advocated a system of Christian education, to make the negro slaves fit for emancipation and to prepare them for freedom, Then, he argued, without bloodshed and the violation of property rights, and with unimpaired benefit to the negro, the desirable end might be reached in the utter extinction of slavery.

Of this appropriate address, so important in the light of coming events, we quote two paragraphs in full. In speaking of existing evils and the remedies for them, he observed: "For the mitigation of these evils, we must, I think, look not only to

Richard B. Cook

particular measures, but to the restoration of sounder general principles. I mean especially that principle on which alone the incorporation of Religion with the State in our Constitution can be defended; that the duties of governors are strictly and peculiarly religious; and that legislatures, like individuals, are bound to carry throughout their acts the spirit of the high truths they have acknowledged. Principles are now arrayed against our institutions; and not by truckling nor by temporizing—not by oppression nor corruption—but by principles they must be met.

"And now, gentlemen, as regards the enthusiasm with which you have rallied round your ancient flag, and welcomed the humble representative of those principles whose emblem it is, I trust that neither the lapse of time nor the seductions of prosperity can ever efface it from my memory. To my opponents, my acknowledgments are due for the good humor and kindness with which they have received me; and while I would thank my friends for their jealous and unwearied exertions in my favor, I briefly but emphatically assure them, that if promises be an adequate foundation of confidence, or experience a reasonable ground of calculation, our victory *is sure*"

The new candidate for Parliamentary honors was "heckled," as it is called, at the hustings, or was interrupted continually while speaking, and questioned by his opponents as to the circumstances of his candidature, his father's connection with slavery, and his own views of capital punishment. From his first appearance in Newark, Mr. Gladstone had been subjected to these examinations and he stood the ordeal well and answered prudently. An instance of this is given. A Radical elector, Mr. Gillson, asked the young Tory candidate if he was the Duke of Newcastle's nominee, and was met by Mr. Gladstone demanding the questioner's definition of the term "nominee." Mr. Gillson replied that he meant a person sent by the Duke of Newcastle to be pushed down the throats of the voters whether they would or not. But Mr. Gladstone was equal to the occasion, and said according to that definition he was not the nominee of the Duke, but came to Newark by the invitation of the Red Club, than whom none were more respectable and intelligent.

This same Red Club was Conservative, and promised to Mr. Gladstone, the thorough Conservative candidate, 650 votes, the whole number within its ranks. He also received the promise of 240 votes of other electors. This was known before the election, so that the result was confidently predicted. On the 11th of December, 1832, the "nomination" was held and the polling or election was held on the two following days, and Mr. Gladstone was chosen by a considerable majority, the votes being, Gladstone, 882; Handley, 793; Wilde, 719. Sergeant Wilde was defeated.

During the public discussions before the election Mr. Gladstone was placed at a great disadvantage. There were three candidates to be heard from and his speech was to be the last in order. Sergeant Wilde made a very lengthy speech, which exhausted the patience of his hearers, who had already stood for nearly seven hours, and showed disinclination to listen to another three hours' address, which, from Mr. Gladstone's talents, they were far from thinking impossible. The Sergeant was condemned for occupying the attention of the electors for such an inordinate length of time, but this did not prevent a scene of outrageous noise and uproar when the Tory candidate rose to speak. The important topic was slavery, but Mr. Gladstone had not proceeded far when the hooting and hissing drowned his voice so that he found it impossible to proceed. When a show of hands was demanded it was declared in favor of Mr. Handley and Sergeant Wilde, but when the election came, it was Mr. Gladstone who triumphed, as has been seen, and who was sent to Parliament as the member from Newark.

In speaking of the manner in which the Parliamentary elections are conducted, an English writer says: "Since 1832, few of those scenes of violence, and even of bloodshed, which formerly distinguished Parliamentary elections in many English boroughs, have been witnessed. Some of these lawless outbreaks were doubtless due to the unpopularity of the

Richard B. Cook

candidates forced upon the electors; but even in the largest towns—where territorial influence had little sway—riots occurred upon which we look back with doubtful amazement. Men holding strong political views have ceased to enforce those views by the aid of brickbats and other dangerous missiles. Yet at the beginning of the present century such arguments were very popular. And to the violence which prevailed was added the most unblushing bribery. Several boroughs, long notorious for extensive bribery, have since been disfranchised. The practice, however, extended to most towns in the kingdom, though it was not always carried on in the same open manner. By a long established custom, a voter at Hull received a donation of two guineas, or four for a plumper. In Liverpool men were openly paid for their votes; and Lord Cochrane stated in the House of Commons that, after his return for Honiton, he sent the town-crier round the borough to tell the voters to go to the chief banker for £10 10s. each. The great enlargement of the constituencies, secured by the Reform Bill of 1832, did much to put an end to this disgraceful condition of things; but to a wider political enlightenment also, some portion of the credit for such a result must be attributed."

What the friends and foes of the new Tory member for Newark thought of his successful canvass and election, it is interesting to learn. When Mr. Gladstone entered upon the contest the question was frequently put, "Who is Mr. Gladstone?" And it was answered, "He is the son of the friend of Mr. Canning, the great Liverpool merchant. He is, we understand, not more than four or five and twenty, but he has won golden opinions from all sorts of people, and promises to be an ornament to the House of Commons." And a few days after his election he addressed a meeting of the Constitutional Club, at Nottingham, when a Conservative journal made the first prophecy as to his future great political fame, saying: "He will one day be classed amongst the most able statesmen in the British Senate." The impression his successful contest made upon the late friends of his school-days may be learned from the following: A short time before the election Arthur Hallam, writing of his friend, "the old *W.E.G.*," says: "I shall be very glad if he gets in.... We want such a man as that. In some things he is likely to be obstinate and prejudiced; but he has a fine fund of high, chivalrous Tory sentiment, and a tongue, moreover, to let it loose with." And after the election he exclaims: "And Gladstone has turned out the Sergeant!... What a triumph for him. He has made his reputation by it; all that remains is to keep up to it."

That one of Mr. Gladstone's Liberal opponents was impressed by his talent and character is shown by the following lines of "descriptive prophecy, perhaps more remarkable for good feeling than for good poetry:"

> "Yet on one form, whose ear can ne'er refuse
> The Muses' tribute, for he lov'd the Muse,
> (And when the soul the gen'rous virtues raise,
> A friendly Whig may chant a Tory's praise,)
> Full many a fond expectant eye is bent
> Where Newark's towers are mirror'd in the Trent.
> Perchance ere long to shine in senates first,
> If manhood echo what his youth rehears'd,
> Soon Gladstone's brows will bloom with greener bays
> Than twine the chaplet of the minstrel's lays;
> Nor heed, while poring o'er each graver line,
> The far, faint music of a flute like mine.
> His was no head contentedly which press'd
> The downy pillow in obedient rest,
> Where lazy pilots, with their canvas furl'd,
> Let up the Gades of their mental world;
> His was no tongue which meanly stoop'd to wear
> The guise of virtue, while his heart was bare;
> But all he thought through ev'ry action ran;
> God's noblest work—I've known one honest man."

Mr. Gladstone spoke at Newark in company with his friend, the Earl of Lincoln, shortly after his election, when another favorable testimony was given, and his address spoken of as "a manly, eloquent speech, replete with sound constitutional sentiments, high moral feeling, and ability of the most distinguished order."

In commenting upon the result of the election a representative of the press of Newark wrote: "We have been told there was no reaction against the Ministry, no reaction in favor of Conservative principles. The delusion has now vanished, and made room for sober reason and reflection. The shadow satisfies no longer, and the return of Mr. Gladstone, to the discomfiture of the learned Sergeant and his friends, has restored the town of Newark to the high rank which it formerly held in the estimation of the friends of order and good government. We venture to predict that the losing candidate in this contest has suffered so severely that he will never show his face in Newark on a similar occasion."

But Mr. Gladstone had made bitter political enemies already, who were not at all reconciled to his election, nor pleased with him. That they were not at all slow to express unbecomingly their bitterness against him, because of their unexpected defeat, the following shows from the *Reflector*: "Mr. Gladstone is the son of Gladstone of Liverpool, a person who (we are speaking of the father) had amassed a large fortune by West India dealings. In other words, a great part of his gold has sprung from the blood of black slaves. Respecting the youth himself— a person fresh from college, and whose mind is as much like a sheet of white foolscap as possible—he was utterly unknown. He came recommended by no claim in the world *except the will of the Duke*. The Duke nodded unto Newark, and Newark sent back the man, or rather the boy of his choice. What! Is this to be, now that the Reform Bill has done its work? Are sixteen hundred men still to bow down to a wooden-headed lord, as the people of Egypt used to do to their beasts, to their reptiles, and their ropes of onions? There must be something wrong—something imperfect. What is it? What is wanting? Why, the Ballot! If there be a doubt of this (and we believe there is a doubt even amongst intelligent men) the tale of Newark must set the question at rest. Sergeant Wilde was met on his entry into the town by almost the whole population. He was greeted everywhere, cheered everywhere. He was received with delight by his friends and with good and earnest wishes for his success by his nominal foes. The voters for Gladstone went up to that candidate's booth (the slave-driver, as they called him) with Wilde's colors. People who had before voted for Wilde, on being asked to give their suffrage said, 'We cannot, we dare not. We have lost half our business, and shall lose the rest if we go against the Duke. We would do anything in our power for Sergeant Wilde and for the cause, but we cannot starve!' Now what say ye, our merry men, touching the Ballot?"

However Mr. Gladstone had won as we have seen the golden opinions of many, and the dreams of his more youthful days were realized when he was sent to represent the people in the House of Commons.

On the 29th of January, 1833, the first Reformed Parliament met, and William E. Gladstone, as the member from Newark, took his seat for the first time in "an assembly which he was destined to adorn, delight and astonish for more than half a century, and over which for a great portion of that period, he was to wield an unequalled and a paramount authority." There were more than three hundred new members in the House of Commons. Lord Althorp led the Whigs, who were largely in the majority and the Tories constituted a compact minority under the skillful leadership of Sir Robert Peel, while the Irish members who were hostile to the ministry followed O'Connell. On the 5th of February the king attended and delivered the speech from the throne in person. This Parliamentary session was destined to become one of the most memorable in history for the importance of the subjects discussed and disposed of, among them the social condition of Ireland, the position of the Irish church, the discontent and misery of the poor in England, and slavery in the British colonies; and for the fact that it was the first Parliament in which William E. Gladstone sat and took part.

There was no reference made to the subject of slavery in the

Richard B. Cook

speech from the throne, but the ministry resolved to consider it. Mr. Stanley, the Colonial Secretary, afterwards fourteenth Earl of Derby and Prime Minister, brought forth, May 14th, 1833, a series of resolutions in favor of the extinction of slavery in the British colonies. "All children of slaves, born after the passage of the Act, and all children of six years old and under, were declared free. But the rest of the slaves were to serve a sort of apprenticeship—three-fourths of their time was for a certain number of years to remain at the disposal of the masters; the other fourth was their own, to be paid for at a fixed rate of wages." The planters were to be duly compensated out of the national treasury.

It was during the discussion of these resolutions that Mr. Gladstone made his maiden speech in Parliament. It was made in answer to what seemed a personal challenge by Lord Howick, Ex-Under Secretary for the colonies, who, opposing gradual emancipation, referred to an estate in Demerara, owned by Mr. Gladstone's father, for the purpose of showing that great destruction of life had taken place in the West Indies owing to the manner in which the slaves were worked. In reply to this Mr. Gladstone said that he would meet some of Lord Howick's statements with denials and others with explanations. He admitted that he had a pecuniary interest in it as a question of justice, of humanity, and of religion. The real cause of the decrease, he said, was owing, not to the increased cultivation of sugar, but to the very large proportion of Africans upon the estate. When it came into his father's possession it was so weak, owing to the large number of negroes upon it, that he was obliged to add two hundred more people to the gang. It was well known that negroes were imported into Demarara and Trinidad up to a later period than into any of the colonies; and he should at a proper time, be able to prove that the decrease on his father's plantation, Vreeden Hoop, was among the old Africans, and that there was an increase going on in the Creole population, which would be a sufficient answer to the charges preferred. The quantity of sugar produced was small compared to that produced on other estates. The cultivation of cotton in

Demarara had been abandoned, and that of coffee much diminished, and the people engaged in these sources of production had been employed in the cultivation of sugar. Besides in Demarara the labor of the same number of negroes, distributed over the year, would produce in that colony a certain quantity of sugar with less injury to the people, than negroes could produce in other colonies, working only at the stated periods of crops.

He was ready to concede that the cultivation was of a more injurious character than others; and he would ask, Were there not certain employments in other countries more destructive of life than others? He would only instance those of painting and working in lead mines, both of which were well known to have that tendency. The noble lord attempted to impugn the character of the gentleman acting as manager of his father's estates; and in making the selection he had surely been most unfortunate; for there was not a person in the colony more remarkable for humanity and the kind treatment of his slaves than Mr. Maclean. Mr. Gladstone, in concluding this able defense of his father, said, that he held in his hand two letters from Mr. Maclean, in which he spoke in the kindest terms of the negroes under his charge; described their state of happiness, content and healthiness—their good conduct and the infrequency of severe punishment—and recommended certain additional comforts, which he said the slaves well deserved.

On the 3d of June, on the resumption of the debate on the abolition of slavery, Mr. Gladstone again addressed the House. He now entered more fully into the charges which Lord Howick had brought against the management of his father's estates in Demarara, and showed their groundlessness. When he had discussed the existing aspect of slavery in Trinidad, Jamaica and other places, he proceeded to deal with the general question. He confessed with shame and pain that cases of wanton cruelty had occurred in the colonies, but added that they would always exist, particularly under the system of slavery; and this was unquestionably a substantial reason why the British Legislature and public should set themselves in good earnest to provide for its extinction; but he maintained that these instances of cruelty could easily be explained by the West Indians, who represented them as rare and isolated cases, and who maintained that the ordinary relation of master and slave was one of kindliness and not of hostility. He deprecated cruelty, and he deprecated slavery, both of which were abhorrent to the nature of Englishmen; but, conceding these things, he asked, "Were not Englishmen to retain a right to their own honestly and legally-acquired property?" But the cruelty did not exist, and he saw no reason for the attack which had recently been made upon the West India interest. He hoped the House would make a point to adopt the principle of compensation, and to stimulate the slave to genuine and spontaneous industry. If this were not done, and moral instruction were not imparted to the slaves, liberty would prove a curse instead of a blessing to them. Touching upon the property question, and the proposed plans for emancipation, Mr. Gladstone said that the House might consume its time and exert its wisdom in devising these plans, but without the concurrence of the Colonial Legislatures success would be hopeless. He thought there was excessive wickedness in any violent interference under the present circumstances. They were still in the midst of unconcluded inquiries, and to pursue the measure then under discussion, at that moment, was to commit an act of great and unnecessary hostility toward the island of Jamaica. "It was the duty of the House to place as broad a distinction as possible between the idle and the industrious slaves, and nothing could be too strong to secure the freedom of the latter; but, with respect to the idle slaves, no period of emancipation could hasten their improvement. If the labors of the House should be conducted to a satisfactory issue, it would redound to the honor of the nation, and to the reputation of his Majesty's Ministers, whilst it would be delightful to the West India planters themselves—for they must feel that to hold in bondage their fellow-men must always involve the greatest responsibility. But let not any man think of carrying this measure by force. England rested her power not upon physical force, but upon her principles, her intellect and virtue; and if this great measure were not placed on a fair basis, or were conducted by violence, he should lament it, as a signal for the ruin of the Colonies and the downfall of the Empire." The attitude of Mr. Gladstone, as borne out by the tenor of his speech, was not one of hostility to emancipation, though he was undoubtedly unfavorable to an immediate and indiscriminate enfranchisement. He demanded, moreover, that the interests of the planters should be duly regarded.

The result of the consideration of these resolutions in the House of Commons was that human slavery in the British Colonies was abolished, and the sum of twenty million pounds, or one hundred million dollars was voted to compensate the slave-owners for their losses. Thus was the work begun by Wilberforce finally crowned with success.

It is an interesting question how Mr. Gladstone's first efforts in Parliament were received. Among his friends his speech was anticipated with lively interest. That morning he was riding in Hyde Park, on his gray Arabian mare, "his hat, narrow-brimmed, high up on the centre of his head, sustained by a crop of thick curly hair." He was pointed out to Lord Charles Russell by a passer-by who said, "That is Gladstone. He is to make his maiden speech to-night. It will be worth hearing."

From the first he appears to have favorably impressed the members of the House. Modest in demeanor, earnest in manner, and fluent in speech, he at once commanded the respect and attention of his fellow-members.

And here is a later testimony as to the early impression made upon his colleagues and contemporaries, when he was twenty-nine years of age, erroneously stated as thirty-five: "Mr. Gladstone, the member for Newark, is one of the most rising young men on the Tory side of the House. His party expect great things from him; and certainly, when it is remembered that his age is only thirty-five, the success of the Parliamentary efforts he has already made justifies their expectations. He is well informed on most of the subjects which usually occupy the attention of the Legislature; and he is happy in turning his information to good account. He is ready on all occasions, which he deems fitting ones, with a speech in favor of the policy advocated by the party with whom he acts. His extempore resources are ample. Few men in the House can improvise better. It does not appear to cost him an effort to speak.... He is a man of very considerable talent, but has nothing approaching to genius. His abilities are much more the result of an excellent education and of mature study than of any prodigality of nature in the distribution of her mental gifts. *I have no idea that he will ever acquire the reputation of a great statesman. His views are not sufficiently profound or enlarged for that; his celebrity in the House of Commons will chiefly depend on his readiness and dexterity as a debater, in conjunction with the excellence of his elocution, and the gracefulness of his manner when speaking....* His style is polished, but has no appearance of the effect of previous preparation. He displays considerable acuteness in replying to an opponent; he is quick in his perception of anything vulnerable in the speech to which he replies, and happy in laying the weak point bare to the gaze of the House. He now and then indulges in sarcasm, which is, in most cases, very felicitous. He is plausible even when most in error. When it suits himself or his party he can apply himself with the strictest closeness to the real point at issue; when to evade the point is deemed most politic, no man can wander from it more widely."

How far these estimates were true we leave to the reader to determine, after the perusal of his life, and in the light of subsequent events.

Mr. Gladstone, after his maiden speech, took an active part in the business of the House during the remainder of the session of 1833. He spoke upon the question of bribery and corruption at Liverpool, and July 8th made an elaborate speech on the Irish Church Temporalities Bill. The condition of Ireland was then, as now, one of the most urgent questions confronting the Ministry. Macaulay "solemnly declared that he would rather live in the midst of many civil wars that he had read of than in some parts of Ireland at this moment." Sydney Smith humorously described "those Irish Protestants whose shutters are bullet-proof; whose dinner-table is regularly spread out with knife, fork, and cocked pistol; salt-cellar and powder-flask; who sleep in sheet-iron nightcaps; who have fought so often and so nobly before their scullery-door, and defended the parlor passage as bravely as Leonidas defended the pass of Thermopylae." Crime was rife and to remedy the serious state of affairs a stringent Coercion Bill was introduced by the government. Mr. Gladstone voted silently for the bill which became a law.

The other bill introduced was that upon the Irish Church, and proposed the reduction of the number of Protestant Episcopal Bishops in Ireland and the curtailment of the income of the Church. This bill Mr. Gladstone opposed in a speech, and he voted against it, but it was passed.

It was in the following session that Mr. Hume introduced his "'Universities Admission Bill,' designed to enable Nonconformists of all kinds to enter the universities, by removing the necessity of subscribing to the thirty-nine articles at matriculation." In the debate that followed Mr. Gladstone soon gave evidence that he knew more about the subject than did the author of the bill. In speaking against the bill, he said in part, "The whole system of the university and of its colleges, both in study and in discipline, aimed at the formation of a moral character, and that aim could not be attained if every student were at liberty to exclude himself from the religious training of the place." And in reply to a remark made by Lord Palmerston in reference to the students going "from wine to prayers, and from prayers to wine," Mr. Gladstone replied, he did not believe that in their most convivial moments they were unfit to enter the house of prayer. This bill was also passed.

It might have been expected that Mr. Gladstone's active participation in the debates in the House of Commons, and the practical ability and debating power he manifested would not escape the attention of the leaders of his party. But the recognition of his merit came sooner than could have been expected. It became evident, towards the close of 1834 that the downfall of the Liberal Ministry was near at hand. Lord Althorp, who had kept the Liberals together, was transferred to the House of Lords, and the growing unpopularity of the Whigs did the rest. The Ministry under Lord Melbourne was dismissed by the king, and a new Cabinet formed by Sir Robert Peel. The new Premier offered Mr. Gladstone the office of Junior Lord of the Treasury, which was accepted.

Truly has an eminent writer said: "When a Prime Minister in difficulties, looking about for men to fill the minor offices of his administration, sees among his supporters a clever and comely young man, eloquent in speech, ready in debate, with a safe seat, an ample fortune, a high reputation at the university, and a father who wields political influence in an important constituency, he sees a Junior Lord of the Treasury made ready to his hand."

Appealing to his constituents at Newark, who, two years before, had sent him to Parliament, he was re-elected. Mr. Handley having retired, Sergeant Wilde was elected with Mr. Gladstone without opposition. Mr. Gladstone was "chaired," or drawn by horses through the town, seated on a chair, after the election, and then addressed the assembled people to the number of 6,000, his speech being received with "deafening cheers."

Shortly after Parliament assembled, Mr. Gladstone was promoted to the office of Under-Secretary for the Colonies. His official chief was Lord Aberdeen, afterwards Prime Minister; and thus began a relation which was destined to greatly affect the destinies of both statesmen.

Mr. Gladstone gave ample proof in his new office of his great abilities and untiring energies.

In March he presented to the House his first bill, which was for the better regulation of the transportation of passengers in merchant vessels to the continent and to the Islands of North America. This bill, which contained many humane provisions, was very favorably received. The new Parliament, which met February 10, 1835, contained a considerable Liberal majority. The old House of Commons had been destroyed by fire during the recess, and the new Commons reassembled in the chamber which had been the House of Lords, and for the first time there was a gallery for reporters in the House.

"A standing order still existed, which forbade the publication of the debates, but the reporters' gallery was a formal and visible recognition of the people's right to know what their representatives were doing in their name." However, the new Ministry was but short-lived, for Sir Robert Peel resigned April 8th, and Mr. Gladstone retired with his chief.

Mr. Gladstone spent the days of his retirement from ministerial office partly in study, and partly in recreation. Being free to follow the bent of his own inclinations, he ordered his life according to his own ideals. He lived in chambers at the Albany, pursued the same steady course of work, proper recreation and systematic devotion, which he had marked out at Oxford. He freely went into society, dined out frequently, and took part in musical parties, much to the edification of his friends who were charmed with the beauty and cultivation of his rich baritone. His friend Monckton Milnes had established himself in London and collected around him a society of young men, interested in politics and religion, and whom he entertained Sunday evenings. But this arrangement "unfortunately," as Mr. Milnes said, excluded from these gatherings the more serious members, such as Acland and Gladstone. Mr. Milnes expressed his opinion of such self-exclusion in these words: "I really think when people keep Friday as a fast, they might make a feast of Sunday." But Mr. Gladstone evidently was not of this opinion, and remained away from these Lord's Day parties. However at other times he met his friends, and received them at his own rooms in the Albany, and on one memorable occasion entertained Wordsworth at breakfast and a few admirers of this distinguished guest.

Mr. Gladstone's relaxations were occasional, and the most of his time was devoted to his Parliamentary duties and study. His constant companions were Homer and Dante, and he at this time, it is recorded, read the whole of St. Augustine, in twenty-two octavo volumes. He was a constant attendant upon public worship at St. James', Piccadilly, and Margaret Chapel, and a careful critic of sermons. At the same time he diligently applied himself to the work of a private member of the House of Commons, working on committees and taking constant part in debate.

In 1836 the question of slavery again came up before Parliament. This time the question was as to the working of the system of negro apprenticeship, which had taken the place of slavery. It was asserted that the system was only slavery under another name. He warmly and ably defended again the West Indian planters. He pleaded that many of the planters were humane men, and defended also the honor of his relatives connected with the traffic so much denounced, when it was assailed. He contended that while the evils of the system had been exaggerated, all mention of its advantages had been carefully withheld. The condition of the negroes was improving. He deprecated the attempt made to renew and perpetuate the system of agitation at the expense of candor and truth. He also at this time spoke on support of authority and order in the government of Canada, and on Church Rates, dwelling upon the necessity of national religion to the security of a state. Mr. Gladstone was not only a Tory but a High Churchman.

King William IV died June 20, 1837, and was succeeded by Queen Victoria. A general election ensued. The Parliament, which had been prorogued by the young queen in person, was dissolved on the 17th of July. Mr. Gladstone, without his consent, was nominated to represent Manchester in the House, but was re-elected for Newark without opposition. He then turned his steps towards Scotland, "to see what grouse he could persuade into his bag." The new Parliament met October 20th, but no business of importance came before it until after the Christmas holidays.

In 1838 a bill was presented in both Houses of Parliament for the immediate abolition of negro apprenticeship. Many harrowing details of the cruelties practiced were cited. Mr. Gladstone returned to the championship of the planters with increased power and success. His long, eloquent and powerful speech of March 30th, although on the unpopular side of the question, is regarded as having so greatly enhanced his reputation as to bring him to the front rank among Parliamentary debaters. Having impassionately defended the planters from the exaggerated charges made against them, he further said: "You consumed forty-five millions of pounds of cotton in 1837 which proceeded from free labor; and, proceeding from slave labor, three hundred and eighteen millions of pounds! And this, while the vast regions of India afford the means of obtaining at a cheaper rate, and by a slight original outlay, to facilitate transport, all that you can require. If, Sir, the complaints against the general body of the West Indians had been substantiated, I should have deemed it an unworthy artifice to attempt diverting the attention of the House from the question immediately at issue, by merely proving that delinquencies existed in other quarters; but feeling as I do that those charges have been overthrown in debate, I think myself entitled and bound to show how capricious are the honorable gentlemen in the distribution of their sympathies among those different objects which call for their application."

Mr. Gladstone, "having turned the tables upon his opponents," concluded by demanding justice, and the motion before the House was rejected.

About one month later Rev. Samuel Wilberforce, afterwards Bishop of Oxford, and of Winchester, wrote to Mr. Gladstone: "It would be an affectation in you, which you are above, not to know that few young men have the weight you have in the House of Commons, and are gaining rapidly throughout the country. Now I do not wish to urge you to consider this as a talent for the use of which you must render an account, for so I know you do esteem it, but what I want to urge upon you is that you should calmly look far before you; see the degree of weight and influence to which you may fairly, if God spares your life and powers, look forward in future years, and thus act *now* with a view to *then*. There is no height to which you may not fairly rise in this country. If it pleases God to spare us violent convulsions and the loss of our liberties, you may at a future day wield the whole government of this land; and if this should be so, of what extreme moment will your *past steps* then be to the real usefulness of your high station.... Almost all our public men act from the merest expediency.... I would have you view yourself as one who may become the head of all the better feelings of this country, the maintainer of its Church and of its liberties, and who must now be fitting himself for this high vocation.... I think my father's life so beautifully shows that a deep and increasing personal religion must be the root of that firm and unwearied consistency in right, which I have ventured thus to press upon you."

Mr. Gladstone began his Parliamentary life as a Tory. Later he developed into a Liberal, a Radical, and yet there is not one who conscientiously doubts his utter honesty. His life has been that of his century—progressive, liberal, humanitarian in its trend.

CHAPTER IV

BOOK ON CHURCH AND STATE

We have now followed Mr. Gladstone in his course until well on the way in his political career, and yet he is but twenty-eight years of age. His personal appearance in the House of Commons at this early stage of his Parliamentary life is thus described: "Mr. Gladstone's appearance and manners are much in his favor. He is a fine looking man. He is about the usual height and of good figure. His countenance is mild and pleasant, and has a highly intellectual expression. His eyes are clear and quick. His eyebrows are dark and rather prominent. There is not a dandy in the House but envies what Truefit would call his 'fine head of jet-black hair.' It is always carefully parted from the crown downwards to his brow, where it is tastefully shaded. His features are small and regular, and his complexion must be a very unworthy witness if he does not possess an abundant stock of health.

"Mr. Gladstone's gesture is varied, but not violent. When he rises he generally puts both his hands behind his back, and having there suffered them to embrace each other for a short time, he unclasps them and allows them to drop on either side. They are not permitted to remain long in that locality before you see them, again closed together and hanging down before him. Their reunion is not suffered to last for any length of time, Again a separation takes place, and now the right hand is seen moving up and down before him. Having thus exercised it a little, he thrusts it into the pocket of his coat, and then

Richard B. Cook

orders the left hand to follow its example. Having granted them a momentary repose there, they are again put into gentle motion, and in a few seconds they are seen reposing *vis-a-vis* on his breast. He moves his face and body from one direction to another, not forgetting to bestow a liberal share of his attention on his own party. He is always listened to with much attention by the House, and appears to be highly respected by men of all parties. He is a man of good business habits; of this he furnished abundant proof when Under-Secretary for the Colonies, during the short-lived administration of Robert Peel."

From this pen picture and other like notices of Mr. Gladstone he must, at that time, have attained great distinction and attracted a good deal of attention for one so young, and from that day to this he has commanded the attention not only of the British Senate and people, but of the world at large. And why? may we ask, unless because of his modest manner and distinguished services, his exalted ability and moral worth.

"The House of Commons was his ground," writes Justin McCarthy. "There he was always seen to the best advantage."

Nevertheless, Mr. Gladstone wrote with the same earnestness and ability with which he spoke. It was early in life that he distinguished himself as an author, as well as an orator and debater in the House of Commons. And it was most natural for him to write upon the subject of the Church, for not only his education led him to the consideration of such themes, but it was within his sphere as an English statesman, for the law of the land provided for the union of the Church and State. It was in 1838, when he was not thirty years of age, that he wrote his first book and stepped at once to the front rank as an author. He had ever been a staunch defender of the Established Church and his first appearance in literature was by a remarkable work in defense of the State Church entitled, "The State in its Relations with the Church." The treatise is thus dedicated: "Inscribed to the University of Oxford, tried and not found wanting through the vicissitudes of a thousand years; in the belief that she is providentially designed to be a fountain of blessings, spiritual, social and intellectual, to this and other countries, to present and future times; and in the hope that the temper of these pages may be found not alien from her own."

This first published book of Mr. Gladstone's was due to the perception that the *status* of the Church, in its connection with the secular power, was about to undergo the severe assaults of the opponents of the Union. There was growing opposition to the recognition of the Episcopal Church as the Church of the State and to taxation of people of other religious beliefs for its support; and this objection was to the recognition and support of any Church by the State. What is called the "American idea"—the entire separation of the Church and State—or as enunciated first by Roger Williams in 1636, in Rhode Island, that the magistrate should have authority in civil affairs only, was becoming more and more the doctrine of dissenters. Preparations were already being made for attacking the national establishment of religion, and with all the fervor springing from conviction and a deep-seated enthusiasm, he came forward to take part in the controversy on Church and State, and as a defender of the Established or Episcopal Church of England.

Some of the positions assumed in this work have since been renounced as untenable, but its ability as a whole, its breadth and its learning could not be denied. It then created a great sensation, and has since been widely discussed. After an examination and a defense of the theory of the connection between Church and State, Mr. Gladstone thus summarizes his principal reasons for the maintenance of the Church establishment:

"Because the Government stands with us in a paternal relation to the people, and is bound in all things not merely to consider their existing tastes, but the capabilities and ways of their improvement; because it has both an intrinsic competency and external means to amend and assist their choice; because to be in accordance with God's mind and will, it must have a religion, and because to be in accordance with its conscience, that religion must be the truth, as held by it under the most solemn and accumulated responsibilities; because this is the only sanctifying and preserving principle of society, as well as to the individual, that particular benefit, without which all others are worse than valueless; we must, therefore, disregard the din of political contention and the pressure of novelty and momentary motives, and in behalf of our regard to man, as well as of our allegiance to God, maintain among ourselves, where happily it still exists, the union between the Church and the State."

Dr. Russell in the following quotation not only accounts for this production from the pen, of Mr. Gladstone, but gives also an outline of the argument:

"Naturally and profoundly religious ... Mr. Gladstone conceived that those who professed the warmest regard for the Church of England and posed as her most strenuous defenders, were inclined to base their championship on mistaken grounds and to direct their efforts towards even mischievous ends. To supply a more reasonable basis for action and to lead this energy into more profitable channels were the objects which he proposed to himself in his treatise of 1838. The distinctive principle of the book was that the State had a conscience. This being admitted, the issue was this: whether the State in its best condition, has such a conscience as can take cognizance of religious truth and error, and in particular whether the State of the United Kingdom at that time was, or was not, so far in that condition as to be under an obligation to give an active and an exclusive support to the established religion of the country.

"The work attempted to survey the actual state of the relations between the State and the Church; to show from history the ground which had been defined for the National Church at the Reformation; and to inquire and determine whether the existing state of things was worth preserving and defending against encroachment from whatever quarter. This question it decided emphatically in the affirmative. Faithful to logic and to its theory, the book did not shrink from applying them to the external case of the Irish Church. It did not disguise the difficulties of the case, for the author was alive to the paradox which it involved. But the one master idea of the system, that the State as it then stood was capable in this age, as it had been in ages long gone by, of assuming beneficially a responsibility for the inculcation of a particular religion, carried him through all. His doctrine was that the Church, as established by law, was to be maintained for its truth; that this was the only principle in which it could be properly and permanently upheld; that this principle, if good in England, was good also for Ireland; that truth is of all possessions the most precious to the soul of man; and that to remove this priceless treasure from the view and the reach of the Irish people would be meanly to purchase their momentary favor at the expense of their permanent interests, and would be a high offense against our own sacred obligations."

We quote also from the opening chapter of the second volume of this work, which treats of the connection subsisting between the State of the United Kingdom and the Church of England and Ireland, and shows Mr. Gladstone's views at that period of his life upon the relations of the Church as affecting Ireland in particular. The passage also indicates the changes that have taken place in his mind since the time when he defended these principles. It also shows the style in which this remarkable book was written and enables us to compare, not only his opinions now and then, but his style in writing then with his style now.

"The Protestant legislature of the British Empire maintains in the possession of the Church property of Ireland the ministers of a creed professed, according to the parliamentary enumeration, of 1835, by one-ninth of its population, regarded with partial favor by scarcely another ninth, and disowned by the remaining seven. And not only does this anomaly meet us full in view, but we have also to consider and digest the fact, that the maintenance of this Church for near three centuries in Ireland has been contemporaneous with a system of partial and abusive government, varying in degree of culpability, but rarely, until of later years, when we have been forced to look at the subject and to feel it, to be exempted in common fairness from the reproach of gross inattention (to say the very least) to the interests of a noble but neglected people.

"But, however formidable at first sight the admissions, which I have no desire to narrow or to qualify, may appear, they in no way shake the foregoing arguments. They do not change the nature of truth and her capability and destiny to benefit mankind. They do not relieve Government of its responsibility, if they show that that responsibility was once unfelt and unsatisfied. They place the legislature of the country in the condition, as it were, of one called to do penance for past offences; but duty remains unaltered and imperative, and abates nothing of her demand on our services. It is undoubtedly competent, in a constitutional view, to the Government of this country to continue the present disposition of Church property in Ireland. It appears not too much to assume that our imperial legislature has been qualified to take, and has taken in point of fact, a sounder view of religious truth than the majority of the people of Ireland in their destitute and uninstructed state. We believe, accordingly, that that which we place before them is, whether they know it or not, calculated to be beneficial to them; and that if they know it not now, they will know it when it is presented to them fairly. Shall we, then, purchase their applause at the expense of their substantial, nay, their spiritual interests?

"It does, indeed, so happen that there are powerful motives on the other side concurring with that which has here been represented as paramount. In the first instance we are not called upon to establish a creed, but only to maintain an existing legal settlement, when our constitutional right is undoubted. In the second, political considerations tend strongly to recommend that maintenance. A common form of faith binds the Irish Protestants to ourselves, while they, upon the other hand, are fast linked to Ireland; and thus they supply the most natural bond of connection between the countries. But if England, by overthrowing their Church, should weaken their moral position, they would be no longer able, perhaps no longer willing, to counteract the desires of the majority tending, under the direction of their leaders (however, by a wise policy, revocable from that fatal course) to what is termed national independence. Pride and fear, on the one hand, are therefore bearing up against more immediate apprehension and difficulty on the other. And with some men these may be the fundamental considerations; but it may be doubted whether such men will not flinch in some stage of the contest, should its aspect at any moment become unfavorable."

Of course the opponents of Mr. Gladstone's views, as set forth in his book, strongly combated his theories. They replied that "the taxation of the State is equal upon all persons, and has for its object their individual, social and political welfare and safety; but that the taxation of one man for the support of his neighbor's religion does not come within the limits of such taxation, and is, in fact, unjust and inequitable."

It was no easy task for Mr. Gladstone, with all his parliamentary duties, to aspire to authorship, and carry his book through the press. In preparing for publication he passed through all the agonies of the author, but was nobly helped by his friend, James R. Hope, who afterwards became Mr. Hope-Scott, Q.C., who read and criticised his manuscript and saw the sheets through the press. Some of the letters from the young Defender of the Faith to his friend contain much that is worth preserving. We give some extracts.

He writes: "If you let them lie just as they are, turning the leaves one by one, I think you will not find the manuscript very hard to make out, though it is strangely cut in pieces and patched.

"I hope its general tendency will meet with your approval; but a point about which I am in doubt, and to which I request your particular attention, is, whether the work or some of the chapters are not so deficient in clearness and arrangement as to require being absolutely rewritten before they can with propriety be published.... Between my eyes and my business I fear it would be hard for me to re-write, but if I could put it into the hands of any other person who could, and who would extract from my papers anything worth having, that might do.

"As regards myself, if I go on and publish, I shall be quite prepared to find some persons surprised, but this, if it should prove so, cannot be helped. I shall not knowingly exaggerate anything; and when a man expects to be washed overboard he must tie himself with a rope to the mast.

"I shall trust to your friendship for frankness in the discharge of your irksome task. Pray make verbal corrections without scruple where they are needed."

Again: "I thank you most cordially for your remarks, and I rejoice to find you act so entirely in the spirit I had anticipated. I trust you will continue to speak with freedom, which is the best compliment as well as the best service you can render me.

"I think it very probable that you may find that V and VI require quite as rigorous treatment as II, and I am very desirous to set both my mind and eyes at liberty before I go to the Continent, which I can now hardly expect to do before the first week in September. This interval I trust would suffice unless you find that the other chapters stand in equal need.

"I entirely concur with your view regarding the necessity of care and of not grudging labor in a matter so important and so responsible as an endeavor to raise one of the most momentous controversies which has ever agitated human opinion,"

Again: "Thanks for your letter. I have been pretty hard at work, and have done a good deal, especially on V. Something yet remains. I must make inquiry about the law of excommunication.... I have made a very stupid classification, and have now amended it; instead of faith, discipline and practice, what I meant was the rule of faith, discipline, and the bearing of particular doctrines upon practice.

"I send back also I and II that you may see what I have done."

The work was successfully issued in the autumn of 1838, and passed rapidly through three editions. How it was received it would be interesting to inquire. While his friends applauded, even his opponents testified to the ability it displayed. On the authority of Lord Houghton, it is said that Sir Robert Peel, the young author's political leader, on receiving a copy as a gift from his follower, read it with scornful curiosity, and, throwing it on the floor, exclaimed with truly official horror: "With such a career before him, why should he write books? That young man will ruin his fine political career if he persists in writing trash like this." However, others gave the book a heartier reception. Crabb Robinson writes in his diary: "I went to Wordsworth this forenoon. He was ill in bed. I read Gladstone's book to him."

December 13, 1838, Baron Bunsen wrote: "Last night at eleven, when I came from the Duke, Gladstone's book was lying on my table, having come out at seven o'clock. It is a book of the time, a great event—the first book since Burke that goes to the bottom of the vital question; far above his party and his time. I sat up till after midnight, and this morning I continued until I had read the whole. Gladstone is the first man in England as to intellectual power, and he has heard higher tones than any one else in the land." And again to Dr. Arnold he writes in high praise of the book, but lamenting its author's entanglement in Tractarian traditions, adds: "His genius will soon free itself entirely and fly towards Heaven with its own wings."

Sir Henry Taylor wrote to the Poet Southey: "I am reading Gladstone's book, which I shall send you if he has not.... His party begin to think of him as the man who will one day be at their head and at the head of the government, and certainly no man of his standing has yet appeared who seems likely to stand in his way. Two wants, however, may lie across his political career—want of robust health and want of flexibility."

Cardinal Newman wrote: "Gladstone's book, as you see, is making a sensation." And again: "The *Times* is again at poor Gladstone. Really I feel as if I could do anything for him. I have not read his book, but its consequences speak for it. Poor fellow! it is so noble a thing."

Lord Macaulay, in the *Edinburgh Review*, April, 1839, in his well-known searching criticism, while paying high tribute to the author's talents and character, said: "We believe that we do him no more than justice when we say that his abilities and demeanor have obtained for him the respect and good will of all parties.... That a young politician should, in the intervals afforded by his Parliamentary avocations, have constructed and propounded, with much study and mental toil, an original theory, on a great problem in politics, is a circumstance which, abstracted from all considerations of the soundness or unsoundness of his opinions, must be considered as highly creditable to him. We certainly cannot wish that Mr. Gladstone's doctrine may become fashionable among public men. But we heartily wish that his laudable desire to penetrate beneath the surface of questions, and to arrive, by long and intent meditation, at the knowledge of great general laws, were much more fashionable than we at all expect it to become."

It was in this article, by Lord Macaulay, that the mow famous words occurred which former Conservative friends of Mr. Gladstone delight to recall in view of his change of political opinions: "The writer of this volume is a young man of unblemished character and of distinguished parliamentary talents; the rising hope of those stern and unbending Tories who follow, reluctantly and cautiously, a leader whose experience and eloquence are indispensable to them, but whose cautious temper and moderate opinions they abhor. It would not be strange if Mr. Gladstone were one of the most unpopular men in England."

Higginson writes: "The hope of the stern and unbending Tories has for years been the unquestioned leader of English Liberals, and though he may have been at times as unpopular as Macaulay could have predicted, the hostility has come mainly from the ranks of those who were thus early named as his friends. But whatever may have been Mr. Gladstone's opinions or affiliations, whoever may have been his friends or foes, the credit of surpassing ability has always been his."

It was remarked by Lord Macaulay that the entire theory of Mr. Gladstone's book rested upon one great fundamental proposition, namely, that the propagation of religious truth is one of the chief ends of government *as* government; and he proceeded to combat this doctrine. He granted that government was designed to protect our persons and our property, but declined to receive the doctrine of paternal government, until a government be shown that loved its subjects, as a father loves his child, and was as superior in intelligence to its subjects as a father was to his children. Lord Macaulay then demonstrated, by appropriate illustrations, the fallacy of the theory that every society of individuals with any power whatever, is under obligation as such society to profess a religion; and that there could be unity of action in large bodies without unity of religious views. Persecutions would naturally follow, or be justifiable in an association where Mr. Gladstone's views were paramount. It would be impossible to conceive of the circumstances in which it would be right to establish by law, as the one exclusive religion of the State, the religion of the minority. The religious teaching which the sovereign ought officially to countenance and maintain is that from which he, in his conscience, believes that the people will receive the most benefit with the smallest mixture of evil. It is not necessarily his own religious belief that he will select. He may prefer the doctrines of the Church of England to those of the Church of Scotland, but he would not force the former upon the inhabitants of Scotland. The critic raised no objections, though he goes on to state the conditions under which an established Church might be retained with advantage. There are many institutions which, being set up, ought not to be rudely pulled down. On the 14th of June, 1839, the question of National Education was introduced in the House of Commons by the Ministry of the day. Lord Stanley opposed the proposal of the government in a powerful speech, and offered an amendment to this effect: "That an address be presented to her Majesty to rescind the order in council for constituting the proposed Board of Privy Council." The position of the government was defended by Lord Morpeth, who, while he held his own views respecting the doctrines of the Roman Catholics and also respecting Unitarian tenets, he maintained that as long as the State thought it proper to employ Roman Catholic sinews, and to finger Unitarian gold, it could not refuse to extend to those by whom it so profited the blessings of education. Speeches were also made by Lord Ashley, Mr. Buller, Mr. O'Connell and others, and in the course of debate reference was freely made to Mr. Gladstone's book on Church and State. Finally Mr. Gladstone rose and remarked, that he would not flinch from a word he had uttered or written upon religious subjects, and claimed the right to contrast his principles, and to try results, in comparison with those professed by Lord John Russell, and to ascertain the effects of both upon the institutions of the country, so far as they operated upon the Established Church in England, in Scotland and in Ireland. It was at this time that a very remarkable scene was witnessed in the House. Turning upon Mr. O'Connell, who had expressed his great fondness for statistics, Mr. Gladstone said the use he had made of them reminded him of an observation of Mr. Canning's, "He had a great aversion to hear of a fact in debate, but what he most distrusted was a figure." He then proceeded to show the inadequacy of the figures presented by Mr. O'Connell. In reply to Lord Morpeth's declaration concerning the duty of the State to provide education for Dissenters so long as it fingered their gold, Mr. Gladstone said that if the State was to be regarded as having no other functions than that of representing the mere will of the people as to religious tenets, he admitted the truth of his principle, but not that the State could have a conscience. It was not his habit to revile religion in any form, but he asked what ground there was for restricting his lordship's reasoning to Christianity. He referred to the position held by the Jews upon this educational question, and read to the House an extract from a recent petition as follows: "Your petitioners feel the deepest gratitude for the expression of her Majesty's most gracious wish that the youth of the country should be religiously brought up, and the rights of conscience respected, while they earnestly hope that the education of the people, Jewish and Christian, will be sedulously connected with a due regard to the Holy Scriptures."

Mr. Gladstone very pertinently asked how the education of the Jewish people, who considered the New Testament an imposture, was "to be sedulously connected with a due regard to the Holy Scriptures," which consisted of the Old and New Testaments? To oblige the Jewish children to read the latter would be directly contrary to the views of the gentlemen on the other side of the House. He would have no child forced to do so, but he protested against paying money from the treasury of the State to men whose business it was to inculcate erroneous doctrines. The debate was concluded, and the government carried its motion by a very small majority. Two years later, when the Jews' Civil Disabilities Bill was before Parliament, Mr. Gladstone again took the unpopular side in the debate and opposed the Bill, which was carried in the House of Commons but defeated in the House of Lords.

Mr. Gladstone published, in 1840, another work, entitled "Church Principles Considered in their Results." It was supplementary to his former book in defense of Church and State, and was written "beneath the shades of Hagley," the house of Lord and Lady Lyttelton, and dedicated "in token of sincere affection" to the author's life-long friend and relative, Lord Lyttelton. He dwelt upon the leading moral characteristics of the English Episcopal Church, their intrinsic value and their adaptation to the circumstances of the times, and defined these characteristics to be the doctrine of the visibility of the Church, the apostolic succession in the ministry, the authority of the Church in matters of faith and the truths symbolized in the sacraments.

In one chapter he strongly attacks Rationalism as a reference of the gospel to the depraved standard of the actual human natures and by no means to its understanding properly so called, as its measure and criterion. He says: "That therefore to rely upon the understanding, misinformed as it is by depraved affections, as our adequate instructor in matters of religion, is most highly irrational." Nevertheless, "the understanding has a great function in religion and is a medium to the affections, and may even correct their particular impulses."

In reference to the question of the reconversion of England to Catholicism, earnestly desired by some, Mr. Gladstone forcibly remarked: "England, which with ill grace and ceaseless efforts at remonstrance, endured the yoke when Rome was in her zenith, and when her powers were but here and there evoked; will the same England, afraid of the truth which she has vindicated, or even with the license which has mingled like a weed with its growth, recur to that system in its decrepitude which she repudiated in its vigor?" If the Church of England ever lost her power, it would never be by submission to Rome, "but by that principle of religions insubordination and self-dependence which, if it refuse her tempered rule and succeed in its overthrow, will much more surely refuse and much more easily succeed in resisting the unequivocally arbitrary impositions of the Roman scheme." Here is the key-note of many of Mr. Gladstone's utterances in after years against the pretentious and aspirations of Rome. The defense of the English Church and its principles and opposition to the Church of Rome have been unchanging features in Mr. Gladstone's religious course. But, in the light of these early utterances, some have criticised severely that legislative act, carried through by him in later years, by which the Disestablishment of the Irish Church was effected. How could the author of "The State in its Relations with the Church" become the destroyer of the fabric of the Irish Church?

To meet these charges of inconsistency Mr. Gladstone issued, in 1868, "A Chapter of Autobiography." The author's motives in putting forth this chapter of autobiography were two—first, there was "the great and glaring change" in his course of action with respect to the Established Church of Ireland, which was not due to the eccentricity or perversion of an individual mind, but to the silent changes going on at the very basis of modern society. Secondly, there was danger that a great cause then in progress might suffer in point of credit, if not of energy and rapidity, from the real or supposed delinquencies of the author.

He stated that "The author had upheld the doctrine that the Church was to be maintained for its truth, and that if the principle was good for England it was good for Ireland too. But he denied that he had ever propounded the maxim *simpliciter* that we were to maintain the establishment. He admitted that his opinion of the Church of Ireland was the exact opposite of what it had been; but if the propositions of his work were in conflict with an assault upon the existence of the Irish Establishment, they were even more hostile to the grounds upon which it was now sought to maintain it. He did not wish to maintain the Church upon the basis usually advanced, but for the benefit of the whole people of Ireland, and if it could not be maintained as the truth it could not be maintained at all."

Mr. Gladstone contended that the Irish Episcopal Church had fallen out of harmony with the spirit and use of the time, and must be judged by a practical rather than a theoretic test. In concluding the author puts antithetically the case for and against the maintenance of the Church of Ireland: "An establishment that does its work in much and has the hope and likelihood of doing it in more; that has a broad and living way open to it into the hearts of the people; that can command the services of the present by the recollections and traditions of the past; able to appeal to the active zeal of the greater portion of the people, and to the respect or scruples of living work and service, and whose adversaries, if she has them, are in the main content to believe that there will be a future for them and their opinions; such an establishment should surely be maintained.

"But an establishment that neither does nor has her hope of doing work, except for a few, and those few the portion of the community whose claims to public aid is the smallest of all; an establishment severed from the mass of the people by an impassable gulf and a wall of brass; an establishment whose good offices, could she offer them, would be intercepted by a long, unbroken chain of painful and shameful recollections; an establishment leaning for support upon the extraneous aid of a State, which becomes discredited with the people by the very act of leading it; such an establishment will do well for its own sake, and for the sake of its creed, to divest itself, as soon as may be, of gauds and trappings, and to commence a new career, in which renouncing at once the credit and the discredit of the civil sanction, and shall seek its strength from within and put a fearless trust in the message that it bears."

Such, then, were the reasons that led the defender of the Irish Church to become its assailant, "That a man should change his opinions is no reproach to him; it is only inferior minds that are never open to conviction."

Mr. Gladstone is a firm Anglican, as we have seen, but the following extract from his address made at the Liverpool College, in December, 1872, gives a fine insight as to the breadth of his Christian sentiments:

"Not less forcibly than justly, you hear much to the effect that the divisions among Christians render it impossible to say what Christianity is, and so destroy all certainty as to the true religion. But if the divisions among Christians are remarkable, not less so is their unity in the greatest doctrines that they hold. Well-nigh fifteen hundred years have passed away since the great controversies concerning the Deity and the person of the Redeemer were, after a long agony, determined. As before that time, in a manner less defined but adequate for their day, so, even since that time, amid all chance and change, more—

aye, many more—than ninety-nine in every hundred Christians have, with one voice, confessed the Deity and incarnation of our Lord as the cardinal and central truth of our religion. Surely there is some comfort here, some sense of brotherhood; some glory due to the past, some hope for the times that are to come."

Mr. Gladstone as Prime Minister of England, during his several administrations, has had a large Church patronage to dispense, in other words, has been called upon, by virtue of his office, to till many vacancies in the Established Church, but it has been truly testified that there has probably never been so laboriously conscientious a distributor of ecclesiastical crown patronage as Mr. Gladstone. In his ecclesiastical appointments he never took politics into consideration. A conspicuous instance of this may be mentioned. When it was rumored that he intended to recommend Dr. Benson, the present Archbishop, for the vacant See of Canterbury, a political supporter called to remonstrate with him. Mr. Gladstone begged to know the ground of his objection. "The Bishop of Truro is a strong Tory," was the answer; "but that is not all. He has joined Mr. Raikes's election committee at Cambridge; and it was only last week that Raikes made a violent personal attack upon yourself." "Do you know," replied Mr. Gladstone, "that you have just supplied me with a strong argument in Dr. Benson's favor? for, if he had been a worldly man or self-seeker he would not have done anything so imprudent."

Mr. Gladstone sympathized more or less with the Nonconformists struggling against the application of university tests and other disabilities from which the Dissenters suffered, but it was not until 1876 that he really discovered the true religions work of the English Nonconformists. The manner in which the Congregationalists, Baptists, Quakers and others rallied to the standard raised in the cause of Bulgarian nationality effected a great change in his attitude towards his Dissenting fellow countrymen. He entertained many of the representative Nonconformist ministers at breakfast, and the fidelity and devotion of Nonconformists generally to the Bulgarian cause left on his mind an impression which has only deepened with the lapse of time. The extent to which this influences him may be gathered from the reply which he made to Dr. Döllinger whilst that learned divine was discussing with him the question of Church and State. Dr. Döllinger was expressing his surprise that Mr. Gladstone could possibly coquette in any way with the party that demanded the severance of Church and State in either Wales or Scotland. It was to him quite incomprehensible that a statesman who held so profoundly the idea of the importance of religion could make his own a cause whose avowed object was to cut asunder the Church from the State. Mr. Gladstone listened attentively to Dr. Döllinger's remarks, and then, in an absent kind of way, said, "But you forget how nobly the Nonconformists supported me at the time of the Eastern Question." The blank look of amazement on Dr. Döllinger's face showed the wide difference between the standpoint of the politician and the ecclesiastic. But Mr. Gladstone knew upon whom to rely in the hour of need, when great moral issues were at stake. The Bishops of the House of Lords had not always done their duty. Lord Shaftesbury, himself a very ardent Churchman, wrote, June 16, 1855, in reference to the Religious Worship Bill: "The Bishops have exhibited great ignorance, bigotry and opposition to evangelical life and action, and have seriously injured their character, influence and position."

Mr. Gladstone never displayed more marked respect for the "Nonconformist conscience" than when, in deference to their earnest appeal, he risked the great split in the Home Rule ranks that followed his repudiation of Mr. Parnell. Mr. Gladstone never hesitated or made the slightest pretense about the matter. If the Nonconformists had been as indifferent as the Churchmen, his famous letter about the Irish leadership would not have been written. "He merely acted, as he himself stated, as the registrar of the moral temperature which made Mr. Parnell impossible. He knew the men who are the Ironsides of his party too well not to understand that if he had remained silent the English Home Rulers would have practically ceased to exist. He saw the need, rose to the occasion and cleared the obstacle which would otherwise have been a fatal impediment to the success of his course. Mr. Gladstone is a practical statesman, and with some instinct divined the inevitable."

Mr. Gladstone's religious belief, as well as his opinion of the Bible and the plan of salvation revealed in the Gospel, are manifest as expressed in the following words from his pen:

"If asked what is the remedy for the deeper sorrows of the human heart—what a man should chiefly look to in his progress through life as the power that is to sustain him under trials and enable him manfully to confront his afflictions—I must point him to something which, in a well-known hymn is called 'the old, old story,' told of in an old, old book, and taught with an old, old teaching, which is the greatest and best gift ever given to mankind."

Another may read the lessons on the Lord's day in Hawarden Church and write and speak in defense of the Established Church of England, but Mr. Gladstone did more—he put his trust in his Lord and Saviour, and believed in his word. Mr. Gladstone was denominationally a member of the Episcopal Church, but religiously he held to views commonly held by all Evangelical Christians, from which the temptations of wealth at home, of college and of politics never turned him.

CHAPTER V

TRAVELS AND MARRIAGE

Mr. Gladstone spent the winter of 1838-9 in Rome. The physicians had recommended travel in the south of Europe for his health and particularly for his eyes, the sight of which had become impaired by hard reading in the preparation of his book. He had given up lamps and read entirely by candle-light with injurious results. He was joined at Rome by his friend, Henry Manning, afterwards Cardinal, and in company they visited Monsignor, afterwards Cardinal, Wiseman, at the English College, on the feast of St. Thomas of Canterbury. They attended solemn mass in honor of that Saint, and the places in the missal were found for them by a young student of the college, named Grant, who afterwards became Bishop of Southwark.

Besides visiting Italy he explored Sicily, and kept a journal of his tour. Sicily is a beautiful and fertile island in the Mediterranean Sea, and is the granary of Rome. His recorded observations show the keenness of his perceptions and the intensity with which he enjoyed the beautiful and wonderful in nature.

Mount Etna, the greatest volcano of Europe, and which rises 10,000 feet above the sea, stirred his soul greatly, and he made an ascent of the mountain at the beginning of the great eruption of 1838. Etna has many points of interest for all classes of scientific men, and not least for the student of arboriculture. It bears at the height of 4000 feet above the level of the sea a wonderful growth—a very large tree—which is claimed by some to be the oldest tree in the world. It is a venerable chestnut, and known as "the father of the forest." It is certainly one of the most remarkable as well as celebrated of trees. It consists not of one vast trunk, but of a cluster of smaller decayed trees or portions of trees growing in a circle, each with a hollow trunk of great antiquity, covered with ferns or ivy, and stretching out a few gnarled branches with scanty foliage. That it is one tree seems to be evident from the growth of the bark only on the outside. It is said that excavations about the roots of the tree showed these various stems to be united at a very small depth below the surface of the ground. It still bears rich foliage and much small fruit, though the heart of the trunk is decayed, and a public road leads through it wide enough for two coaches to drive abreast. Travelers have differed in their measurements of this stupendous growth. Admiral Smyth, who takes the lowest estimate, giving 163 feet, and Brydone giving, as the highest, 204 feet. In the middle of the cavity a hut is built, for the accommodation of those who collect and preserve the chestnuts. One of the Queens of Arragon is reported to have taken shelter in this tree, with her mounted suite of one hundred persons; but, "we may, perhaps, gather from this that mythology is not confined to the lower latitudes."

Further up the mountain is another venerable chestnut, which, with more reason, probably, may be described without fear of contradiction as the largest chestnut tree in the world. It rises from one solid stem to a remarkable height before it branches. At an elevation of two feet from the earth its circumference was found by Brydone to be seventy-six feet. These trees are reputed to have flourished for much more than a thousand years. Their luxuriant growth is attributed in part to the humid atmosphere of the Bosco, elevated above the scorching, arid region of the coast, and in part to the great richness of the soil. The luxuriance of the vegetation on the slopes of Etna attracts the attention of every traveler; and Mr. Gladstone remarked upon this point: "It seems as though the finest of all soils were produced from the most agonizing throes of nature, as the hardiest characters are often reared amidst the severest circumstances. The aspect of this side of Sicily is infinitely more active and the country is cultivated as well as most parts of Italy."

He and his party started on the 30th of October, and found the path nearly uniform from Catania, but the country bore a volcanic aspect at every step. At Nicolosi their rest was disturbed by the distant booming of the mountain. From this point to the Bosco the scenery is described as a dreary region, but the tract of the wood showed some beautiful places resembling an English park, with old oaks and abundant fern. "Here we found flocks browsing; they are much exposed to sheep-stealers, who do not touch travelers, calculating with justice that men do not carry much money to the summit of Etna." The party passed the Casa degli Inglesi, which registered a temperature of 31°, and then continued the ascent on foot for the crater. A magnificent view of sunrise was here obtained.

"Just before we reached the lip of the crater the guide exultingly pointed out what he declared to be ordinarily the greatest sight of the mountain, namely, the shadow of the cone of Etna, drawn with the utmost delicacy by the newly-risen sun, but of gigantic extent; its point at this moment rested on the mountains of Palermo, probably one hundred miles off, and the entire figure was visible, the atmosphere over the mountains having become and continuing perfectly and beautifully transparent, although in the hundreds of valleys which were beneath us, from the east to the west of Sicily, and from the mountains of Messina down to Cape Passaro, there were still abundant vapors waiting for a higher sun to disperse them; but we enjoyed in its perfection this view of the earliest and finest work of the greater light of heaven, in the passage of his beams over this portion of the earth's surface. During the hour we spent on the summit, the vision of the shadow was speedily contracting, and taught us how rapid is the real rise of the sun in the heavens, although its effect is diminished to the eye by a kind of foreshortening."

The writer next describes in vivid and powerful language the scene presented to the view at the very mouth of the crater. A large space, one mile in circumference, which a few days before had been one fathomless pit, from which issued masses of smoke, was now absolutely filled up to within a few feet of the brim all round. A great mass of lava, a portion of the contents of this immense pit, was seen to detach itself by degrees from one behind. "It opened like an orange, and we saw the red-hot fibres stretch in a broader and still broader vein, until the mass had found a support on the new ground it occupied in front; as we came back on our way down this had grown black." A stick put to it took fire immediately. Within a few yards of this lava bed were found pieces of ice, formed on the outside of the stones by Frost, "which here disputes every inch of ground with his fierce rival Fire."

Mr. Gladstone and his fellow-travelers were the first spectators of the great volcanic action of this year. From the highest peak attainable the company gazed upon the splendid prospect to the east spread out before them, embracing the Messina Mountains and the fine kindred outline of the Calabrian coast, described by Virgil in the third book of the Aeneid. Mr. Gladstone graphically describes the eruption which took place and of which he was the enraptured witness. Lava masses of 150 to 200 pounds weight were thrown to a distance of probably a mile and a half; smaller ones to a distance even more remote. The showers were abundant and continuous, and the writer was impressed by the closeness of the descriptions in Virgil with the actual reality of the eruption witnessed by himself. On this point he observes:

"Now how faithfully has Virgil (Ae. iii, 571, et seq.) comprised these particulars, doubtless without exaggeration, in his fine description! First, the thunder-clap, or crack—

'Horrificis juxta tonat Aetna ruinis.'

Secondly, the vibration of the ground to the report—

'Et, fessum quoties mutet latus, intremere omnem
Murmure Trinacriam.'

Thirdly, the sheet of flame—

'Attolitque globos flarmmarum, et sidera lambit.'

Fourthly, the smoke—

'Et coelum subtexere fumo.'

Fifthly, the fire shower—

'Scopulos avulsaque viscera montis
Erigit erucatans, liquefactaque saxa sub auras
Cum gemitu glomerat, fundoque exae tuat imo.'

Sixthly the column of ash—

'Atram prorumpit ad aethera nubem
Turbine fumantem piceo et candente favilla.'

And this is within the limits of twelve lines. Modern poetry has
its own merits, but the conveyance of information is not,
generally speaking, one of them. What would Virgil have
thought of authors publishing poems with explanatory notes
(to illustrate is a different matter), as if they were so many
books of conundrums? Indeed this vice is of very late years."

The entire description, of which this is but an extract, is very
effective and animated, and gives with great vividness the first
impressions of a mind susceptible to the grand and imposing
aspects of nature.

"After Etna," says Mr. Gladstone in his diary, "the temples are
certainly the great charm and attraction of Sicily. I do not
know whether there is any one among them which, taken
alone, exceeds in beauty that of Neptune, at Paestum; but they
have the advantage of number and variety, as well as of highly

interesting positions. At Segesta the temple is enthroned in a perfect mountain solitude, and it is like a beautiful tomb of its religion, so stately, so entire; while around, but for one solitary house of the keeper, there is nothing, absolutely nothing, to disturb the apparent reign of Silence and of Death.... The temples enshrine a most pure and salutary principle of art, that which connects grandeur of effect with simplicity of detail; and, retaining their beauty and their dignity in their decay, they represent the great man when fallen, as types of that almost highest of human qualities—silent yet not sullen, endurance."

While sojourning at Rome Mr. Gladstone met Lord Macaulay. Writing home from Rome in the same year, Lord Macaulay says: "On Christmas Eve I found Gladstone in the throng, and I accosted him, as we had met, though we had never been introduced to each other. He received my advances with very great *empressement* indeed, and we had a good deal of pleasant talk." And again he writes: "I enjoyed Italy immensely; far more than I had expected. By-the-by, I met Gladstone at Rome. We talked and walked together in St. Peter's during the best part of an afternoon. He is both a clever and an amiable man."

Among the visitors at Rome the winter that Mr. Gladstone spent in the eternal city were the widow and daughters of Sir Stephen Richard Glynne, of Hawarden Castle, Flintshire, Wales. He had already made the acquaintance of these ladies, having been a friend of Lady Glynne's eldest son at Oxford, and having visited him at Hawarden in 1835. He was thrown much into their society while at Rome, and became engaged to the elder of Lady Glynne's daughters, Catharine Glynne. It is strange to relate that some time before this when Miss Glynne met her future husband at a dinner-party, an English minister sitting next to her had thus drawn her attention to Mr. Gladstone: "Mark that young man; he will yet be Prime Minister of England." Miss Glynne and her sister were known as "the handsome Miss Glynnes."

Richard B. Cook

William E. Gladstone and Catharine Glynne were married July 25, 1839, at Hawarden Castle. At the same time and place Miss Mary Glynne was married to George William, fourth Lord Lyttleton, with whom Mr. Gladstone was on the most intimate terms of friendship until his lordship's untoward and lamented death. The brother of these ladies was Sir Stephen Glynne, the then owner of Hawarden. Mrs. Gladstone was "in her issue heir" of Sir Stephen Glynne, who was ninth and last baronet of that name.

The marriage ceremony has been thus described by an eye-witness:

"For some time past the little town of Hawarden has been in a state of excitement in consequence of the anticipated nuptials of the two sisters of Sir Stephen Glynne, Bart., M.P., who have been engaged for some time past to Lord Lyttelton and to Mr. W. Ewart Gladstone. Thursday last (July 25th) was fixed upon for the ceremony to take place; but in consequence of the Chartists having attacked Lord Lyttelton's mansion in Worcestershire, it was feared that the marriage would be delayed. All anxieties on this subject were put an end to by orders being issued to make ready for the ceremony, and the Hawarden folks lost no time in making due preparations accordingly. The church was elegantly and profusely decorated with laurels, while extremely handsome garlands, composed of the finest flowers, were suspended from the venerable roof. About half-past ten a simultaneous rising of the assembled multitude and the burst of melody from the organ announced that the fair brides had arrived, and all eyes were turned towards the door to witness the bridal *cortege*. In a few minutes more the party arrived at the communion table and the imposing ceremony commenced. At this period the *coup d'oeil* was extremely interesting. The bridal party exhibited every elegance of costume; while the dresses of the multitude, lit up by the rays of a brilliant sunlight, filled up the picture. The Rev. the Hon. G. Neville performed the ceremony. At its conclusion the brides visited the rectory, whence they soon afterwards set out—Lord and Lady Lyttelton to their seat in

Worcestershire, and Mr. and Mrs. Gladstone on a visit to Sir Richard Brooke, Norton Priory Mansion, in Cheshire. The bridal party having returned to the castle, the good folks of Hawarden filled up the day with rambling over Sir Stephen Glynne's delightful park, to which free access was given to all comers; and towards evening a dance on the green was got up."

It is to be remarked that by his marriage Mr. Gladstone became allied with the house of Grenville, a family of statesmen, which, directly or in its ramifications, had already supplied England with four Prime Ministers. Baron Bunsen, who made his acquaintance that year, writes that he "was delighted with the man who is some day to govern England if his book is not in the way."

Mrs. Gladstone is widely and deservedly known for her many philanthropic enterprises, but even better, perhaps, has proved herself to be a noble and devoted wife and mother. She has cheered by her sympathy her illustrious husband in his defeats as well as in his triumphs, in the many great undertakings of his political career, and been to him all the late Viscountess Beaconsfield was to Mr. Gladstone's Parliamentary rival. As a mother, she nursed and reared all her children, and ever kept them in the maternal eye, carefully watching over and tending them. One of the most interesting buildings at Hawarden is Mrs. Gladstone's orphanage, which stands close to the castle. Here desolate orphans are well cared for, and find, until they are prepared to enter on the conflict and to encounter the cares of life, a happy home.

Mrs. Gladstone, although in many respects an ideal wife, was never able to approach her husband in the methodical and business-like arrangement of her affairs. Shortly after their wedding, the story runs, Mr. Gladstone seriously took in hand the tuition of his handsome young wife in book-keeping, and Mrs. Gladstone applied herself with diligence to the unwelcome task. Some time after she came down in triumph to her husband to display her domestic accounts and her correspondence, all docketed in a fashion which she supposed would excite the admiration of her husband. Mr. Gladstone cast his eye over the results of his wife's labor and exclaimed in despair: "You have done them all wrong, from beginning to end!" His wife, however, has been so invaluable a helpmeet in other ways that it seems somewhat invidious to recall that little incident. She had other work to do, and she wisely left the accounts to her husband and his private secretaries.

The union of Mr. and Mrs. Gladstone has been blessed by eight children, all of whom save two still survive. There were four sons, the eldest, William Henry, was a member of the Legislature, and the second, the Rev. Stephen Edward Gladstone, is rector of Hawarden. The third son is named Henry Neville and the fourth Herbert John Gladstone. The former is engaged in commerce and the latter is the popular member for Leeds. The eldest daughter, Anne, is married to Rev. E.C. Wickham, A.M., headmaster of Wellington College; and the second, Catharine Jessy Gladstone, died in 1850; the third daughter, Mary, is married to Rev. W. Drew, and the fourth, Helen Gladstone, is principal of Newnham College. As Sir John Gladstone had the pleasure of seeing his son William Ewart become a distinguished member of Parliament, so Mr. Gladstone in his turn was able to witness his eldest son take his seat in the British Senate.

It was a sad bereavement when the Gladstones were called upon to part with their little daughter, Catharine Jessy, April 9, 1850, between four and five years old. Her illness was long and painful, and Mr. Gladstone bore his part in the nursing and watching. He was tenderly fond of his little children and the sorrow had therefore a peculiar bitterness. But Mr. Gladstone has since had another sad experience of death entering the family circle. July 4, 1891, the eldest son, William Henry Gladstone, died. The effect upon the aged father was greatly feared, and the world sympathized with the great statesman and father in his sad trial, and with the afflicted family. In a letter dated July 9, the day after the interment, Mr. Gladstone wrote:

"We, in our affliction are deeply sensible of the mercies of God. He gave us for fifty years a most precious son. He has now only hidden him for a very brief space from the sight of our eyes. It seems a violent transition from such thoughts to the arena of political contention, but the transition may be softened by the conviction we profoundly hold that we, in the first and greatest of our present controversies, work for the honor, well-being and future peace of our opponents not less than for our own."

When away from the trammels of office, Mr. Gladstone taught his elder children Italian. All the sons went to Eton and Oxford, and the daughters were educated at home by English, French and German governesses. A close union of affection and sentiment has always been a marked characteristic of this model English family. Marriage and domestic cares, however, made little difference in Mr. Gladstone's mode of life. He was still the diligent student, the constant debater and the copious writer that he had been at Eton, at Oxford and in the Albany.

In the early days of their married life, Mr. and Mrs. Gladstone lived in London with Lady Glynne, at 13 Carlton House Terrace. Later they lived at 6 Carlton Gardens, which was made over to them by Sir John Gladstone; then again at 13 Carlton House Terrace; and when Mr. Gladstone was in office, at the official residence of the Prime Minister, Downing Street. In 1850 Mr. Gladstone succeeded to his patrimony, and in 1856 he bought 11 Carlton House Terrace, which was his London house for twenty years; and he subsequently lived for four years at 73 Harley Street. During the parliamentary recess Mr. and Mrs. Gladstone divided their time between Fasque, Sir John Gladstone's seat in Kincardineshire, and Hawarden Castle, which they shared with Mrs. Gladstone's brother, Sir Stephen Glynne, till in his death in 1874, when it passed into their sole possession. In 1854 Mrs. Gladstone's brother added to the castle a new wing, which he especially dedicated to his illustrious brother-in-law, and which is fondly known as "The Gladstone Wing." And Mr. Gladstone, having only one country house, probably spent as much time at

Hawarden as any other minister finds it possible to devote to residence out of London.

Hawarden, usually pronounced Harden, is the name of a large market-town, far removed from the centre and seat of trade and empire, in Flintshire, North Wales, six miles southwest from the singular and ancient city of Chester, of which it may be called a suburb. It is not pretty, but a clean and tolerably well-built place, with some good houses and the usual characteristics of a Welsh village. The public road from Chester to Hawarden, which passes by the magnificent seat of the Duke of Westminster, is not, except for this, interesting to the stranger. There is a pedestrian route along the banks of the river Dee, over the lower ferry and across the meadows. But for the most part the way lies along dreary wastes, unadorned by any of the beautiful landscape scenery so common in Wales. Broughton Hall, its pleasant church and quiet churchyard, belonging to the Hawarden estate, are passed on the way. The village lies at the foot of the Castle, and outside of the gates of Hawarden Park. The parish contains 13,000 acres, and of these the estate of Mr. Gladstone consists of nearly 7000. The road from the village for the most part is dreary, but within the gates the park is as beautiful as it is extensive. Richly wooded, on both sides of its fine drive are charming vistas opening amongst the oaks, limes and elms. On the height to the left of the drive is the ancient Hawarden Castle, for there are two—the old and the new—the latter being the more modern home of the proprietor.

The ancient Castle of Hawarden, situated on an eminence commanding an extensive prospect, is now in ruins. What, however, was left of the old Castle at the beginning of the century stands to-day a monument of the massive work of the early masons. The remnant, which ages of time and the Parliamentary wars and the strange zeal of its first owner under Cromwell for its destruction, allowed to remain, is in a marvelous state of preservation, and the masonry in some places fifteen feet thick. There is a grandeur in the ruin to be enjoyed, as well as a scene of beauty from its towers. The old

Castle, like the park itself, is open to the public without restriction. Only two requests are made in the interests of good order. One is that visitors entering the park kindly keep to the gravel walks, while the other is that they do not inscribe their names on the stone-work of the ancient ruin, which request has been unheeded.

This ancient Castle was doubtless a stronghold of the Saxons in very early times, for it was found in the possession of Edwin of Mercia at the Norman Conquest, and was granted by William the Conqueror to his nephew, Hugh Lupus. In later times Prince Llewelyn was Lord of Hawarden, of which he was dispossessed by his brother, David. It was only after Wales was conquered that Hawarden became an English stronghold, held against the Welsh.

The Castle had its vicissitudes, both as to its condition and proprietorship, for many years, even generations. Somewhere between 1267 and 1280 the Castle had been destroyed and rebuilt. It was rebuilt in the time of Edward I or Edward II, and formed one link in the chain by which the Edwards held the Welsh to their loyalty. Its name appears in the doomsday-book, where it is spelled Haordine. It was presented by King Edward to the House of Salisbury. Then the Earls of Derby came into possession, and they entertained within its walls Henry VII in the latter part of the fifteenth century. During the Parliamentary wars it was held at first for the Parliament, and was taken by siege in 1643. The royalists were in possession two years later, and at Christmas time, in 1645, Parliament ordered that the Castle be dismantled, which was effectively done. The latest proprietor of those times was James, Earl of Derby. He was executed and the estates were sold. They were purchased by Sergeant Glynne, Lord Chief Justice of England under Cromwell, from whom in a long line of descent they were inherited, upon the death of the last baronet, Sir Stephen Glynne, in 1874, by the wife of William E. Gladstone. Sergeant Glynne's son, Sir William, the first baronet, when he came into possession, was seized with the unaccountable notion of further destroying the old Castle, and

Richard B. Cook

by the end of the seventeenth century very little remained beyond what stands to-day.

Hawarden is supposed to be synonymous with the word Burg-Ardden, Ardin, a fortified mound or hill. It is usually supposed to be an English word, but of Welsh derivation, and is no doubt related to dinas, in Welsh the exact equivalent to the Saxon *burg*. The Welsh still call it Penarlas, a word the etymology of which points to a period when the lowlands of Saltney were under water, and the Castle looked over a lake. The earlier history of the Castle goes back to the time when it was held by the ancient Britons, and stood firm against Saxon, Dane, or whatever invading foe sought to deprive the people of their heritage in the soil. On the invasion of William, as we have seen, it was in the possession of Edwin, sovereign of Deira. "We find it afterwards," says another account, "in the possession of Roger Fitzvalarine, a son of one of the adventurers who came over with the Conqueror. Then it was held, subordinately, by the Monthault, or Montalt, family, the stewards of the palatinate of Chester. It is remarkable, as we noticed in our story of Hughenden Manor, that as the traditions of that ancient place touched the memory of Simon de Montfort, the great Earl of Leicester, so do they also in the story of the old Castle of Hawarden. Here Llewelyn, the last native prince of Wales, held a memorable conference with the Earl. With in the walls of Hawarden was signed the treaty of peace between Wales and Cheshire, not long to last; here Llewelyn saw the beautiful daughter of De Montfort, whose memory haunted him so tenderly and so long. Again we find the Castle in the possession of the Montalt family, from whom it descended to the Stanleys, the Earl of Derby.... Here the last native princes of Wales, Llewelyn and David, attempted to grasp their crumbling sceptre, Here no doubt halted Edward I, 'girt with many a baron bold;' here the Tudor prince, Henry VII, of Welsh birth, visited in the later years of the fifteenth century; and this was the occasion upon which it passed into the family whose representatives had proclaimed him monarch on Bosworth field. But when James, Earl of Derby, was beheaded, after the battle of Worcester, in 1651, the estate was purchased under the Sequestration Act by Sergeant Glynne, whose portrait hangs over the mantleshelf of the drawing-room; 'but,' says Mrs. Gladstone, in calling our attention to it, 'he is an ancestor of whom we have no occasion to be and are not proud.'"

This remark of Mrs. Gladstone's may be explained by the following from the pen of a reputable author: "Sergeant Glynne, who flourished (literally flourished) during the seventeenth century, was a most unscrupulous man in those troubled times. He was at first a supporter of Charles I, then got office and preferment under Cromwell, and yet again, like a veritable Vicar of Bray, became a Royalist on the return of Charles II. The Earl of Derby, who was taken prisoner at the battle of Worcester, in 1661, was executed, and his estates forfeited. Of these estates Sergeant Glynne managed to get possession of Hawarden; and though on the Restoration all Royalists' forfeited estates were ordered to be restored, Glynne managed somehow to remain in possession of the property."

It is very probable that Hawarden Castle was no exception to those cruel haunts of feudal tyranny and oppression belonging to the days of its power. Many years ago, when the rubbish was cleared away beneath the Castle ruin, a flight of steps was found, at the foot of which was a door, and a draw-bridge, which crossed a long, deep chasm, neatly faced with freestone; then another door leading to several small rooms, all, probably, places of confinement; and those hollows, now fringed with timber trees, in those days constituted a broad, deep fosse.

The old Hawarden Castle, a curious ruin covered with moss and ivy, like many other ancient piles of stone in historic England, is a reminder of a past and warlike age, when an Englishman's home had to be a castle to protect him and his family from his enemies. But times have changed for the better, and long immunity from internal foes and invading armies has had its peaceful effects upon the lands and the homes of men. As the grounds of Hawarden show the remarkable cultivation produced by long periods of peaceful

Richard B. Cook

toil, so the ancient castle has given way for the modern dwelling, a peaceful abode whose only protecting wall is that with which the law surrounds it.

Modern Hawarden Castle is a castle only in name. The new "Castle" has been the home of the Glynns' for generations, and ever since the marriage of Mr. Gladstone and Miss Glynn has been the dwelling of the Gladstones. Mr. Gladstone has greatly improved the Hawarden estate and the castle has not been overlooked. Among the improvements to the castle may be named the additions to the library and the Golden Wedding Porch.

The new Castle was begun in 1752, by Sir John Glynne, who "created a stout, honest, square, red-brick mansion;" which was added to and altered in the Gothic style in 1814. The Glynnes lived in Oxfordshire till early in the eighteenth century, when they built themselves a small house, which was on the site of the present Castle. The new Hawarden Castle stands in front of the massive ruin of the old Castle, which has looked down on the surrounding country for six centuries. A recent writer speaking of the new structure as a sham Castle, with its plaster and stucco, and imitation turrets, says: "It would not have been surprising if the old Castle had, after the manner of Jewish chivalry, torn its hair of thickly entwined ivy, rent its garments of moss and lichen, and fallen down prostrate, determined forever to shut out the sight of the modern monstrosity."

However, the author somewhat relents and thus describes the modern edifice:

"The aspect of the house is very impressive and imposing, as it first suddenly seems to start upon the view after a long carriage-drive through the noble trees, if not immediately near, but breaking and brightening the view on either hand; yet, within and without, the house seems like its mighty master— not pensive but rural; it does not even breathe the spirit of quiet. Its rooms look active and power-compelling, and we could not but feel that they were not indebted to any of the aesthetic inventions and elegancies of furniture for their charm. Thus we have heard of one visitor pathetically exclaiming, 'Not one *dado* adorns the walls!' Hawarden is called a Castle, but it has not, either in its exterior or interior, the aspect of a Castle. It is a home; it has a noble appearance as it rises on the elevated ground, near the old feudal ruin which it has superseded, and looks over the grand and forest-like park, the grand pieces of broken ground, dells and hollows, and charming woodlands."

The traditional history of Hawarden Church, as well as that of the Castle, travels back to a very remote antiquity, and is the central point of interest to many a tragedy, and some of a very grotesque character. For instance, for many ages the inhabitants of Hawarden were called "Harden Jews," and for this designation we have the following legendary account. In the year 946, during the reign of Cynan ap Elisap Anarawd, King of Gwynedd North, there was a Christian temple at Harden, and a rood-loft, in which was placed an image of the Virgin Mary, with a very large cross in her hands, which was called "holy rood." During a very hot and dry summer the inhabitants prayed much and ardently for rain, but without any effect. Among the rest, Lady Trowst, wife of Sytsyllt, governor of Harden Castle, went also to pray, when, during this exercise, the holy rood fell upon her head and killed her. Such behavior upon the part of this wooden Virgin could be tolerated no longer. A great tumult ensued in consequence, and it was concluded to try the said Virgin for murder, and the jury not only found her guilty of wilful murder, but of inattention in not answering the prayers of innumerable petitioners. The sentence was hanging, but Span, of Mancot, who was one of the jury, opposed this act saying it was best to drown, since it was rain they prayed for. This was fiercely opposed by Corbin, of the gate, who advised that she should be laid on the sands by the river. So, this being done, the tide carried the lady, floating gently, like another lady, Elaine, upon its soft bosom, and placed her near the walls of Caerleon (now Chester), where she was found next day, says the legend, drowned and dead. Here the inhabitants of Caerleon buried her. Upon this occasion, it is said, the river, which had until then been called the Usk, was changed to Rood Die, or Rood Dee. We need not stay here to analyze some things belonging to locality and etymology, which appear to us somewhat anachronistic and contradictory in this ancient and queer legend.

Hawarden Church is a fairly large structure, externally a plain old brick building with a low tower and a dwarf spire, standing in the midst of a large population of graves. There is preserved in the annals of the Church a list of the rectors of Hawarden as far back as 1180.

About forty years ago a fire broke out in the Church, and when all was over, very little was left of the original structure except the walls. It was restored with great expedition, and was re-opened within the same year. The present building is a restoration to the memory of the immediate ancestor, from whom the estate is derived by the present family. It is the centre of hard, earnest work, done for an exceptionally large parish. But the Church population is occasionally recruited from all the ends of the earth.

It is here that the Gladstone family worship on the plain, uncushioned pew, near the lectern and opposite the pulpit. When the estates came into the hands of the Glynnes the living was bestowed upon a member of the family. The Rector is Rev. Stephen Gladstone, second son of the Premier. He is not a great preacher, but he is quietly earnest and instructive. Mr. Gladstone was up early on Sunday mornings and seldom failed to be in his pew at Church. Crowds filled the Church Sunday, morning and evening, week after week, many of them strangers, to see the Prime Minister of England, and behold him leave his pew and, standing at the reading-desk, go through his part of the service—that of reading the lessons for the day, in this obscure village Church. After church Mr. Gladstone went to the rectory with his family, with his cloak only over his shoulders, when the weather required, and as he walked along the path through the churchyard would bow to the crowds that stood on either side uncovered to greet him as he passed by. The two brothers, until recently, lived at the rectory, and the whole family seemed to live in the most beautiful harmony together.

Both Mr. and Mrs. Gladstone attribute much of his health to the fact that he will have his Sabbath to himself and his family, undisturbed by any of the agitations of business, the cares of State, or even the recreations of literature and scholastic study. This profound public regard for the day of rest, whether in London or at Hawarden, awakens a feeling of admiration and puts us in mind of his great predecessor in statesmanship, Cecil, Lord Burleigh, who, when he arrived at Theobalds on a Saturday evening would throw off his cloak or chain of office and exclaim, "Lie there and rest, my good lord treasurer."

One of the main points of interest at the home of Mr. Gladstone is the library. There is not a room in Hawarden Castle in which there is not an abundance of books, which are not all collected in the library, but distributed all over the house. Where other people have cabinets for curiosities, china, etc., there are here shelves and cases full of books. In ante-room and bed-room dressing-room and nursery they are found, not by single volumes, but in serried ranks; well-known and useful books. But it is in the library where Mr. Gladstone has collected by years of careful selection, a most valuable and large array of books, from all parts of the world, upon every subject. These books are classified and so arranged as to be of immediate use. All those on one particular subject are grouped together.

Mr. Gladstone was a familiar figure in the book stores, and especially where rare, old books were to be found, and he seldom failed to return home with some book in his pocket. Mrs. Gladstone is said to have gone through his pockets often upon his return home, and sent back many a volume to the book-seller, that had found its way to the pocket of her husband, after a hasty glance at its title. He kept himself

Richard B. Cook

informed of all that was going on in the literary, scientific and artistic worlds, receiving each week a parcel of the newest books for his private readings. Every day he looked over several book-sellers's catalogues, and certain subjects were sure of getting an order.

Hawarden library gave every evidence of being for use, and not show. Mr. Gladstone knew what books he had and was familiar with their contents. Some books were in frequent use, but others were not forgotten. He could put his hand on any one he wanted to refer to. At the end of a volume read he would construct an index of his own by which he could find passages to which he wished to refer.

There are few stories that Mr. Gladstone told with greater relish than one concerning Sir Antonio Panizzi, who many years ago visited the library at Hawarden. Looking round the room and at its closely packed shelves, he observed in a patronizing tone, "I see you have got some books here." Nettled at this seemingly slighting allusion to the paucity of his library, Mr. Gladstone asked Panizzi how many volumes he thought were on the shelves. Panizzi replied: "From five to six thousand." Then a loud and exulting laugh rang round the room as Mr. Gladstone answered: "You are wrong by at least two thousand, as there are eight thousand volumes and more before you now." Since then the library has grown rapidly.

The fate of this large library was naturally a matter of much consideration to Mr. Gladstone. It was particularly rich in classical and theological works, so it occured to its owner to form a public library under a trusteeship, for the benefit of students, under the care of the Rector of Hawarden, or some other clergyman. So he caused to be erected at a cost to him of about $5,000, a corrugated iron building on a knoll just outside Hawarden Church. The name of this parish library is "The St. Deiniol's Theological and General Library of Hawarden." In 1891, Mr. Gladstone had deposited about 20,000 volumes upon the shelves in this new building, with his own hands, which books were carried in hand-carts from the castle. Since that time thousands have been added to this valuable collection.

It was a happy thought of Mr. Gladstone to found a theological library in the immediate vicinity of Hawarden; also to have connected with it a hostel where students could be boarded and lodged for six dollars a week and thus be enabled to use the library in the pursuit of their studies. Mr. Gladstone has endowed the institution with $150,000. Rev. H. Drew, the son-in-law of Mr. Gladstone, is warden and librarian.

Richard B. Cook

CHAPTER VI

ENTERS THE CABINET

We come now to another memorable period in the life of William E. Gladstone. This period, beginning with 1840, has been styled "a memorable decade" in the history of Parliament. His marriage and the publication of his first book were great events in his eventful life, but the young and brilliant statesman was soon to enter the British Cabinet. He was before long to demonstrate that he not only possessed the arts of the fluent and vigorous Parliamentary debater, but the more solid qualities pertaining to the practical statesman and financier. In following his course we will be led to observe the early stages of his changing opinions on great questions of State, and to trace the causes which led to his present advanced views as well as to his exalted position. The estimation in which he was then held may be indicated by the following, from one of his contemporaries, Sir Stafford Northcote, afterwards Lord Iddesleigh, and who subsequently succeeded him as leader of the House of Commons: "There is but one statesman of the present day in whom I feel entire confidence, and with whom I cordially agree, and that statesman is Mr. Gladstone. I look upon him as the representative of the party, scarcely developed as yet, though secretly forming and strengthening, which will stand by all that is dear and sacred in my estimation, in the struggle which I believe will come ere *very* long between good and evil, order and disorder, the Church and the world, and I see a very small band collecting round him, and ready to fight manfully under his leading."

In 1840 Mr. Gladstone crossed swords with the distinguished historian and Parliamentary debater, Lord Macaulay, in debate in the House of Commons on the relations of England with China. The speech of Mr. Gladstone was remarkable for its eloquent expression of anxiety that the arms of England should never be employed in unrighteous enterprises. Sir James Graham moved a vote of censure of the ministry for "want of foresight and precaution," and "especially their neglect to furnish the superintendent at Canton with powers and instructions calculated to provide against the growing evils connected with the contraband traffic in opium, and adapted to the novel and difficult situation in which the superintendent was placed." Mr. Gladstone, on the 8th of April, spoke strongly in favor of the motion, and said if it failed to involve the ministry in condemnation they would still be called upon to show cause for their intention of making war upon China. Answering the speech of Lord Macaulay of the previous evening, Mr. Gladstone said: "The right honorable gentleman opposite spoke last night in eloquent terms of the British flag waving in glory at Canton, and of the animating effects produced on the minds of our sailors by the knowledge that in no country under heaven was it permitted to be insulted. But how comes it to pass that the sight of that flag always raises the spirit of Englishmen? It is because it has always been associated with the cause of justice, with opposition to oppression, with respect to national rights, with honorable commercial enterprises; but now, under the auspices of the noble lord, that flag is hoisted to protect an infamous contraband traffic, and if it were never to be hoisted except as it is now hoisted on the coast of China, we should recoil from its sight with horror, and should never again feel our hearts thrill, as they now thrill with emotion, when it floats proudly and magnificently on the breeze." The ministry escaped censure when the vote was taken by a bare majority.

In the summer of 1840 Mr. Gladstone, accompanied by Lord Lyttleton, went to Eton to examine candidates of the Newcastle Scholarship, founded by his political friend, the Duke of Newcastle. Mr. Gladstone had the pleasure in this examination of awarding the Newcastle medal to Henry Fitzmaurice Hallam, the youngest brother of his own beloved friend and son of the historian Hallam. One of the scholars he examined writes: "I have a vivid and delightful impression of Mr. Gladstone sitting in what was then called the library, on an *estrade* on which the head master habitually sate, above which was placed, about 1840, the bust of the Duke of Newcastle and the names of the Newcastle scholars.... When he gave me a Virgil and asked me to translate Georg. ii, 475, *seq.*, I was pleasantly surprised by the beautiful eye turning on me with the question, 'What is the meaning of *sacra fero?*' and his look of approval when I said, 'Carry the sacred vessels in the procession.'"

"I wish you to understand that Mr. Gladstone appeared not to me only, but to others, as a gentleman wholly unlike other examiners or school people. It was not as *a politician* that we admired him, but as a refined Churchman, deep also in political philosophy (so we conjectured from his quoting Burke on the Continual State retaining its identity though made up of passing individuals), deep also in lofty poetry, as we guessed from his giving us, as a theme for original Latin verse, 'the poet's eye in a fine frenzy,' etc. When he spoke to us in 'Pop' as an honorary member, we were charmed and affected emotionally: his voice was low and sweet, his manner was that of an elder cousin: he seemed to treat us with unaffected respect; and to be treated with respect by a man is the greatest delight for a boy. It was the golden time of 'retrograding transcendentalism,' as the hard-heads called the Anglo-Catholic symphony. He seemed to me then an apostle of unworldly ardor, bridling his life."

The Whig administration, which for some time had been growing very unpopular, was defeated and went out of power in 1841. From the very beginning of the session their over-throw was imminent. Among the causes which rendered the ministry obnoxious to the country, and led to their downfall, may be named the disappointment of both their dissenting English supporters and Irish allies; their financial policy had proved a complete failure and dissatisfied the nation; and the deficit in the revenue this year amounted to no less a sum than two millions and a half pounds. Every effort to remedy the financial difficulties offered by the ministry to the House was rejected, Hence it was felt on all sides that the government of the country must be committed to stronger hands. Accordingly, in May, Sir Robert Peel proposed a resolution in the House of Commons to the effect that the ministry did not possess sufficiently the confidence of the House to carry through measures deemed essential for the public welfare; and that their continuance in office was, under the circumstances, at variance with the Constitution, For five days this resolution was discussed, but Mr. Gladstone took no part in the debate. The motion of Sir Robert Peel passed by a majority vote of one, and on the 7th of June Lord John Russell announced that the ministry would at once dissolve Parliament and appeal to the country. Parliament was prorogued by the Queen in person June 22d, and the country was soon in the turmoil of a general election. By the end of July it was found that the ministry had been defeated and with greater loss than the Tories even had expected. The Tories had a great majority of the new members returned. The Liberal seats gained by the Tories were seventy-eight, while the Tory seats gained by Liberals were only thirty-eight, thus making a Tory majority of eighty. Mr. Gladstone was again elected at Newark, and was at the head of the poll; with Lord John Manners, afterwards Duke of Rutland, as his colleague.

The new Parliament met in August, and the ministers were defeated, in both Houses, on the Address and resigned. Sir Robert Peel was called upon by the Queen to form a new ministry, and Mr. Gladstone was included by his leader in the administration. In appearing on the hustings at Newark Mr. Gladstone said that there were two points upon which the British farmer might rely—the first being that adequate protection would be given him, and, second, that protection would be given him through the means of the sliding scale. The duties were to be reduced and the system improved, but the principle was to be maintained. "There was no English

Richard B. Cook

statesman who could foresee at this period the results of that extraordinary agitation which, in the course of the next five years, was destined to secure the abrogation of the Corn Laws."

There is a tradition that, having already conceived a lively interest in the ecclesiastical and agrarian problems of Ireland, Mr. Gladstone had set his affections on the Chief Secretaryship. But Sir Robert Peel, a consummate judge of administrative capacity, had discerned his young friend's financial aptitude, and the member for Newark became vice-president of the Board of Trade and master of the Mint.

Although in the midst of engrossing cares of office as vice-president of the Board of Trade, yet Mr. Gladstone found time to renew his old interest in ecclesiastical concerns. In the fall of 1841 an English Episcopal Bishopric was established at Jerusalem, Mr. Gladstone dined with Baron Bunsen on the birthday of the King of Prussia, when, as reported by Lord Shaftesbury, he "stripped himself of a part of his Puseyite garments, spoke like a pious man, rejoiced in the bishopric of Jerusalem, and proposed the health of Alexander, the new Bishop of that see. This is delightful, for he is a good man, a clever man and an industrious man." And Baron Bunsen, speaking of the same occasion, said, "Never was heard a more exquisite speech, It flowed like a gentle, translucent stream. We drove back to town in the clearest starlight; Gladstone continuing with unabated animation to pour forth his harmonious thoughts in melodious tone." And Mr. Gladstone himself writes later; "Amidst public business, quite sufficient for a man of my compass, I have, during the whole of the week, perforce, been carrying on with the Bishop of London and with Bunsen a correspondence on, and inquisition into, the Jerusalem design, until I almost reel and stagger under it."

And still later he writes: "I am ready individually to brave misconstruction for the sake of union with any Christian men, provided the terms of the union be not contrary to sound principle; and perhaps in this respect might go further, at least in one of the possible directions, than you. But to declare the living constitution of a Christian Church to be of secondary moment is of course in my view equivalent to a denial of a portion of the faith—and I think you will say it is a construction which can not fairly be put upon the design, as far as it exists in fixed rules and articles. It is one thing to attribute this in the way of unfavorable surmise, or as an apprehension of ultimate developments—it is another to publish it to the world as a character ostentatiously assumed."

We have evidence also that at this time he was not permitted to forget that he was an author, for he thus writes, April 6, 1842, to his publisher: "Amidst the pressure of more urgent affairs, I have held no consultation with you regarding my books and the sale or no sale of them. As to the third edition of the 'State in its Relations,' I should think that the remaining copies had better be got rid of in whatever summary or ignominious mode you may deem best. They must be dead beyond recall. As to the others, I do not know whether the season of the year has at all revived the demand; and would suggest to you whether it would be well to advertise them a little. I do not think they find their way much into the second-hand shops. With regard to the fourth edition, I do not know whether it would be well to procure any review or notice of it, and I am not a fair judge of its merits, even in comparison with the original form of the work; but my idea is that it is less defective, both in the theoretical and in the historical development, and ought to be worth the notice of those who deemed the earlier editions worth their notice and purchase; that it would really put a reader in possession of the view it was intended to convey, which I fear is more than can with any truth be said of its predecessors. I am not, however, in any state of anxiety or impatience; and I am chiefly moved to refer these suggestions to your judgment from perceiving that the fourth edition is as yet far from having cleared itself."

It was from this time that a marked change was observable in the subjects of Mr. Gladstone's Parliamentary addresses. "Instead of speaking on the corporate conscience of the State and the endowments of the Church, the importance of

Christian education and the theological unfitness of the Jews to sit in Parliament, he was solving business-like problems about foreign tariffs and the exportation of machinery; waxing eloquent over the regulation of railways and a graduated tax on corn; subtle on the momentary merits of half-farthings and great in the mysterious lore of quassia and cocculus indicus."

In the short session of Parliament, in 1841, that which followed the accession of Sir Robert Peel to the office of Prime Minister, he was questioned by his opponents as to his future policy. The Premier declined to state the nature of the measures he intended to present, or which he contemplated making, in the intervening months of the recess of Parliament so near at hand. He wanted time for the arrangement of his plans and the construction of his political programme. An effort was made to embarrass the administration by refusing to vote the necessary supplies, until inquiry should be made into the existing distress, but it was defeated. Three weeks later Parliament was dissolved by Royal commission. In the following sitting of Parliament several measures of high practical character were presented.

Sir Robert Peel acceded to office in very critical times. The condition of the country was truly lamentable. Distress and discontent were widespread and the difficulties of the government were greatly enhanced by popular tumults. The Free Trade agitation was already making great headway in the land, and when the Premier brought forward his new sliding scale of duties in the House of Commons it was denounced by Mr. Cobden as an insult to a suffering people. The Premier said that he considered the present not an unfavorable time for discussing the corn laws; that there was no great stock on hand of foreign growth to alarm the farmers; that the recess had been marked by universal calm; that there was no popular violence to interrupt legislation; and that there was a disposition to view any proposal for the adjustment of the question with calmness and moderation.

The Premier's view of the situation did not seem to be wholly in accord with the well-known facts, for the Queen even, on her appearance at the London theatres, had been hooted, and the Prime Minister himself was burnt in effigy during a riot at Northampton; great excitement prevailed throughout the country, and Lord John Russell moved as an amendment "That this House, considering the evils which have been caused by the present corn laws and especially by the fluctuation of the graduated or sliding scale, is not prepared to adopt the measure of her Majesty's government, which is founded on the same principles and is likely to be attended by similar results."

It was incumbent upon Mr. Gladstone to lead the opposition to this motion. He showed that the proposed plan was not founded on the same principle of the existing one, except that both involved a sliding scale; that the present distress was caused by fluctuation of the seasons and not by the laws; that high prices of food were chargeable to successive failures of the crops; that these unavoidable fluctuations were not aggravated by the corn laws; that Sir Robert Peel's plan of working was far superior to that of Lord John Russell; that the drains upon the currency, caused by bad harvests, were not to be prevented by a fixed duty; that a uniform protection could not be given to corn, as to other articles, because at high prices of corn no duty could be maintained, and that, therefore, at low prices, it was but just to give a duty which would be an effectual protection. The debate which followed was characterized by vigorous speeches from Mr. Roebuck and Lord Palmerston. Lord John Russell's amendment was lost by a large majority. A motion presented by Mr. Villiers, the Free Trade advocate, for the immediate repeal of the corn laws was also lost by a majority of over three hundred.

On the 11th of March Sir Robert Peel introduced his budget. The budget for 1842 was produced under depressing circumstances. There was a deficit of £2,750,000, or about $15,000,000, and taxation upon articles of consumption had been pushed to its utmost limit. Peel was a great financier, but the fiscal difficulties by which he was now surrounded were enough to appall the most ingenious of financial ministers.

Mr. Gladstone rendered the Premier invaluable service in the preparation both of his budget and of his tariff scheme. The merit of the budget was its taxation of wealth and the relief of the manufacturing industry. The second branch of the financial plan, the revised tariff—a customs duties scheme— was very important, and it was understood to be mainly the work of Mr. Gladstone. Out of nearly 1200 duty-paying articles, a total abolition, or a considerable reduction, was made in no fewer than 750. This was certainly a great step towards the freedom of manufacturers, Sir Robert Peel's boast that he had endeavored to relieve manufacturing industries was more than justified by this great and comprehensive measure. The very best means for relieving the manufacturing industries had been devised.

But while this great relief to industry was welcomed the Opposition did not relax their efforts for the abolition of the corn laws, which were continued into the session of 1843. Sir Robert Peel acknowledged, amidst loud cheers from the Opposition, that all were agreed in the general rule that we should purchase in the cheapest market and sell in the dearest; but he added, "If I propose a greater change in the corn laws than that which I submit to the consideration of the House I should only aggravate the distress of the country, and only increase the alarm which prevails among important interests." Mr. Hume hailed with joy the appearance of the Premier and his colleagues as converts to the principles of Free Trade; Mr. Gladstone replied, that, whoever were the authors of the principles on which the government measures rested, he must protest against the statement that the ministry came forward as converts to principles which they had formerly opposed.

During the progress of the debate of 1842, on the revised Tariff Bill, Mr. Gladstone's labors were very great. He was called upon to explain or defend the details of the scheme, and had something to say about every article of consumption included in, or excluded from, the list. He spoke one hundred and twenty-nine times, chiefly on themes connected with the new fiscal legislature. He demonstrated his capacity for grasping all the most complicated details of finance, and also the power of comprehending the scope and necessities of the commercial interests of the country. No measure with which his name has since been connected has done him more credit. He spoke incessantly, and amazed the House by his mastery of details, his intimate acquaintance with the commercial needs of the country, and his inexhaustible power of exposition. On March 14th Greville wrote, "Gladstone has already displayed a capacity which makes his admission into the Cabinet indispensable." A commercial minister had appeared on the scene, and the shade of Hoskisson had revived.

Though engrossed in schemes of practical legislation, and in all the excitements and interests of office, he could, as he has ever done during his long career, turn aside for the discourse on social and educational questions with much earnestness and eloquence, as if they, and only they, possessed his mind. In January, 1843, he spoke at the opening of the Collegiate Institute of Liverpool, and delivered a powerful plea for the better education of the middle classes, which was one of the most forcible speeches he ever delivered. He said:

"We believe that if you could erect a system which should present to mankind all branches of knowledge save the one that is essential, you would only be building up a Tower of Babel, which, when you had completed it, would be the more signal in its fall, and which would bury those who had raised it in its ruins. We believe that if you can take a human being in his youth, and if you can make him an accomplished man in natural philosophy, in mathematics, or in the knowledge necessary for the profession of a merchant, a lawyer, or a physician; that if in any or all of these endowments you could form his mind—yes, if you could endow him with the science and power of a Newton, and so send him forth—and if you had concealed from him, or, rather, had not given him a knowledge and love of the Christian faith—he would go forth into the world, able indeed with reference to those purposes of

Richard B. Cook

science, successful with the accumulation of wealth for the multiplication of more, but 'poor, and miserable, and blind, and naked' with reference to everything that constitutes the true and sovereign purposes of our existence—nay, worse, worse—with respect to the sovereign purpose—than if he had still remained in the ignorance which we all commiserate, and which it is the object of this institution to assist in removing."

It was admitted on all hands that great fiscal reforms had been conceived and executed; and speaking of the session of 1842, a writer, not favorable to the Tories, wrote: "The nation saw and felt that its business was understood and accomplished, and the House of Commons was no longer like a sleeper under a nightmare. The long session was a busy one. The Queen wore a cheerful air when she thanked Parliament for their effectual labors. The Opposition was such as could no longer impede the operations of the next session. The condition of the country was fearful enough, but something was done for its future improvement, and the way was now shown to be open for further beneficent legislation."

The corn law reformers renewed their efforts, led by Lord Howick, as soon as the parliamentary session of 1843 opened. An inquiry by the whole House was demanded into the causes of the long continued manufacturing depression referred to in the Queen's speech. Mr. Gladstone replied that while the Opposition proposed to repeal the corn laws, they offered no measure of relief in their place. The corn laws were at the root of the distress in the country, but the difficulty was to unite the ranks of the Opposition in opinion as to what ought to follow the repeal of the corn laws. The question between the government and the Opposition was not really so great as the latter wished to make out. It was simply as to the amount of relaxation the country could bear in the duties. It was the intention of the First Lord of the Treasury to attain his object "by increasing the employment of the people, by cheapening the prices of the articles of consumption, as also the articles of industry, by encouraging the means of exchange with foreign nations, and thereby encouraging in return an extension of the export trade; but besides all this, if he understood the measure of the government last year, it was proposed that the relaxation should be practically so limited as to cause no violent shock to existing interests, such as would have the tendency of displacing that labor which should be employed, and which, if displaced, would be unable to find another field." The measure of the previous year had nothing but a beneficial effect, but the repeal of the corn laws would displace a vast mass of labor. Lord Howick's motion was defeated and so were others offered by Mr. Villiers and Lord John Russell, by diminishing majorities, and Mr. Gladstone protested against the constant renewal of uneasiness in the country by successive motions of this kind in Parliament.

The year 1843 was one destined to witness a great advance in Mr. Gladstone's progress towards the front rank among statesmen. June 10th, Lord Ripon, who was President of the Board of Trade, left this place for the Board of Control, and Mr. Gladstone was appointed to the position, and thus became a member of the Cabinet at the age of thirty-three Mr. Gladstone now became in name what he had been already in fact—the President of the Board of Trade. He states that "the very first opinion which he was ever called upon to give in Cabinet" was an opinion in favor of withdrawing the bill providing education for children in factories; to which vehement opposition was offered by the Dissenters, on the ground that it was too favorable to the Established Church. It seemed that his position was assured and yet in October he wrote to a friend: "Uneasy, in my opinion, must be the position of every member of Parliament who thinks independently in these times, or in any that are likely to succeed them; and in proportion as a man's course of thought deviates from the ordinary lines his seat must less and less resemble a bed of roses." Mr. Gladstone possibly felt when he penned these lines that the time was at hand when his convictions would force him to take a position that would array against him some of his most ardent friends.

During the session of 1844 Mr. Gladstone addressed the

House on a variety of subjects, including rail ways, the law of partnership, the agricultural interest, the abolition of the corn laws, the Dissenters' Chapel Bill and the sugar duties. One very valuable bill he had carried was a measure for the abolition of restrictions on the exportation of machinery. Another was the railway bill, to improve the railway system, by which the Board of Trade had conditional power to purchase railways which had not adopted a revised scale of tolls. The bill also compulsorily provided for at least one third-class train per week-day upon every line of railway, to charge but one penny a mile, regulated the speed of traveling, compelled such trains to stop at every station, and arranged for the carrying of children under three years of age for nothing and those under twelve at reduced fares. This measure, conceived so distinctly in the interests of the poorer classes, met with considerable opposition at first from the various railway companies, but it was ultimately passed into law. These were measures passed in the spirit of reform, though by a Conservative government.

There was another matter legislated upon which shows how Mr. Gladstone's mind was undergoing changes in the direction of religious toleration. Lady Hewley had originally founded and given to Calvinistic Independents certain charities which had gradually passed to Unitarians, who were ousted from their benefits. A bill was proposed to vest property left to Dissenting bodies in the hands of that religions body with whom it had remained for the preceding twenty years. The measure was passed, but when it was discussed in the House of Commons Mr. Gladstone said that it was a bill which it was incumbent upon the House to endorse; that there was no contrariety between his principles of religious belief and those on which legislation in this case ought to proceed; that there was a great question of justice, viz., whether those who were called Presbyterian Dissenters, and who were a century and a half ago of Trinitarian opinions, ought not to be protected at the present moment in possession of the chapels which they held, with the appurtenances of those chapels? On the question of substantial justice he pronounced the strongest affirmative opinion. "After this speech there were those who thought, and expressed their hope and belief in words, that the 'champion of Free Trade' would ere long become the advocate of the most unrestricted liberty in matters of religion. Their hope, if sanguine as to its immediate fulfillment, was far from groundless."

However, in December of the same year Mr. Gladstone wrote to his friend Archdeacon, afterwards Bishop Wilberforce, about the prospects of the Church of England: "I rejoice to see that your views on the whole are hopeful. For my part I heartily go along with you. The fabric consolidates itself more and more, even while the earthquake rocks it; for, with a thousand drawbacks and deductions, love grows larger, zeal warmer, truth firmer among us. It makes the mind sad to speculate upon the question how much better all might have been; but our mourning should be turned into joy and thankfulness when we think also how much worse it *was*."

The next event in the life of Mr. Gladstone is marked by a momentous change in his political position. Scarcely had Parliament met in January, 1845, when it was announced to the astonishment of everyone that Mr. Gladstone had resigned his place as President of the Board of Trade in the Cabinet. He set a good deal of speculation at rest by the announcement made in his speech on the address of the Queen, that his resignation was due solely to the government intentions with regard to Maynooth College. Before, however, he had resigned, Mr. Gladstone had completed a second and revised tariff, carrying further the principles of the revision of 1842.

In the session of 1844 Sir Robert Peel, in response to the requests of Irish members, had promised that the Government would take up the question of academical education in Ireland, with the view of bringing it more nearly to the standard of England and Scotland, increasing its amount and improving its quality. In fulfillment of this pledge the government, at the beginning of the session of 1845, proposed to establish non-sectarian colleges in Ireland, and to increase the appropriation to Maynooth. The College of Maynooth, which was established for the education of Roman Catholic priests and laymen, had fallen into poverty and decay. In order to gratify the Irish, the government offered to increase the grant already made from $45,000 to $150,000 a year. This appropriation was not to be subject to any annual vote, and the affairs of the College were to be executed by the Board of Works. These proposals placed Mr. Gladstone in a position of great difficulty. He must either support Sir Robert Peel's measure, or retire from the Cabinet into isolation, if not subject to the imputation of eccentricity. He took council with his friends, Archdeacon Manning and Mr. Hope, who advised him to remain, and with Lord Stanley who warned him that his resignation must be followed by resistance of the proposals of the government, which would involve him in a storm of religious agitation. But Mr. Gladstone persisted in his intention, in what seemed like giving up his brilliant prospects, but said it would not necessarily be followed by resistance to the proposal about Maynooth.

Mr. Gladstone said that the proposed increase in the Maynooth endowment and the establishment of non-sectarian colleges were at variance with views he had written and uttered upon the relations of the Church and State. "I am sensible how fallible my judgment is," said Mr. Gladstone, "and how easily I might have erred; but still it has been my conviction that although I was not to fetter my judgment as a member of Parliament by a reference to abstract theories, yet, on the other hand, it was absolutely due to the public and due to myself that I should, so far as in me lay, place myself in a position to form an opinion upon a matter of so great importance, that should not only be actually free from all bias or leaning with respect to any consideration whatsoever, but an opinion that should be unsuspected. On that account I have taken a course most painful to myself in respect to personal feelings, and have separated myself from men with whom and under whom I have long acted in public life, and of whom I am bound to say, although I have now no longer the honor of serving my most gracious Sovereign, that I continue to regard them with unaltered sentiments both of public regard and private attachment."

Then again he said: "My whole purpose was to place myself in a position in which I should be free to consider any course without being liable to any just suspicion on the ground of personal interest. It is not profane if I now say, '*with a great price obtained I this freedom.*' The political association in which I stood was to me at the time the *alpha* and *omega* of public life. The government of Sir Robert Peel was believed to be of immovable strength. My place, as President of the Board of Trade, was at the very kernel of its most interesting operations; for it was in progress from year to year, with continually waxing courage, towards the emancipation of industry, and therein towards the accomplishment of another great and blessed work of public justice. Giving up what I highly prized, aware that

> male sarta
> Gratia nequicquam coit, et rescinditur.

I felt myself open to the charge of being opinionated and wanting in deference to really great authorities, and I could not but know that I should inevitably be regarded as fastidious and fanciful, fitter for a dreamer, or possibly a schoolman, than for the active purposes of public life in a busy and moving age."

There were some of his party angry and others who thought that there was something almost Quixotic in Mr. Gladstone's honorable resignation, because so soon as he felt himself free he gave his support to the Maynooth Bill and also to the scheme for the extension of academical education in Ireland, which latter was described by Sir R. Inglis as a "gigantic scheme of godless education." In Greville's "Memoirs" we find: "Gladstone's explanation is ludicrous. Everybody said that he had only succeeded in showing that his resignation was unnecessary. He was criticised as the possessor of a kind of supernatural virtue that could scarcely be popular with the slaves of party, and he was considered whimsical, fantastic, impracticable, a man whose 'conscience was so tender that he could not go straight,' a visionary not to be relied on—in fact, a character and intellect useless to the political manager." "I am greatly alarmed at Gladstone's resignation. I fear it foretells measures opposed to the Church truth," wrote Wilberforce; and Peel told Gladstone beforehand that his reasons for his resignation would be considered insufficient. But Mr. Gladstone's resignation, when understood, elicited the liveliest expressions of regret from friend and foe, as well as the most flattering testimonies as to his ability and character. His chief, Sir Robert Peel, and Lord John Russell, the leader of the Opposition, were alike complimentary in their remarks.

Dr. Russell, the biographer of Mr. Gladstone, says: "Mr. Gladstone's retirement, by impairing his reputation for common sense, threatened serious and lasting injury to his political career, But the whirligig of time brought its revenges even more swiftly than usual. A conjunction of events arose in which he was destined to repair the mischief which the speculative side had wrought; but for the moment the speculative side was uppermost."

Mr. Gladstone was fast leaving his Toryism behind. To show how far his views had changed in the course of seven years, it may be said that in his speech on these measures he observed how that exclusive support to the Established Church was a doctrine that was being more and more abandoned. Mr. Burke considered it contrary to wise policy to give exclusive privileges to a negative creed like that of Protestantism. They could not prove their religious scruples for denying this grant to Roman Catholics, because they gave their votes of money to almost every Dissenting seat. He hoped the concession now made— which was a great and liberal gift, because unrestricted and given in a spirit of confidence—would not lead to the renewal of agitation in Ireland by Mr. O'Connell. It might be well for him to reflect that agitation was a two-edged sword. Being conformable to justice and not contrary to principle, he hoped the measure proposed would pass into a law.

W. T. Stead, in a recent article, said, in relation to Mr.

Gladstone's retirement from the Cabinet, that "It is ridiculous to pretend, with Mr. Gladstone's career before us, that his course has been swayed by calculating self-interest. He has been the very madman of politics from the point of view of Mr. Worldly Wiseman. 'No man,' said he, the other day, 'has ever committed suicide so often as I,' and that witness is true. The first and perhaps the most typical of all his many suicides was his resignation of his seat in Sir Robert Peel's Cabinet, not because he disapproved of the Maynooth Grant, but because, as he had at one time written against it, he was determined that his advocacy of it should be purged of the last taint of self-interest. As Mr. George Russell rightly remarks, 'This was an act of Parliamentary Quixotism too eccentric to be intelligible. It argued a fastidious sensitiveness of conscience, and a nice sense of political propriety so opposed to the sordid selfishness and unblushing tergiversation of the ordinary place-hunter as to be almost offensive.' But as Mr. Gladstone was then, so he has been all his life—the very Quixote of conscience. Judged by every standard of human probability, he has ruined himself over and over and over again. He is always ruining himself, and always rising, like the Phoenix, in renewed youth from the ashes of his funeral pyre. As was said in homely phrase some years ago, he 'always keeps bobbing up again.' What is the secret of this wonderful capacity of revival? How is it that Mr. Gladstone seems to find even his blunders help him, and the affirmation of principles that seem to be destructive to all chance of the success of his policy absolutely helps him to its realization?"

From a merely human standpoint it is inexplicable. But

> 'If right or wrong in this God's world of ours
> Be leagued with higher powers,'

then the mystery is not so insolvable. He believed in the higher powers. He never shrank from putting his faith to the test; and on the whole, who can deny that for his country and for himself he has reason to rejoice in the verification of his working hypothesis?

Richard B. Cook

'We walk by faith and not by sight,' he said once; 'and by no one so much as by those who are in politics is this necessary.' It is the evidence of things not seen, the eternal principles, the great invisible moral sanctions that men are wont to call the laws of God, which alone supply a safe guide through this mortal wilderness.

'Men of a thousand shifts and wiles, look here!
See one straightforward conscience put in pawn
To win a world; see the obedient sphere
By bravery's simple gravitation drawn!
Shall we not heed the lesson taught of old,
And by the Present's lips repeated still?
In our own single manhood to be bold,
Fortressed in conscience and impregnable.'

"Mr. Gladstone has never hesitated to counter at sharp right angles the passion and the fury of the day. Those who represent him as ever strong upon the strong side, wilfully shut their eyes to half his history. He challenged Lord Palmerston over the Don Pacifico question, and was believed to have wrecked himself almost as completely as when in 1876 he countered even more resolutely the fantastic Jingoism of Lord Beaconsfield. It is easy for those who come after and enter into the spoils gained by sacrifices of which they themselves were incapable to describe the Bulgarian agitation as an astute party move. The party did not think so. Its leaders did not think so. Some of those who now halloo loud enough behind Mr. Gladstone were then bitter enough in their complaint that he had wrecked his party. One at least, who was constrained to say the other thing in public, made up for it by bitter and contemptuous cavilings in private. Now it is easy to see that Lord Beaconsfield was mistaken and that Mr. Gladstone held the winning card all along. But no one knew it at the time when the card had to be played, certainly not Mr. Gladstone himself. He simply saw his duty a dead sure thing, and, like Jim Bludsoe on the burning boat, 'He went for it there and then.' It turned up trumps, but no one knew how heavy were the odds against it save those who went through the stress and the strain of that testing and trying time by his side."

In the summer of 1845 Mr. Gladstone proposed to his intimate friend, Mr. J.R. Hope, that they should spend the month of September in a working tour in Ireland, giving evidence of his characteristic desire always to come in personal contact with any question that he had to discuss. He suggests "their eschewing all grandeur, and taking little account even of scenery, compared with the purpose of looking, from close quarters, at the institutions for religion and education of the country, and at the character of the people. It seems ridiculous to talk of supplying the defects of second-hand information by so short a trip; but although a longer time would be much better, yet even a very contracted one does much when it is added to an habitual, though indirect, knowledge." The projected trip, however, had to be abandoned.

Towards the close of the year 1845 Mr. Gladstone issued a pamphlet entitled "Remarks upon recent Commercial Legislation," in which he not only discussed the salutary effects of the late commercial policy, but used arguments clearly showing that he was advancing to the position of a free-trader. His general conclusion was that English statesmen should use every effort to disburden of all charges, so far as the law was concerned, the materials of industry, and thus enable the workman to approach his work at home on better terms, as the terms in which he entered foreign markets were altered for the worse against him.

While Mr. Gladstone was so willing to deal generously more than ever before with the Irish Roman Catholics, his confidence in the Established Episcopal Church of Ireland was growing less. "I am sorry," he wrote to Bishop Wilberforce, "to express my apprehension that the Irish Church is not in a large sense efficient; the working results of the last ten years have disappointed me. I may be answered, Have faith in the ordinance of God; but then I must see the seal and signature, and these, how can I separate from ecclesiastical descent? The title, in short, is questioned, and vehemently, not only by the

Radicalism of the day, but by the Roman Bishops, who claim to hold succession of St. Patrick, and this claim has been alive all along from the Reformation, so that lapse of years does nothing against it."

The name of Dr. Döllinger, the distinguished reformed Roman Catholic, has been mentioned already in connection with that of Mr. Gladstone. In the fall of 1845 Mr. Gladstone went to Munich and paid his first visit to Dr. Döllinger. For a week he remained in daily intercourse with this eminent divine, and the foundation was laid of a friendship which was sustained by repeated visits and correspondence, and which lasted until the doctor's death in 1890.

In the winter of 1845 Mr. Gladstone met with a painful accident that resulted in a permanent injury to his hand. He was by no means what is termed a sportsman, yet he was somewhat fond of shooting. His gun was prematurely discharged while he was loading it, and shattered the first finger of his left hand, so that amputation was necessary.

CHAPTER VII

MEMBER FOR OXFORD

"Mr. Gladstone's career," says his biographer, G.W.E. Russell, "naturally divides itself into three parts. The first of them ends with his retirement from the representation of Newark. The central part ranges from 1847 to 1868. Happily the third is still incomplete." The first division, according to Dr. Russell, of this remarkable life, we have considered, and we now pass on to the development of the second period. The causes which led up to Mr. Gladstone's retirement from the representation for Newark to that of Oxford we will now proceed to trace.

The agitation by the ablest orators against the corn laws had been going on for ten years, when an announcement was made in the "Times" of December 4, 1845, that Parliament would be convened the first week in January, and that the Queen's address would recommend the immediate consideration of the corn laws, preparatory to their total abolition. This startling news took the other daily papers by surprise, for there had been recently a lull in the agitation, and several of them contradicted it positively. Yet the newspapers had noticed the unusual occurrence of four cabinet meetings in one week. The original statement was confirmed. The ministry was pledged to support the measure. The hour had come, the doom of the corn laws was sealed. Mr. Gladstone's thoughts and labors for some years past had been leading him away from Protection, in which he had been brought up, in the direction of Free Trade; and although he was unable to participate in the last part of the struggle in Parliament, because he was not a member of the House, he was yet in harmony with Sir Robert Peel, and indeed is said to have converted the Premier to Free Trade views. Such a change of views was not the sudden impulse of an hour. The next step was to announce his changed convictions. And so upon other occasions in his life, his attitude on the question of the corn laws led to his separation from some old and greatly cherished political and personal friends, and among the first to disapprove of his new departure must have been his own father, who would think his son was going to ruin the country.

The Duke of Buccleuch and Lord Stanley informed Sir Robert Peel that they could not support a measure for the repeal of the corn laws, and Sir Robert Peel, being doubtful whether he could carry through the proposed measure in the face of such opposition, tendered his resignation as premier to the Queen. Lord John Russell was called upon to form a new ministry, but, having failed in this, the Queen desired Sir Robert Peel to withdraw his resignation, and resume the head of the government again.

It was found when the list of the new Peel Cabinet was published, that Mr. Gladstone was a member of it; having accepted the office of Colonial Secretary, in the place of Lord Stanley, who had resigned because not in sympathy with the proposed movement and of repeal. Accepting office in a ministry pledged to repeal the corn laws led to the retirement of Mr. Gladstone from the House of Commons as the representative for Newark. The Duke of New Castle, the patron and friend of Mr. Gladstone, was an ardent Protectionist, and could not sanction the candidature of a supporter of Free Trade principles. His patronage was therefore necessarily withdrawn from Mr. Gladstone. Indeed, the Duke had turned his own son, Lord Lincoln, out of the representation of Nottinghamshire for accepting office under Sir Robert Peel, and he naturally showed no mercy to the brilliant but wayward politician, whom his favor had made member for Newark. Besides, Mr. Gladstone felt he held opposite principles from those he held when elected, and that unless the constituency had changed with him, he could no longer honorably continue to represent them, even if the influence and friendship of the Duke permitted it.

Accordingly he did not offer himself for re-election, but retired and issued an address to the electors of Newark, dated January 5, 1846, of which the following is an extract: "By accepting the office of Secretary of State for the Colonies, I have ceased to be your representative in Parliament. On several accounts I should have been peculiarly desirous at the present time of giving you an opportunity to pronounce your constitutional judgment on my public conduct, by soliciting at your hands a renewal of the trust which I have already received from you on five successive occasions, and held during a period of thirteen years. But as I have good reason to believe that a candidate recommended to your favor through local connections may ask your suffrages, it becomes my very painful duty to announce to you on that ground alone my retirement from a position which has afforded me so much of honor and of satisfaction." Mr. Gladstone further goes on to explain that he accepted office because he held that "it was for those who believed the Government was acting according to the demands of public duty to testify that belief, however limited their sphere might be, by their co-operation." He had acted "in obedience to the clear and imperious call of public obligation."

It was in this way that Mr. Gladstone became a voluntary exile from the House of Commons during this important season, and took no part in the debates, his personal powerful advocacy being lost in the consideration of the great measure before the House. He was a member of the Cabinet, but not of the House of Commons. It was no secret, however, that he was the most advanced Free Trader in the Peel Cabinet, and that the policy of the government in regard to this great measure of 1846 was to a large extent moulded by him.

It is also known that his representations of the effects of Free Trade on the industry of the country and the general well-being of the people strengthened the Premier in his resolve to sweep away the obnoxious corn laws. His pamphlet on recent commercial legislation had prepared the way for the later momentous changes; and to Mr. Gladstone is due much of the credit for the speedy consummation of the Free Trade policy of the Peel Ministry. Mr. Gladstone may be regarded as the pioneer of the movement.

Just at this time a calamity occurred in Ireland which furnished Sir Robert Peel an additional argument for the prompt repeal of the corn laws; namely, a prospective famine, owing to the failure of the potato crop. With threatened famine in Ireland, such as had never been experienced, the Prime Minister saw clearly that corn must be admitted into the country free of duty. The Anti-Corn Law League was growing powerful and even irresistible, while both in England and Ireland many landlords of influence, who did not belong to the League, were in sympathy with the movement started by the Premier and ready to extend to him a hearty support.

But the friends of Protection did not leave the Premier without opposition. Knowing that Sir Robert Peel's personal influence was greater than that of any minister who had "virtually governed the empire," they used every means at their comm- and, fair and unfair, to defeat the bill. However, their efforts were destined to failure. Some contended that the presentation and passage of the corn law repeal bill ought to be left to the Liberals. But Free Trade had not received the support of every member of the Liberal party, and Sir Robert Peel was in a position to carry out the measure, and it was not in accordance with the wisdom of practical politics to halt. Indeed, at this very juncture, Mr. Cobden wrote to the Premier that he had the power, and that it would be disastrous to the country for him to hesitate. Writing from Edinburgh, Lord John Russell announced his conversion to total and immediate repeal of the corn laws. Sir Robert Peel hesitated no longer, but, feeling that the crisis had arrived, determined to grapple with it. It was duty to country before and above fancied loyalty to party to be considered. It is strange what remedies some men deem sensible, suggested to prevent famine in Ireland.

"Obviously the Government was in difficulties. What those difficulties were it was not hard to guess. In the previous autumn it had become known that, after a long season of sunless wet, the potatoes had everywhere been attacked by an obscure disease. The failure of this crop meant an Irish famine. The steps suggested to meet this impending calamity were strange enough. The head of the English peerage recommended the poor to rely on curry-powder as a nutritious and satisfying food. Another duke thought that the government could show no favor to a population almost in a state of rebellion, but that individuals might get up a subscription. A noble lord, harmonizing materialism and faith, urged the government to encourage the provision of salt fish, and at the same time to appoint a day of public acknowledgment of our dependence on Divine goodness. The council of the Royal Agricultural Society, numbering some of the wealthiest noblemen and squires in England, were not ashamed to lecture the laborers on the sustaining properties of thrice-boiled bones."

When Parliament assembled the Premier entered into an explanation of the late ministerial crisis, and unfolded his projected plans. He said that the failure of the potato crop had led to the dissolution of the late government, that matters now could brook no further delay; that prompt action must now be taken on the Corn Laws; that the progress of reason and truth demanded it; that his opinions on the subject of Protection had undergone a great change; that the experience of the past three years confirmed him in his new views; that he could not conceal the knowledge of his convictions, however much it might lay him open to the charge of inconsistency; that, though accused of apathy and neglect, he and his colleagues were even then engaged in the most extensive and arduous inquiries into the true state of Ireland; and that, as these inquiries progressed, he has been forced to the conclusion that the protection policy was unsound and consequently untenable.

It is worthy of note that Mr. Disraeli, the future Parliamentary rival of Mr. Gladstone, took part, as a member of the House of Commons, in the discussion of the question under consideration. The following words show his attitude: "To the opinions which I have expressed in this House in favor of Protection I adhere. They sent to this House, and if I had relinquished them I should have relinquished my seat also." "It would be an unprofitable talk," writes Barnett Smith, "to unravel the many inconsistencies of Lord Beaconsfield's career; but with regard to this deliverance upon Protection, the curious in such matters may turn back to the records of 1842, when they will discover that at that time he was quite prepared to advocate measures of a Free Trade character. But we must pass on from this important question of the Corn Laws, with the angry controversy to which it gave rise. Sir Robert Peel brought forward his measure, and after lengthened debate in both Houses, it became law, and grain was admitted into English ports under the new tariff."

After all their success in carrying through the important Corn Law Repeal scheme, the ministry of Sir Robert Peel was doomed to fall upon an Irish question. The very day that brought their victory in the passage of the Corn Law Repeal Act in the House of Lords saw the defeat of the ministry in the House of Commons on their bill for the suppression of outrage in Ireland. Sir Robert Peel found himself in a minority of 73 and therefore tendered his resignation. It was accepted and Sir Robert Peel went out of office forever. Lord John Russell was sent for by the Queen, and he succeeded in forming a Whig Ministry.

Mr. Gladstone's return to the Cabinet of Sir Robert Peel, as we have seen, cost him his seat in the House of Commons. It was not until the brief session of 1847, that he appeared again in Parliament. The Queen dissolved Parliament in person, July, 23d. The election succeeding turned in many instances upon ecclesiastical questions, and especially upon the Maynooth grant.

It was announced early in 1847 that one of the two members of the House of Commons for the University of Oxford intended to retire at the next general election. Mr. Canning had pronounced the representation of the university as the most coveted prize of public life, and Mr. Gladstone himself confessed that he "desired it with an almost passionate fondness." Mr. Gladstone, as a graduate of Oxford, was looked upon not only by his contemporaries, but by his seniors and those who came after him, with feelings of enthusiastic admiration. The feeling then was reciprocal, and he was proposed for the vacant seat. Sir R. N. Inglis was secure in his seat, and so the contest lay between Mr. Gladstone and Mr. Round, who was of the ultra-Protestant and Tory school. The contest excited the keenest interest and was expected on all hands to be very close.

Mr. Gladstone in his address to the electors of his *Alma Mater* confessed that in the earlier part of his public life he had been an advocate for the exclusive support of the national religion of the state, but it had been in vain; the time was against him. He said: "I found that scarcely a year passed without the adoption of some fresh measure involving the national recognition and the national support of various forms of religion, and, in particular, that a recent and fresh provision had been made for the propagation from a public chair of Arian or Socinian doctrines. The question remaining for me was whether, aware of the opposition of the English people, I should set down as equal to nothing, in a matter primarily connected not with our own but with their priesthood, the wishes of the people of Ireland; and whether I should avail myself of the popular feeling in regard to the Roman Catholics for the purpose of enforcing against them a system which we had ceased by common consent to enforce against Arians—a system, above all, of which I must say that it never can be conformable to policy, to justice or even to decency, when it has become avowedly partial and one-sided in its application."

This address intensified the determination of those opposed to Mr. Gladstone to defeat him. A great portion of the press was, however, in his favor. Some of the journals that were enthusiastic for Mr. Gladstone were very bitter against Mr. Round. Mr. Gladstone's distinguished talent and industry were lauded, as well as his earnest attachment to the Church of England. He had, however, renounced the exclusiveness of his politico-ecclesiastical principles, and no longer importuned Parliament to ignore all forms of religion but those established by law, or which were exactly coincident with his own belief. "His election," declared one journal, "unlike that of Mr. Round, while it sends an important member to the House of Commons, will certainly be creditable, and may be valuable to the university; and we heartily hope that no negligence or hesitation among his supporters may impede his success." Even outside of church circles the election was regarded with great interest.

The nomination took place July 29th. After the usual ceremony, the voting commenced in convocation-house, which was densely crowded. So great was the pressure of the throng that men fainted and had to be carried out. Mr. Coleridge, afterward Lord Coleridge, was the secretary of Mr. Gladstone's committee. Distinguished men, among them Sir Robert Peel, his colleague in the Cabinet, came from a great distance to "plump" for Mr. Gladstone. The venerable Dr. Routh, then nearly ninety-two years old, came forth from his retirement at Magdalen College to vote for him. Mrs. Gladstone, according to Mr. Hope-Scott, was an indefatigable canvasser for her husband. At the close of the poll the vote stood: Inglis, 1700; Gladstone, 997; Round, 824. Of course Sir Robert Inglis, with his "prehistoric Toryism," stood at the head. To the supporters of Mr. Gladstone and Mr. Round must be added 154 who were paired. Mr. Gladstone received a majority of 173 over his ultra-Protestant opponent. The total number of those polled exceeded that registered at any previous election, showing the intense and general interest in the result.

This period of Mr. Gladstone's life has been very properly styled by one of his biographers, as the transition period. "On one side the Conservative Free-trader clings fondly and tenaciously to the Toryism of his youth, on another, he is reaching out toward new realms of Liberal thought and action. He opposes marriage with a deceased wife's sister on theological and social grounds, asserting roundly that such marriage is 'contrary to the law of God, declared for three thousand years and upwards.' He deprecates the appointment of a Commission to enquire into the Universities, because it will deter intending benefactors from effecting their munificent intentions. He argues for a second chamber in Australian legislatures, citing, perhaps a little unfortunately, the constitutional example of contemporary France. In all these utterances it is not hard to read the influence of the traditions in which he was reared, or of the ecclesiastical community which he represents in Parliament."

"Yet even in the theological domain a tendency towards Liberalism shows itself. His hatred of Erastianism is evinced by his gallant but unsuccessful attempt to secure for the clergy and laity of each colonial diocese the power of self-government. Amid the indignant protests of his Tory allies, and in opposition to his own previous speech and vote, he vindicates the policy of admitting the Jews to Parliament. He defends the establishment of diplomatic relations with the Court of Rome; he supports the alteration of the parliamentary oath; and, though he will not abet an abstract attack on Church Rates, he contends that their maintainance involves a corresponding duty to provide accommodation in the church for the very poorest of the congregation."

"On the commercial side his Liberalism is rampant. With even fanatical faith he clings to Free Trade as the best guarantee for our national stability amid the crash of the dynasties and constitutions which went down in '48. He thunders against the insidious dangers of reciprocity. He desires, by reforming the laws which govern navigation, to make the ocean, 'that great highway of nations, as free to the ships that traverse its bosom as to the winds that sweep it.'"

Richard B. Cook

"And so the three years—1847, 1848, 1849—rolled by, full of stirring events in Europe and in England, in Church and in State, but marked by no special incidents in the life of Mr. Gladstone. For him these years were a period of mental growth, of transition, of development. A change was silently proceeding, which was not completed for twenty years, if, indeed, it has been completed yet. 'There have been,' he wrote in later days to Bishop Wilberforce, 'two great deaths, or transmigrations of spirit, in my political existence—one, very slow, the breaking of ties with my original party.' This was now in progress. The other will be narrated in due course."

One of the features of the general election of 1847 that excited the wildest popular comment was the election of Baron Rothschild for the City of London. There was nothing illegal in the election of a Jew, but he was virtually precluded from taking his seat in the House of Commons, because the law required every member to subscribe not only to the Christian religion, but to the Protestant Episcopal faith. To obviate this difficulty, Lord John Russell, soon after Parliament assembled, offered a resolution affirming the eligibility of Jews to all functions and offices to which Roman Catholics were admissible by law. Sir R.H. Inglis opposed the resolution and Mr. Gladstone, his colleague, supported it.

Mr. Gladstone inquired whether there were any grounds for the disqualification of the Jews which distinguished them from any other classes in the community. They contended for a "Christian Parliament, but the present measure did not make severance between politics and religion, it only amounted to a declaration that there was no necessity for excluding a Jew, as such, from an assembly in which every man felt sure that a vast and overwhelming majority of its members would always be Christian. It was said that by admitting a few Jews they would un-Christianize Parliament; that was true in word, but not in substance." He had no doubt that the majority of the members who composed it would always perform their obligations on the true faith of a Christian. It was too late to say that the measure was un-Christian, and that it would call down the vengeance of heaven. When he opposed the last law of the removal of Jewish disabilities, he foresaw that if he gave the Jew municipal, magisterial and executive functions, we could not refuse him legislative functions any longer. "The Jew was refused entrance into the House because he would then be a maker of the law; but who made the maker of the law? The constituencies; and into these constituencies had been admitted the Jews. Now were the constituencies Christian constituencies? If they were, was it probable that the Parliament would cease to be a Christian Parliament?"

Mr. Gladstone admitted the force of the prayer in Bishop Wilberforce's petition, that in view of this concession measures should be taken to give greater vigor to the Church, and thus operate to the prevention of an organic change in the relations between Church and State. In concluding his defence of Lord John Russell's resolution Mr. Gladstone expressed the opinion that if they admitted Jews into Parliament, prejudice might be awakened for awhile, but the good sense of the people would soon allay it, and members would have the consolation of knowing that in case of difficulty they had yielded to a sense of justice, and by so doing had not disparaged religion or lowered Christianity, but rather had elevated both in all reflecting and well-regulated minds. The logic of this speech could not be controverted, though Mr. Newdegate declared that Mr. Gladstone would never have gained his election for the University of Oxford had his sentiments on the Jewish question been then known. The resolution of Lord John Russell was carried by a large majority, whereupon he announced first a resolution, and then a bill, in accordance with its terms.

The year 1848 was a year of excitement and revolution. All Europe was in a state of agitation, and France by a new revolution presented another one of her national surprises. The news of a revolution in France caused the greatest perturbation throughout England, and disturbances in the capital of the country. Great demonstrations were made at Trafalgar Square and Charing Cross, March 6th, but the meetings assumed more of a burlesque than of a serious character. In Glasgow and other parts of the country there were serious riots. Shops were sacked, and the military was called out to quell the disturbance, which was not effected until the soldiers fired with fatal results upon the rioters. There were uprisings and mob violence also at Manchester, Edinburgh, Newcastle, but they were of a less formidable character. A Chartist meeting was held on Kennington Common, March 13th, but, though the meeting had been looked forward to with great apprehensions by all lovers of law and order, yet it passed off without the serious results anticipated.

Though great preparations were made in view of the demonstration, yet, fortunately it passed off without loss of life. The meeting however had furnished a pretext for the gathering of a lawless mob, although but few were politically concerned in it. It was deemed necessary, to provide against every emergency, so special constables in great numbers were sworn in previous to the meetings, and it is interesting to observe that amongst the citizens who came forward in London to enroll themselves as preservers of the peace of society were William Ewart Gladstone, the Duke of Norfolk, the Earl of Derby, and Prince Louis Napoleon, afterwards Emperor of France.

The people were becoming dissatisfied with the government of the country, particularly with its financial measures. A deficiency of two million pounds appeared, and additional taxation would be necessary owing to the Caffre War. It was therefore proposed to continue the income tax for five years and increase it slightly. Owing to the distress in Ireland it was not proposed to extend the operation of this measure to that country. The property tax was defended on the same principles laid down by Mr. Pitt, and in 1842, by Sir Robert Peel. But this scheme was bitterly opposed and many attributed the depressed condition of the finances to free trade. Sir Robert Peel decided to support the proposed tax for three years. Mr. Disraeli desired the success of Sir Robert Peel's policy, and described himself as a "free-trader, but not a free-booter of the

Manchester school;" and he dubbed the blue-book of the Import Duties Committee "the greatest work of imagination that the nineteenth century has produced." He said that the government, by acting upon it, and taking it for a guide, resembled a man smoking a cigar on a barrel of gunpowder.

This epigrammatic speech of Mr. Disraeli brought Mr. Gladstone to his feet. He said, by way of introduction, that he could not hope to sustain the lively interest created by the remarkable speech of his predecessor—a display to which he felt himself unequal—he would pass over the matters of a personal description touched upon by the honorable gentleman, and confine himself to defending the policy which had been assailed. Mr. Gladstone then demonstrated, by a series of elaborate statistics, the complete success of Sir Robert Peel's policy. He also said, that the confidence of the public would be greatly shaken by an adverse vote, and he alluded to the unsettled condition of affairs in the Cabinet. "I am sure," said Mr. Gladstone, "that this House of Commons will prove itself to be worthy of the Parliaments which preceded it, worthy of the Sovereign which it has been called to advise, and worthy of the people which it has been chosen to represent, by sustaining this nation, and enabling it to stand firm in the midst of the convulsions that shake European society; by doing all that pertains to us for the purpose of maintaining social order, the stability of trade, and the means of public employment; and by discharging our consciences, on our own part, under the difficult circumstances of the crisis, in the perfect trust that if we set a good example to the nations—for whose interests we are appointed to consult—they, too, will stand firm as they have in other times of almost desperate emergency; and that through their good sense, their moderation, and their attachment to the institutions of the country, we shall see these institutions still exist, a blessing and a benefit to prosperity, whatever alarms and whatever misfortunes may unfortunately befall other portions of civilized Europe."

"It was fortunate for the future interests of the country," says Dr. Smith, his biographer, "that the proposals of the government were at this juncture supported by a great majority of the House of Commons. In a moment of unreasoning panic there was some danger of the adoption of a reactionary policy—a step that would have lost to the country those blessings which it subsequently enjoyed as the outcome of Free Trade."

May 15, Mr. Labouchere, President of the Board of Trade, proposed a plan for the modification of the navigation laws. Reserving the coasting trade and fisheries of Great Britain and the Colonies, it was proposed "to throw open the whole navigation of the country, of every sort and description." But the Queen claimed the right of putting such restrictions as she saw fit upon the navigation of foreign countries, if those countries did not meet England on equal terms; and that each colony should be allowed to throw open its coasting trade to foreign countries. Mr. Gladstone made a lengthy speech, examining closely the operation of existing laws, and showing the necessity for their repeal. With regard to the power claimed by the Queen in Council, with a view to enforcing reciprocity, Mr. Gladstone said, "I confess it appears to me there is a great objection to conferring such a power as that which is proposed to be given to the Queen in Council." He contended also for a gradual change in the laws. The policy of excluding the coasting trade from the measure he also condemned. "It would have been much more frank to have offered to admit the Americans to our coasting trade if they would admit us to theirs." If England and America concurred in setting an example to the world, he hoped we should "live to see the ocean, that great highway of nations, as free to the ships that traverse its bosom as the winds that sweep it. England would then have achieved another triumph, and have made another powerful contribution to the prosperity of mankind." The bill was postponed until the following year.

During the session of 1848 Mr. Gladstone spoke upon the proposed grant of Vancouver's Island to the Hudson's Bay Company; and upon the Sugar Duties Bill; but the most important speech delivered by him at that time was upon a measure to legalize diplomatic relations with the Court of Rome. It was objected that thus recognizing the spiritual governor of Rome and of all the Roman Catholic population of the world, would neither conciliate the affections of the Protestants, nor satisfy the wishes of the Roman Catholics, who had denounced it strongly to the Pope.

Mr. Gladstone took broad and comprehensive views of the question. To some features of the Bill he was opposed, but was in favor of its principle. It was unfortunate as to time, owing to the condition of affairs in Italy. England must take one of two positions. If she declined political communication with the See of Rome, she had no right to complain of any steps which the Pope might take with respect to the administration of his own ecclesiastical affairs; but an act so directly in contravention of the laws of the land as the partitioning of the country into archbishoprics and bishoprics was a most unfortunate proceeding; wrong because it was generally and justly offensive to the feelings of the people of England, and totally unnecessary, as he believed, for Roman Catholic purposes, but also because it ill assorted with the grounds on which the Parliament was invited by the present bill to establish definite relations with the See of Rome. For one hundred years after the Reformation the Pope was actually in arms for the purpose of recovering by force his lost dominions in this country. It was only natural, therefore, that we should have prohibited relations with the See of Rome when it attacked the title of the Sovereign of these realms, but there was no such reason for continuing the prohibition at the present moment.

Those who have studied Mr. Gladstone's career carefully attest that this speech would have been impossible from his lips ten years before the time it was delivered; and early in the next session of Parliament he delivered another speech which furnishes us an example of the growth of his liberal views in matters of conscience. Lord John Russell proposes further relief upon the matter of oaths to be taken by members of Parliament. Mr. Gladstone said that the civil political claims of the Jew should not be barred, and he deprecated the tendency to degenerate formalism in oaths, but he was glad that the words, "on the true faith of a Christian" in respect to all Christian members of the House of Commons had been retained. He also, later in the session, favored correcting the enormous evils growing out of the Church rate system, with taxation of all the further support of the State Church. He did not believe in imposing an uncompensated burden upon any man. Every man contributing his quota was entitled to demand a free place in the house of his Maker. "But the centre and best parts of the Church were occupied by pews exclusively for the middle classes, while the laboring classes were jealously excluded from almost every part of light and hearing in the Churches, and were treated in a manner most painful to reflect upon."

When Mr. Labouchere re-introduced the ministerial bill for the repeal of the Navigation Laws, in the session of 1849, Mr. Gladstone supported generally the measure in a full and exhaustive speech. He favored the bill with certain modifications. The Marquis of Granby expressed fears at the consequences of the change proposed, and Mr. Gladstone answered him: "The noble Marquis," he observed, "desired to expel the vapours and exhalations that had been raised with regard to the principle of political economy, and which vapours and exhalations I find for the most part in the fears with which those changes are regarded. The noble Marquis consequently hoped that the Trojan horse would not be allowed to come within the walls of Parliament. But however applicable the figures may be to other plans, it does not, I submit, apply to the mode of proceeding I venture to recommend to the House, because we follow the precedent of what Mr. Huskisson did before us. Therefore more than one moiety of the Trojan horse has already got within the citadel— it has been there for twenty-five years, and yet what has proceeded from its bowels has only tended to augment the rate of increase in the progress of your shipping. Therefore, let us not be alarmed by vague and dreamy ratiocinations of evil, which had never been wanting on any occasion, and which never will be wanting so long as this is a free State, wherein every man can find full vent and scope for the expression, not only of his principles, but of his prejudices and his fears. Let us not be deterred by those apprehensions from giving a calm and serious examination to this question, connected as it is with the welfare of our country. Let us follow steadily the light of experience, and be convinced that He who preserved us during the past will also be sufficient to sustain us during all the dangers of the future."

Mr. Disraeli seized the opportunity to make a caustic speech, in which he fiercely attacked both Mr. Labouchere and Mr. Gladstone, and alluded sarcastically to their "great sacrifices," and said that the latter was about to give up that good development of the principle of reciprocity which the House had waited for with so much suspense. Mr. Gladstone replied, "I am perfectly satisfied to bear his sarcasm, good humoured and brilliant as it is, while I can appeal to his judgment as to whether the step I have taken was unbecoming in one who conscientiously differs with him on the freedom of trade, and has endeavoured to realize it; because, so far from its being the cause of the distress of the country, it has been, under the mercy of God, the most signal and effectual means of mitigating this distress, and accelerating the dawn of the day of returning prosperity."

Mr. Gladstone spoke also during the session upon the subject of Colonial Reform which came before the House on several occasions, and especially in connection with riots in Canada; and on a bill for the removal of legal restrictions against marriage with a deceased wife's sister. He opposed the latter measure upon theological, social, and moral grounds, and begged the House to repeat the almost entire sentiment of the country respecting the bill. To do otherwise would be to inflict upon the Church the misfortune of having anarchy introduced among its ministers. He hoped they would do all that in them lay to maintain the strictness of the obligations of marriage, and the purity of the hallowed sphere of domestic life. The bill was rejected.

In the Parliamentary session of 1850 one of the chief topics of discussion was the great depression of the agricultural interests of the country. The country was at peace, the revenues were in a good condition, foreign trade had increased, but the farmers still made loud complaints of the disastrous condition, which they attributed to free-trade measures, which they contended had affected the whole of the agricultural interests. Consequently, February 19th, Mr. Disraeli moved for a committee of the whole House to consider such a revision of the Poor Laws of the United Kingdom as might mitigate the distress of the agricultural classes. Some thought that this was a movement against free-trade, but Mr. Gladstone courted the fullest investigation, and seeing no danger in the motion, voted for it. However, the motion of Mr. Disraeli was lost.

Mr. Gladstone likewise favored the extension of the benefits of Constitutional government to certain of the colonies,—for example as set forth in the Australian Colonies Government Bill; and twice during the session he addressed the House on questions connected with slavery, and upon motion of Mr. Haywood for an inquiry into the state of the English and Irish universities, and the government unexpectedly gave their consent to the issuing of a Royal Commission for the purpose. Mr. Gladstone said that any person who might be deliberating with himself whether he would devote a portion of his substance for prosecuting the objects of learning, civilization and religion, would be checked by the prospect that at any given time, and under any given circumstances, a minister, who was the creature of a political majority, might institute a state inquiry into the mode in which the funds he might devise were administered. It was not wise to discourage eleemosynary establishments. It would be better for the Crown to see what could be done to improve the colleges by administering existing laws.

In reviewing the past ten years we exclaim, truly has the period from 1841 to 1850, in the political life of Mr. Gladstone, been called a memorable decade.

It was in the year 1850, as we have seen, that the Gladstones were plunged into domestic sorrow by the death of their little daughter, Catharine Jessy; and it was this same year that brought to Mr. Gladstone another grief from a very different source. This second bereavement was caused by the withdrawal of two of his oldest and most intimate friends, the Archdeacon of Chichester and Mr. J. R. Hope, from the Protestant Episcopal Church of England and their union with the Roman Catholic Church. Mr. Hope, who became Hope-Scott on succeeding to the estate of Abbotsford, was the gentleman who helped Mr. Gladstone in getting through the press his book on Church and State, revising, correcting and reading proof. The Archdeacon, afterwards Cardinal Manning, had, from his undergraduate days, exercised a powerful influence over his contemporaries. He was gifted with maturity of intellect and character, had great shrewdness, much tenacity of will, a cogent, attractive style, combined with an impressive air of authority, to which the natural advantages of person and bearing added force. Besides having these qualifications for leadership, he had fervid devotion, enlarged acquaintance with life and men, and an "unequalled gift of administration;" though a priest, he was essentially a statesman, and had at one time contemplated a political career. He was Mr. Gladstone's most trusted counsellor and most intimate friend.

The cause, or rather occasion for these secessions from the Church of England to the Church of Rome, is thus related: "An Evangelical clergyman, the Rev. G. C. Gorham, had been presented to a living in the diocese of Exeter; and that truly formidable prelate, Bishop Phillpotts, refused to institute him, alleging that he held heterodox views on the subject of Holy Baptism. After complicated litigation, the Judicial Committee of the Privy Council decided, on March 8, 1850, that the doctrine held by the incriminated clergyman was not such as to bar him from preferment in the Church of England. This decision naturally created great commotion in the Church. Men's minds were rudely shaken. The orthodoxy of the Church of England seemed to be jeopardized, and the supremacy of the Privy Council was in a matter touching religious doctrine felt to be an intolerable burden."

Mr. Gladstone, as well as others, was profoundly agitated by these events, and June 4th he expressed his views in a letter to Dr. Blomfield, Bishop of London. The theme of his letter was, "The Royal Supremacy, viewed in the light of Reason, History and the Constitution." He contended that the Royal Supremacy, as settled at the Reformation, was not inconsistent with the spiritual life and inherent jurisdiction of the Church, but the recent establishment of the Privy Council as the ultimate court of appeal in religious causes was "an injurious and even dangerous departure from the Reformation settlement."

In this letter Mr. Gladstone said, in summing up: "I find it no part of my duty, my lord, to idolize the Bishops of England and Wales, or to place my conscience in their keeping. I do not presume or dare to speculate upon their particular decisions; but I say that, acting jointly, publicly, solemnly, responsibly, they are the best and most natural organs of the judicial office of the Church in matters of heresy, and, according to reason, history and the constitution, in that subject-matter the fittest and safest counsellors of the Crown."

But this view regarding the Church of England did not suit some minds, and among them the two friends with whom Mr. Gladstone had, up to this time, acted in religious matters. These troubles in the Church so powerfully affected them that they withdrew.

The following quotation shows Mr. Gladstone's firmness in regard to his own choice of the Protestant Christianity over and above Catholicism, In a letter, written in 1873, to Mrs. Maxwell-Scott, of Abbotsford, the daughter of his friend Hope, he thus writes of an interview had with her father: "It must have been about this time that I had another conversation with him about religion, of which, again, I exactly recollect the spot. Regarding (forgive me) the adoption of the Roman religion by members of the Church of England as nearly the greatest calamity that could befall Christian faith in this country, I rapidly became alarmed when these changes began; and very long before the great luminary, Dr. Newman, drew after him, it may well be said, 'the third part of the stars of Heaven.' This alarm I naturally and freely expressed to the man upon whom I most relied, your father."

Richard B. Cook

CHAPTER VIII

THE NEAPOLITAN PRISONS

In considering Mr. Gladstone's exposure of the cruelties practiced in the prisons of Naples, we are confronted with his attitude in the House of Commons just before, in a case where the same principles seemed to be involved, and in which Mr. Gladstone took the directly opposite course. We refer to the Don Pacifico case. Both were at first merely personal questions, but finally became international. Mr. Gladstone to many appeared to take an inconsistent course in these seemingly similar cases, in that while opposing national intervention in the affairs of Don Pacifico, he tried to stir up all Europe for the relief of the sufferers in the Neapolitan prisons. "It is not a little remarkable that the statesman who had so lately and so vigorously denounced the 'vain conception that we, forsooth, have a mission to be the censors of vice and folly, of abuse and imperfection, among the other countries of the world,' should now have found himself irresistibly impelled by conscience and humanity to undertake a signal and effective crusade against the domestic administration of a friendly power."

The most memorable debate in the new chamber of the House of Commons, which was first occupied in 1850, was that associated with the name of Don Pacifico. It is however conceded that the circumstances from which it all proceeded were comparatively trivial in the extreme. Don Pacifico was a Maltese Jew and a British subject, dwelling at Athens. He had made himself distasteful to the people of Athens, and consequently his house was destroyed and robbed by a mob, April 4, 1847. He appealed to the government at Athens for redress, demanding over $150,000 indemnity for the loss of his property, among which "a peculiarly sumptuous bedstead figured largely." Don Pacifico's claim was unheeded, probably because it was exorbitant and the Greek government was poor. Lord Palmerston was then the Foreign Secretary of the English Government. He was rash and independent in his Foreign policy, and often acted, as the Queen complained, without consultation and without the authority of the Sovereign.

The Foreign Secretary had had other quarrels with the Government at Athens. Land belonging to an English resident in Athens had been seized without sufficient compensation; Ionian subjects of the English Crown had suffered hardships at the hands of the Greek authorities, and an English Midshipman had been arrested by mistake. Lord Palmerston looked upon these incidents, slight as they were in themselves, as indicative of a plot on the part of the French Minister against the English, and especially as the Greek Government was so dilatory in satisfying the English claims. "This was enough. The outrage on Don Pacifico's bedstead remained the head and front of Greek offending, but Lord Palmerston included all the other slight blunders and delays of justice in one sweeping indictment; made the private claims into a national demand, and peremptorily informed the Greek Government that they must pay what was demanded of them within a given time. The Government hesitated, and the British fleet was ordered to the Piraeus, and seized all the Greek vessels which were found in the waters. Russia and France took umbrage at this high-handed proceeding and championed Greece. Lord Palmerston informed them it was none of their business and stood firm. The French Ambassador was withdrawn from London, and for awhile the peace of Europe was menaced." The execution of the orders of Lord Palmerston was left with Admiral Sir William Parker, who was first to proceed to Athens with the English fleet, and failing to obtain satisfaction was to blockade the Piraeus, which instructions he faithfully obeyed.

The debate began in Parliament June 24, 1850. The stability of the Whig administration, then in power, depended upon the results. In the House of Lords, Lord Stanley moved a resolution, which was carried, expressing regret that "various claims against the Greek Government, doubtful in point of justice and exaggerated in amount, have been enforced bycoercive measures, directed against the commerce and people of Greece, and calculated to endanger the continuance of our friendly relations with foreign powers." A counter-resolution was necessary in the House of Commons to offset the action of the Lords, so a Radical, Mr. Roebuck, much to the surprise of many, came to the defense of the Government and offered the following motion, which was carried: "That the principles which have hitherto regulated the foreign policy of Her Majesty's Government are such as were required to preserve untarnished the honor and dignity of this country, and, in times of unexampled difficulty, the best calculated to maintain peace between England and the various nations of the world."

The debate which followed, and which was prolonged over four nights, was marked on both sides by speeches of unusual oratorical power and brilliancy. The speeches of Lord Palmerston, Sir Robert Peel, Mr. Cockburn, Mr. Cobden, Mr. Disraeli and Mr. Gladstone were pronounced as remarkable orations. Sir Robert Peel made a powerful speech against the Ministers, which was made memorable not only for its eloquence, but because it was his last. Lord Palmerston defended himself vigorously in a speech of five hours' duration. "He spoke," said Mr. Gladstone, "from the dusk of one day to the dawn of the next." He defended his policy at every point. In every step taken he had been influenced by the sole desire that the meanest, the poorest, even the most disreputable subject of the English Crown should be defended by the whole might of England against foreign oppression. He reminded them of all that was implied in the Roman boast, *Civis Romanus sum*, and urged the House to make it clear that a

British subject, in whatever land he might be, should feel confident that the watchful eye and the strong arm of England could protect him. This could not be resisted. *Civis Romanus sum* settled the question.

Mr. Gladstone's reply was a masterpiece. It was exhaustive and trenchant, and produced a great effect. He first spoke upon the position of the Government and the constitutional doctrines which they had laid down in regard to it, and then severely condemned the conduct of the Premier for being so heedless of the censure of the House of Lords and in trying to shield himself behind the precedents which are in reality no precedents at all. With reference to the Greek question, he repudiated precedents which involved the conduct of strong countries against weak ones. The Greek Government had put no impediment in the way of arbitration. Instead of trusting and trying the tribunals of the country and employing diplomatic agency simply as a supplemental resource, Lord Palmerston had interspersed authority of foreign power, in contravention both of the particular stipulations of the treaty in force between Greece and England and of the general principles of the law of nations. He had thus set the mischievous example of abandoning the methods of law and order, and resorted to those of force. Non-interference had been laid down as the basis of our conduct towards other nations, but the policy of Lord Palmerston had been characterized by a spirit of active interference.

Mr. Gladstone's words were in part as follows: "Does he [Lord Palmerston] make the claim for us [the English] that we are to be lifted upon a platform high above the standing-ground of all other nations?... It is indeed too clear ... that he adopts, in part, the vain conception that we, forsooth, have a mission to be the censors of vice and folly, of abuse and imperfection among the other countries of the world; that we are to be the universal schoolmasters, and that all those who hesitate to recognize our office can be governed only by prejudice or personal animosity, and shall have the blind war of diplomacy forthwith declared against them."

Again: "Let us recognize, and recognize with frankness, the equality of the weak with the strong; the principles of brotherhood among nations, and of their sacred independence. When we are asking for the maintenance of the rights which belong to our fellow-subjects, resident in Greece, let us do as we would be done by, and let us pay all respect to a feeble State and to the infancy of free institutions.... Let us refrain from all gratuitous and arbitrary meddling in the internal concerns of other States, even as we should resent the same interference if it were attempted to be practiced toward ourselves."

In this address Mr. Gladstone evinces his inclination to appeal to the higher and nobler nature of man, to the principles of brotherhood among nations, to the law of God and nature, and to ask as a test of the foreign policy of the government, not whether it is striking, or brilliant, or successful, but whether it is right.

This speech of Mr. Gladstone's was recognized as the finest he had delivered in Parliament, and its power was acknowledged by both sides of the House, by political opponent and friend. Lord Chief Justice Cockburn, then a member of the House, referring in a speech the following evening to Mr. Gladstone and his remarkable speech, uttered these words: "I suppose we are now to consider him as the representative of Lord Stanley in the House—Gladstone *Vice* Disraeli, am I to say, resigned or superseded?" The government was sustained.

We have already stated that it was during this memorable debate that Sir Robert Peel made his last speech.—On the following day, 29th of June, 1850, Sir Robert called at Buckingham Palace for the purpose of leaving his card. On proceeding up Constitution Hill on horse back he met one of Lady Dover's daughters, and exchanged salutations. Immediately afterwards his horse became restive and shying towards the rails of the Green Park, threw Sir Robert sideways on his left shoulder. Medical aid was at hand and was at once administered. Sir Robert groaned when lifted and when asked whether he was much hurt replied, "Yes, very much." He was conveyed home where the meeting with his family was very affecting, and he swooned in the arms of his physician. He was placed upon a sofa in the dining-room from which he never moved. His sufferings were so acute that a minute examination of his injuries could not be made. For two or three days he lingered and then died, July 2d. An examination made after death revealed the fact that the fifth rib on the left side was fractured, the broken rib pressing on the lung, producing effusion and pulmonary engorgement. This was probably the seat of the mortal injury, and was where Sir Robert complained of the greatest pain.

The news of Sir Robert's death produced a profound sensation throughout the land. Great and universal were the tokens of respect and grief. There was but one feeling,—that England had lost one of her most illustrious statesmen. Even those who had been in opposition to his views, alluded to the great loss the nation had sustained and paid a fitting tribute to his memory. The House of Commons, on motion of Mr. Hume July 3d, at once adjourned. In the House of Lords the Duke of Wellington and Lord Brougham spoke in appreciative words of the departed statesman. "Such was the leader whom Mr. Gladstone had faithfully followed for many years."

Supporting Mr. Hume's motion, Mr. Gladstone said: "I am quite sure that every heart is much too full to allow us, at a period so early, to enter upon a consideration of the amount of that calamity with which the country has been visited in his, I must even now say, premature death; for though he has died full of years and full of honors, yet it is a death which our human eyes will regard as premature; because we had fondly hoped that, in whatever position he was placed, by the weight of his character, by the splendor of his talents, by the purity of his virtues, he would still have been spared to render to his countrymen the most essential services. I will only, sir, quote those most touching and feeling lines which were applied by one of the greatest poets of this country to the memory of a man great indeed, but yet not greater than Sir Robert Peel:"

'Now is the stately column broke,
The beacon light is quenched in smoke;
The trumpet's silver voice is still;
The warder silent on the hill.'

"Sir, I will add no more—in saying this I have, perhaps, said too much. It might have been better had I confined myself to seconding the motion. I am sure the tribute of respect which we now offer will be all the more valuable from the silence with which the motion is received, and which I well know has not arisen from the want, but from the excess of feeling on the part of members of this House."

Upon the death of Sir Robert Peel began the disintegration of the party distinguished by his name—Peelites. Some of its members united with the Conservatives, and others, such as Sir James Graham, Sidney Herbert, and Mr. Gladstone held themselves aloof from both Whigs and Tories. Conservative traditions still exercised considerable influence over them, but they could not join them, because they were already surrendering to strong liberal tendencies. It is said that Mr. Gladstone at this time, and for a decade thereafter, until the death of Sir James Graham, was greatly indebted to this statesman, not only for the growth of his liberal principles, but for his development as a practical statesman. Sir James wielded great influence over his contemporaries generally, because of his great knowledge of Parliamentary tactics, and the fact that he was the best educated and most thoroughly accomplished statesman of his age. "If he could be prevailed upon to speak in the course of a great debate, his speech was worth fifty votes," so great was his influence and power. "However great may have been the indebtedness of Mr. Gladstone to Sir James Graham, if the former had not been possessed of far wider sympathies—to say nothing of superior special intellectual qualities—than his political mentor, he never could have conceived and executed those important legislative acts for which his name will now chiefly be remembered."

The other case occupying the attention of Parliament, to

which we have alluded, we must now consider—Mr. Gladstone and the prisons of Naples. Owing to the illness of one of his children, for whom a southern climate was recommended, Mr. Gladstone spent several months of the Winter of 1850-1 in Naples. His brief visit to this city on a purely domestic mission was destined to assume an international importance. It came to his knowledge that a large number of the citizens of Naples, who had been members of the Chamber of Deputies, an actual majority of the representatives of the people, had been exiled or imprisoned by King Ferdinand, because they formed the opposition party to the government, and that between twenty and thirty thousand of that monarch's subjects had been cast into prison on the charge of political disaffection. The sympathies of Mr. Gladstone were at once enlisted in behalf of the oppressed Neapolitans. At first Mr. Gladstone looked at the matter only from a humanitarian and not from a political aspect, and it was only upon the former ground that he felt called and impelled to attempt the redress of the wrongs which were a scandal to the name of civilisation in Europe. And it was not long before England and the Continent were aroused by his denunciations of the Neapolitan system of government. Mr. Gladstone first carefully ascertained the truth of the statements made to him in order to attest their accuracy, and then published two letters on the subject addressed to the Earl of Aberdeen. These letters were soon followed by a third. In the first of these letters, dated April 7, 1851, he brings an elaborate, detailed and horrible indictment against the rulers of Naples, especially as regards their prisons and the treatment of persons confined in them for political offenses. He disclaimed any thought of having gone to Naples for the purpose of political criticism or censorship, to look for defects in the administration of the government, or to hear the grievances of the people, or to propagate ideas belonging to another country. But after a residence of three or four months in their city he had returned home with a deep feeling of the duty upon him to make some endeavor to mitigate the horrors in the midst of which the government of Naples was carried on.

There were chiefly three reasons that led him to adopt the present course: "First, that the present practices of the Government of Naples, in reference to real or supposed political offenders, are an outrage upon religion, upon civilization, upon humanity and upon decency. Secondly, that these practices are certainly, and even rapidly, doing the work of Republicanism in that country—a political creed which has little natural or habitual root in the character of the people. Thirdly, that as a member of the Conservative party in one of the great family of European nations, I am compelled to remember that party stands in virtual and real, though perhaps unconscious alliance with all the established Governments of Europe as such; and that, according to the measure of its influence, they suffer more or less of moral detriment from its reverses, and derive strength and encouragement from its successes."

He passed over the consideration of the all important question whether the actual Government of the Two Sicilies was one with or without a title, one of law or one of force, and came to the real question at issue. His charge against the Neapolitan Government was not one of mere imperfection, not corruption in low quarters, not occasional severity, but that of incessant, systematic, deliberate violation of the law by the power appointed to watch over and maintain it.

Mr. Gladstone, with impassionate language, thus formulates his fearful indictment: "It is such violation of human and written law as this, carried on for the purpose of violating every other law, unwritten and eternal, human and divine; it is the wholesale persecution of virtue, when united with intelligence, operating upon such a scale that entire classes may with truth be said to be its object, so that the Government is in bitter and cruel, as well as utterly illegal hostility to whatever in the nation really lives and moves, and forms the mainspring of practical progress and improvement; it is the awful profanation of public religion, by its notorious alliance in the governing powers with the violation of every moral rule under the stimulants of fear and vengeance; it is the perfect prostitution of the judicial office which has made it, under veils only too threadbare and transparent, the degraded recipient of the vilest and clumsiest forgeries, got up wilfully and deliberately, by the immediate advisers of the Crown, for the purpose of destroying the peace, the freedom, aye, and even, if not by capital sentences, the life of men among the most virtuous, upright, intelligent, distinguished and refined of the whole community; it is the savage and cowardly system of moral as well as in a lower degree of physical torture, through which the sentences obtained from the debased courts of justice are carried into effect.

"The effect of all this is a total inversion of all the moral and social ideas. Law, instead of being respected, is odious. Force and not affection is the foundation of government. There is no association, but a violent antagonism between the idea of freedom and that of order. The governing power, which teaches of itself that it is the image of God upon earth, is clothed in the view of the overwhelming majority of the thinking public with all the vices for its attributes. I have seen and heard the strong expression used, 'This is the negation of God erected into a system of Government.'"

It was not merely the large numbers imprisoned unjustly, to which public attention was directed, that called for righteous indignation and made Mr. Gladstone's words create such a sensation in Europe, but the mode of procedure was arbitrary in the extreme. The law of Naples required that personal liberty should be inviolable, except under warrant from a court of justice. Yet in utter disregard of this law the authorities watched the people, paid domiciliary visits, ransacked houses, seized papers and effects, and tore up floors at pleasure under pretense of searching for arms, imprisoned men by the score, by the hundred, by the thousand without any warrant whatever, sometimes without even any written authority whatever, or anything beyond the word of a policeman, constantly without any statement whatever of the nature of the offense. Charges were fabricated to get rid of inconvenient persons. Perjury and forgery were resorted to in order to establish charges, and the whole mode of conducting trials was a burlesque of justice.

He thus describes the dungeons of Naples, in which some of the prisoners were confined for their political opinions: "The prisons of Naples, as is well known, are another name for the extreme of filth and horror. I have really seen something of them, but not the worst. This I have seen, my Lord: the official doctors not going to the sick prisoners, but the sick prisoners, men almost with death on their faces, toiling up stairs to them at that charnel-house of the Vicaria, because the lower regions of such a palace of darkness are too foul and loathsome to allow it to be expected that professional men should consent to earn bread by entering them." Of some of those sufferers Mr. Gladstone speaks particularly. He names Pironte, formerly a judge, Baron Porcari, and Carlo Poerio, a distinguished patriot. The latter he specially speaks of as a refined and accomplished gentleman, a copious and elegant speaker, a respected and blameless character, yet he had been arrested and condemned for treason. Mr. Gladstone says: "The condemnation of such a man for treason is a proceeding just as conformable to the laws of truth, justice, decency, and fair play, and to the common sense of the community—in fact, just as great and gross an outrage on them all—as would be a like condemnation in this country of any of our best known public men—Lord John Russell, or Lord Lansdowne, or Sir James Graham, or yourself."

There was no name dearer to Englishmen than that of Poerio to his Neapolitan fellow-countrymen. Poerio was tried and condemned on the sole accusation of a worthless character named Jerrolino. He would have been acquitted nevertheless, by a division of four to five of his judges, had not Navarro (who sat as a judge while directly concerned in the charge against the prisoner), by the distinct use of intimidation, procured the number necessary for a sentence. A statement is furnished on the authority of an eye-witness, as to the inhumanity with which invalid prisoners were treated by the Grand Criminal Court of Naples; and Mr. Gladstone minutely describes the manner of the imprisonment of Poerio and six of his incarcerated associates. Each prisoner bore a weight of chain amounting to thirty-two pounds and for no purpose whatever were these chains undone. All the prisoners were confined, night and day, in a small room, which may be described as amongst the closest of dungeons; but Poerio was after this condemned to a still lower depth of calamity and suffering. "Never before have I conversed," says Mr. Gladstone, speaking of Poerio, "and never probably shall I converse again, with a cultivated and accomplished gentleman, of whose innocence, obedience to law, and love of his country, I was as firmly and as rationally assured as your lordship's or that of any other man of the very highest character, whilst he stood before me, amidst surrounding felons, and clad in the vile uniform of guilt and shame." But he is now gone where he will scarcely have the opportunity even of such conversation. I cannot honestly suppress my conviction that the object in the case of Poerio, as a man of mental power sufficient to be feared, is to obtain the scaffold's aim by means more cruel than the scaffold, and without the outcry which the scaffold would create.

Mr. Gladstone said that it was time for the veil to be lifted from scenes more fit for hell than earth, or that some considerable mitigation should be voluntarily adopted. This letter was published in 1851—the year of the great Exposition in London—and a copy was sent to the representative of the Queen in every court of Europe. Its publication caused a widespread indignation in England, a great sensation abroad, and profoundly agitated the court of Naples.

In the English Parliament Sir De Lacy Evans put the following question to the Foreign Secretary: "If the British Minister at the court of Naples had been instructed to employ his good offices in the cause of humanity, for the diminution of these lamentable severities, and with what result?" In reply to this question Lord Palmerston accepted and adopted Mr. Gladstone's statement, which had been confirmed from other quarters, expressing keen sympathy and humanitarian feeling with the cause which he had espoused, but Lord Palmerston pointed out that it was impossible to do anything in a matter which related entirely to the domestic affairs of the Government at Naples. He said: "Instead of confining himself to those amusements that abound in Naples, instead of diving into volcanoes, and exploring excavated cities, we see him going into courts of justice, visiting prisons, descending into dungeons, and examining great numbers of the cases of unfortunate victims of illegality and injustice, with the view afterwards to enlist public opinion in the endeavor to remedy those abuses." This announcement by the Foreign Secretary was warmly applauded by the House. "A few days afterwards Lord Palmerston was requested by Prince Castelcicala to forward the reply of the Neapolitan Government to the different European courts to which Mr. Gladstone's pamphlet had been sent. His lordship, with his wonted courage and independent spirit, replied that he 'must decline being accessory to the circulation of a pamphlet which, in my opinion, does no credit to its writer, or the Government which he defends, or to the political party of which he professes to be the champion.' He also informed the Prince that information received from other sources led him to the conclusion that Mr. Gladstone had by no means overstated the various evils which he had described; and he [Lord Palmerston] regretted that the Neapolitan Government had not set to work earnestly and effectually to correct the manifold and grave abuses which clearly existed."

The second paper of Mr. Gladstone upon the same subject was a sequel to the first. His wish was that everything possible should be done first in the way of private representation and remonstrance, and he did not regret the course he had taken, though it entailed devious delays. In answer to the natural inquiry why he should simply appear in his personal capacity through the press, instead of inviting to the grave and painful question the attention of the House of Commons, of which he was a member, he said, that he had advisedly abstained from mixing up his statements with any British agency or influences which were official, diplomatic, or political. The claims and interests which he had in view were either wholly null and valueless, or they were broad as the extension of the human race and long-lived as its duration.

As to his general charges he had nothing to retract. His representations had not been too strongly stated, for the most disgraceful circumstances were those which rested upon public notoriety, or upon his own personal knowledge. It had been stated that he had overestimated the number of prisoners, and he would give the Neapolitan Government the full benefit of any correction. But the number of political prisoners *in itself*, was a secondary feature of the case, for "if they were fairly and legally arrested, fairly and legally treated before trial—fairly and legally tried, that was the main matter. For the honor of human nature men would at first receive some statements with incredulity. Men ought to be slow to believe that such things could happen, and happen in a Christian country, the seat of almost the oldest European civilization." But those thus disposed in the beginning he hoped would not close their minds to the reception of the truth, however painful to believe. The general probability of his statements could not, unfortunately be gainsaid.

Many replies were made to Mr. Gladstone's pamphlet that were violent and abusive. They appeared not only in Naples, Turin, and Paris, but even in London.

All these answers, were in truth no replies at all, for they did not disprove the facts. These professed corrections of Mr. Gladstone's statements did not touch the real basis of the question. It was necessary to say something if possible by way of defense, or justice, which had as yet not been done.

There was one reply that was put forth that Mr. Gladstone felt demanded some attention, namely, the official answer of the Neapolitan Government to his charges. To this he replied in a letter, in 1852. In his reply he placed, point by point, the answers in the scales along with his own accusations. There was in the Neapolitan answers to the letters really a tacit

Richard B. Cook

admission of the accuracy of nine-tenths of Mr. Gladstone's statements, Mr. Gladstone enumerated the few retractions which he had to make, which were five in number. That the prisoner, Settembrine, had not been tortured and confined to double chains for life, as was currently reported and believed; that six judges had been dismissed at Reggio upon presuming to acquit a batch of political prisoners, required modifying to three; that seventeen invalids had not been massacred in the prison of Procida during a revolt, as stated; and that certain prisoners alleged to have been still incarcerated after acquittal had been released after the lapse of two days. These were all the modifications he had to make in his previous statements. And as to the long list of his grave accusations, not one of them rested upon hearsay. He pointed out how small and insignificant a fraction of error had found its way into his papers. He fearlessly reasserted that agonizing corporal punishment was inflicted by the officials in Neapolitan prisons, and that without judicial authority. As to Settembrine, the political prisoner named, he was incarcerated in a small room with eight other prisoners, one of whom boasted that he had murdered, at various times, thirty-five persons. Several of his victims had been his prison companions, and "the murders of this Ergastolo" had exceeded fifty in a single year. It was true that at the massacre at Procida the sick had not been slain in the prisons, yet prisoners who hid under beds were dragged forth and shot in cold blood by the soldiery after order had been restored. The work of slaughter had been twice renewed, and two officers received promotion or honors for that abominable enormity.

Mr. Gladstone found in the reply of the Government of Naples no reason to retract his damaging statements in reference to Neapolitan inhumanity, on the other hand he discovered grounds for emphasizing his accusations. And as to his statement regarding the number of the sufferers from Neapolitan injustice and cruelty, he defended at length his statement as to the enormous number of the prisoners.

It was clear to all candid minds that all the replies had failed to prove him wrong in any of his substantial changes, which retained their full force. "The arrow has shot deep into the mark," observed Mr. Gladstone, "and cannot be dislodged. But I have sought, in once more entering the field, not only to sum up the state of the facts in the manner nearest to exactitude, but likewise to close the case as I began it, presenting it from first to last in the light of a matter which is not primarily or mainly political, which is better kept apart from Parliamentary discussion, which has no connection whatever with any peculiar idea or separate object or interest of England, but which appertains to the sphere of humanity at large, and well deserves the consideration of every man who feels a concern for the well-being of his race, in its bearings on that well-being; on the elementary demands of individual domestic happiness; on the permanent maintenance of public order; on the stability of thrones; on the solution of that great problem, which, day and night, in its innumerable forms must haunt the reflections of every statesman, both here and elsewhere, how to harmonize the old with the new conditions of society, and to mitigate the increasing stress of time and change upon what remains of this ancient and venerable fabric of the traditional civilization of Europe."

Mr. Gladstone also said, that the question had been asked, whether a government "could be induced to change its policy, because some individual or other had by lying accusations held it up to the hatred of mankind," yet he had the satisfaction of knowing that upon the challenge of a mere individual, the government of Naples had been compelled to plead before the tribunal of general opinion, and to admit the jurisdiction of that tribunal. It was to public sentiment that the Neapolitan Government was paying deference when it resolved on the manly course of a judicial reply; and he hoped that further deference would be paid to that public sentiment in the complete reform of its departments and the whole future management of its affairs.

After a consideration of the political position of the throne of the Two Sicilies, in connection with its dominions on the mainland, Mr. Gladstone thus concluded his examination of the official reply of the Neapolitan Government: "These pages have been written in the hope that, by thus making, through the press, rather than in another mode, that rejoinder to the Neapolitan reply which was doubtless due from me, I might still, as far as depended on me, keep the question on its true ground, as one not of politics but of morality, and not of England but of Christendom and of mankind. Again I express the hope that this may be my closing word. I express the hope that it may not become a hard necessity to keep this controversy alive until it reaches its one only possible issue, which no power of man can permanently intercept. I express the hope that while there is time, while there is quiet, while dignity may yet be saved in showing mercy, and in the blessed work of restoring Justice to her seat, the Government of Naples may set its hand in earnest to the work of real and searching, however quiet and unostentatious, reform; that it may not become unavoidable to reiterate these appeals from the hand of power to the one common heart of mankind; to produce these painful documents, those harrowing descriptions, which might be supplied in rank abundance, of which I have scarcely given the faintest idea or sketch, and which, if laid from time to time before the world, would bear down like a deluge every effort at apology or palliation, and would cause all that has recently been made known to be forgotten and eclipsed in deeper horrors yet; lest the strength of offended and indignant humanity should rise up as a giant refreshed with wine, and, while sweeping away these abominations from the eye of Heaven, should sweep away along with them things pure and honest, ancient, venerable, salutary to mankind, crowned with the glories of the past and still capable of bearing future fruit."

The original purpose of these letters, though at first not gained, was unmistakable in the subsequent revolution which created a regenerated, free and united Italy. The moral influence of such an exposure was incalculable and eventually irresistible. The great Italian patriot and liberator of Italy, General Garibaldi, was known to say that Mr. Gladstone's protest "sounded the first trumpet call of Italian liberty." If France and England had unitedly protested against the Neapolitan abuse of power and violation of law, such a protest would have been heard and redress granted, but such joint action was not taken. The letters reached the fourteenth edition and in this edition Mr. Gladstone said that by a royal decree, issued December 27, 1858, ninety-one political prisoners had their punishment commuted into perpetual exile from the kingdom of the two Sicilies, but that a Ministerial order of January 9, 1859, directed that they should be conveyed to America; that of these ninety-one persons no less than fourteen had died long before in dungeons, and that only sixty-six of them embarked January 16, 1859, and were taken to Cadiz, where they were shipped on board an American sailing vessel, which was to have carried them to New York, but eventually landed them at Cork. "Eleven men were kept behind, either because it was afterwards thought advisable not to release them, as in the case of Longo and Delli Franci, two artillery officers, who were still in the dungeons of Gaeta. Whenever the prisoners were too sick to be moved, as was the case with Pironti, who was paralytic; or because they were in some provincial dungeons too remote from Naples." Such was the fate of some of the patriots officially liberated by Ferdinand's successor, Francis II.

The charges of Mr. Gladstone against the Neapolitan Government met with confirmation from another source nearer home. In 1851 Mr. Gladstone translated and published Farini's important and bulky work, entitled, "The Roman State, from 1815 to 1850." The author, Farini, addressed a note to his translator, in which he said that he had dedicated the concluding volume of his work to Mr. Gladstone, who, by his love of Italian letters, and by his deeds of Italian charity, had established a relationship with Italy in the spirit of those great Italian writers who had been their masters in eloquence, in civil philosophy and in national virtue, from Dante and Macchivelli down to Alfieri and Gioberti. Signor Farini endorsed the charges made by Mr. Gladstone against the Neapolitan Government. He wrote: "The scandalous trials for high treason still continue at Naples; accusers, examiners, judges, false witnesses, all are bought; the prisons, those tombs of the living, are full; two thousand citizens of all ranks and conditions are already condemned to the dungeons, as many to confinement, double that number to exile; the majority guilty of no crime but that of having believed in the oaths made by Ferdinand II. But, in truth, nothing more was needed to press home the indictment."

At the period of Mr. Gladstone's visit to Naples there was a growing sentiment throughout Italy for Italian independence and union. The infamous measures adopted by the King of Naples to repress in his own dominions every aspiration after freedom, only succeeded in making the people more determined and the liberty for which they sighed surer in the end. His system of misgovernment went on for a few years longer and was the promoting cause of the revolutionary movements which continually disturbed the whole Italian peninsula. A conference was held in Paris upon the Italian question, which failed to accomplish anything, against which failure Count Cavour addressed a protest to the French and British Governments in April, 1856. Afterwards the King of Naples and his Ministers were remonstrated with, but this was of no avail, only drawing forth an assertion that the sovereign had the right to deal with his own subjects as he pleased. France and England finally withdrew their representatives from Naples, and the storm soon afterwards broke. The brilliant success of Garibaldi in 1860 filled Francis II with terror. He was now, like all evil men, ready to make the most lavish promises of liberal reform to escape the consequences of his misdeeds. However, his repentance came too late. The victorious Garibaldi issued a decree ultimately, stating that the Two Sicilies, which had been redeemed by Italian blood, and which had freely elected him their dictator, formed an integral part of one and indivisable Italy, under the constitutional King Victor Emmanuel and his descendants. Francis II was dethroned and expelled from his kingdom by the legitimate fruits of his own hateful policy and that of his predecessor. "Count Cavour was the brain as Garibaldi was the hand of that mighty movement which resulted in the unity of Italy," says an English writer, "but as Englishmen we may take pride in the fact that not the least among the precipitating causes of this movement was the fearless exposure by Mr. Gladstone of the cruelties and tyrannies of the Neapolitan Government."

CHAPTER IX

THE FIRST BUDGET

The precise date at which Mr. Gladstone became a Liberal cannot be determined, but during the Parliamentary sessions of 1851 and 1852 he became finally alienated from the Conservative party, although he did not enter the ranks of the Liberals for some years afterward. He himself stated that so late as 1851 he had not formally left the Tory party, nevertheless his advance towards Liberalism is very pronounced at this period. It is well for us to trace the important events of these two sessions, for they also lead up to the brilliant financial measures of 1853, which caused Mr. Gladstone's name to be classed with those of Pitt and Peel. Mr. Gladstone's trusted leader was dead, and he was gradually coming forward to take the place in debate of the fallen statesman.

When Mr. Gladstone returned home from Italy he found England convulsed over renewed papal aggressions. The Pope had, in the preceding September, issued Letters Apostolic, establishing a Roman Catholic Hierarchy in England, and in which he had mapped out the whole country into papal dioceses. This act of aggression produced a storm of public indignation. It was regarded by the people generally as an attempt to wrest from them their liberties and enslave them. It was looked upon by the Protestants indignantly as an attack upon the Reformed Faith. Anglicans resented it as an act which practically denied the jurisdiction and authority of the Church of England, established already by law. Englishmen, faithfully devoted to the British Constitution, which guaranteed the Protestant Religion, were incensed by this interference with the prerogative of the Crown; while all ardent patriots were influenced by the unwarranted and unsolicited interference of a foreign potentate. Every element of combustion being present, meetings were held everywhere, inflammatory speeches were made on every public occasion, and patriotic resolutions were passed. Pulpit and platform rang with repeated cries of "No Popery," and echoed at the Lord Mayor's banquet, at the Guildhall, and even at Covent Garden Theatre in Shakesperian strains. The Prime Minister, Lord John Russell, published his famous Durham letter, addressed to the Bishop of Durham, rebuking and defying the Pope, and charging the whole High Church Party of the Church of England with being the secret allies and fellow-workers of Rome.

In the beginning of the Parliamentary session of 1851 Lord John Russell moved for permission to bring in a bill to counteract the aggressive policy of the Church of Rome, on account of which aggression of the Pope the whole country was well-nigh in a condition of panic. The measure was debated for four days, and was entitled the Ecclesiastical Faiths Bill. It was designed to prevent the assumption by Roman Catholic prelates of titles taken from any territory or place in England. Severe penalties were attached to the use of such titles, and all acts done by, and requests made to, persons under them were to be void. The bill was not well received by some, being thought, on one side too mild and on the other as too stringent. Mr. Disraeli and Mr. Gladstone both opposed it; the latter because the change was wanted by English Catholics rather than by the Vatican. He condemned the vanity and boastful spirit of the papal documents, but contended that his fellow Catholic countrymen should not suffer for that. The difficulty of applying it to Ireland, where the system objected to already existed, was pointed out. However the preliminary motion was passed by 395 votes against 63, "this enormous majority," says an English author, "attesting the wide-spread fear of Romish machinations." The measure became a law, but

Richard B. Cook

it was a dead letter, and was quietly repealed twenty years afterwards at Mr. Gladstone's request.

Before, however, the bill was passed a ministerial crisis had intervened. During this session other difficulties were encountered by the Ministry. The financial as well as this ecclesiastical question was a problem. The Conservatives were strong and compact, and enjoyed the adhesion of the Peelites, while the Ministerial party was to a great extent demoralized. Mr. Disraeli, owing to the deep distress that prevailed in the agricultural districts, renewed his motion upon the burdens on land and the inequalities of taxation, and consequently he presented a resolution that it was the duty of the government to introduce measures for the alleviation of the distress without delay. The government admitted the distress, but denied that it was increasing. They attempted to prove that pauperism had decreased in all parts of the kingdom—England, Ireland and Scotland. Commerce was in a most prosperous condition, while the revenues had reached the unexampled amount of $350,000,000. "Sir James Graham stigmatized the motion as an attempt to turn out the administration, to dissolve Parliament, and to return to Protection." The Ministry was sustained by a small majority, and was successful in some measures, but soon suffered several minor defeats and finally was forced to retire.

One of the successful measures was that introduced by Mr. Loche King, and opposed by Lord John Russell, for assimilating the country franchise to that of the boroughs. The budget of the government introduced January 17th was unpopular. It demanded a renewed lease for three years of the obnoxious income-tax, but promised a partial remission of the window duties, which was a tax upon every window in a house, together with some relief to the agriculturists. The first budget having been rejected a second financial statement was offered later in the session. It imposed a house-tax, withdrew the bonus to agriculturists, repealed the window-tax, but re-demanded the income-tax for three years. The main features of the budget were acceptable to the House, but the Government suffered defeat on minor financial questions, which tendered still further to diminish the popularity of the ministry.

Upon the resignation of Lord John Russell and his Cabinet, in February, 1851, Lord Stanley was called upon to form a new administration, and Mr. Gladstone was invited to become a member of the Cabinet. Lord Stanley having failed, Lord Aberdeen was invited to form a new Cabinet, by the Queen, with like results. Both these gentlemen having declined the task of forming a new administration, Lord John Russell and his colleagues resumed office, but the reconstructed ministry was soon to receive a fatal blow through Lord Palmerston, the foreign Secretary.

On the 2d of December, 1851, Louis Napoleon, Prince President of the French Republic, by a single act of lawless violence, abolished the constitution, and made himself Dictator. The details of this monstrous deed, and of the bloodshed that accompanied it, created a profound sensation in England. The Queen was very anxious that no step should be taken and no word said by her ministry which could be construed into an approval by the English government of what had been done. Indeed the Queen who knew the failing of her Foreign Secretary to act hastily in important matters of State without the consent or advice of Queen or Cabinet, questioned the Premier and was assured that nothing had been done in recognition of the new government in Paris. Indeed the Cabinet had passed a resolution to abstain from the expression of opinions in approval or disapproval of the recent *coup d'état* in France. But it soon leaked out that Lord Palmerston who thought he understood full well the foreign relations of England, and what her policy should be, had both in public dispatches and private conversation spoken favorably of the policy adopted by Louis Napoleon. He had even expressed to Count Walewski, the French Ambassador in London, his entire approval of the Prince President's act. This was too much for the Queen, who had as early as the August before, in a memorandum sent to the Premier, imperatively protested against the crown's being ignored by the Foreign Secretary, so

Richard B. Cook

Lord Palmerston was dismissed from office by Lord John Russell, Christmas Eve, 1851. He bore his discharge with meekness, and even omitted in Parliament to defend himself in points where he was wronged. But Justin McCarthy says: "Lord Palmerston was in the wrong in many if not most of the controversies which had preceded it; that is to say, he was wrong in committing England as he so often did to measures which had not the approval of the sovereign or his colleagues."

In February following, 1852, Lord Palmerston enjoyed, as he expressed it, his "tit-for-tat with Johnny Russell" and helped the Tories to defeat his late chief in a measure for reorganizing the militia as a precaution against possible aggression from France. The ministry had not saved itself by the overthrow of Lord Palmerston.

Upon the retirement of Lord John Russell from office, in 1852, the Earl of Derby, formerly Lord Stanley, succeeded him as Prime Minister. Mr. Gladstone was invited to become a member of the new Tory Cabinet, but declined, whereupon Lord Malmesbury dubiously remarked, November 28th: "I cannot make out Gladstone, who seems to me a dark horse." Mr. Disraeli was chosen Chancellor of the Exchequer, and became Leader in the House of Commons, entering the Cabinet for the first time. "There was a scarcely disguised intention to revive protection." It was Free Trade or Protection, and the Peelites defended their fallen leader, Peel. "A makeshift budget" was introduced by Mr. Disraeli and passed. It was destined, it seems, that the Derby Administration was not to be supported, but to be driven out of power by Mr. Gladstone, who was to cross swords before the nation with his future parliamentary rival, Disraeli.

Mr. Disraeli seemed now bent upon declaring the Free Trade Policy of Sir Robert Peel a failure. Mr. Disraeli's power of forgetfulness of the past is one of the most fortunate ever conferred upon a statesman. During the debate he declared that the main reason why his party had opposed Free Trade was not that it would injure the landlord, nor the farmer, but that "it would prove injurious to the cause of labor." "He also said, though interrupted by cries of astonishment and of 'Oh, oh!' that not a single attempt had been made in the House of Commons to abrogate the measure of 1846." Mr. Sidney Herbert, who was wounded to the quick by the assaults on Sir Robert Peel, rose to defend the great Conservative statesman. His speech contained one passage of scathing invective addressed to Mr. Disraeli.

Mr. Herbert said: "The memory of Sir Robert Peel requires no vindication—his memory is embalmed in the grateful recollection of the people of this country; and I say, if ever retribution is wanted—for it is not words that humiliate, but deeds—if a man wants to see humiliation, which God knows is always a painful sight, he need but look there!"—and upon this Mr. Herbert pointed with his finger to Mr. Disraeli sitting on the Treasury Bench. The sting of invective is truth, and Mr. Herbert certainly spoke daggers if he used none; yet the Chancellor of the Exchequer sat impassive as a Sphinx.

Parliament was dissolved soon after the formation of the new government, July 1, 1852, and during the recess, September 14, 1852, the Duke of Wellington passed away and a public funeral was given the victor of Waterloo.

On the assembling of Parliament Mr. Gladstone delivered a eulogy on the Duke, drawing special lessons from his illustrious career, which had been prolonged to a green old age. Mr. Gladstone said: "While many of the actions of his life, while many of the qualities he possessed, are unattainable by others, there are lessons which we may all derive from the life and actions of that illustrious man. It may never be given to another subject of the British Crown to perform services so brilliant as he performed; it may never be given to another man to hold the sword which was to gain the independence of Europe, to rally the nations around it, and while England saved herself by her constancy, to save Europe by her example; it may never be given to another man, after having attained such eminence, after such an unexampled series of victories, to show equal moderation in peace as he has shown greatness in war, and to devote the remainder of his life to the cause of internal and external peace for that country which he has so well served; it may never be given to another man to have equal authority, both with the Sovereign he served and with the Senate of which he was to the end a venerated member; it may never be given to another man after such a career to preserve, even to the last, the full possession of those great faculties with which he was endowed, and to carry on the services of one of the most important departments of the State with unexampled regularity and success, even to the latest day of his life. These are circumstances, these are qualities, which may never occur again in the history of this country. But these are qualities which the Duke of Wellington displayed, of which we may all act in humble imitation: that sincere and unceasing devotion to our country; that honest and upright determination to act for the benefit of the country on every occasion; that devoted loyalty, which, while it made him ever anxious to serve the Crown, never induced him to conceal from the Sovereign that which he believed to be the truth; that devotedness in the constant performance of duty; that temperance of his life, which enabled him at all times to give his mind and his faculties to the services which he was called on to perform; that regular, consistent, and unceasing piety by which he was distinguished at all times of his life; these are qualities that are attainable by others, and these are qualities which should not be lost as an example."

At this session of Parliament Mr. Disraeli brought forward his second budget in a five hour speech. The new Chancellor of the Exchequer proposed to remit a portion of the taxes upon malt, tea, and sugar, but to counterbalance these losses he also proposed to extend the income-tax and house-tax. The debate, which was very personal, was prolonged several days, and Mr. Disraeli, towards its close, bitterly attacked several members, among them Sir James Graham, whom Mr. Gladstone not only defended, but in so doing administered a scathing rebuke to the Chancellor for his bitter invective and personal abuse. Mr. Gladstone's speech at the close of Mr. Disraeli's presentation was crushing, and was generally regarded as giving the death-blow to this financial scheme.

Mr. Gladstone told Mr. Disraeli that he was not entitled to charge with insolence men of as high position and of as high character in the House as himself, and when the cheers which had interrupted him had subsided, concluded: "I must tell the right honorable gentleman that he is not entitled to say to my right honorable friend, the member for Carlisle, that he regards but does not respect him. And I must tell him that whatever else he has learnt—and he has learnt much—he has not learnt to keep within those limits of discretion, of moderation, and of forbearance that ought to restrain the conduct and language of every member in this House, the disregard of which, while it is an offence in the meanest amongst us, is an offence of tenfold weight when committed by the leader of the House of Commons."

The thrilling scene enacted in the House of Commons on that memorable night is thus described: "In the following month the Chancellor of the Exchequer produced his second budget. It was an ambitious and a skillful attempt to reconcile conflicting interests, and to please all while offending none. The government had come into office pledged to do something for the relief of the agricultural interests. They redeemed their pledge by reducing the duty on malt. This reduction created a deficit; and they repaired the deficit by doubling the duty on inhabited houses. Unluckily, the agricultural interests proved, as usual, ungrateful to its benefactors, and made light of the reduction on malt; while those who were to pay for it in double taxation were naturally indignant. The voices of criticism, 'angry, loud, discordant voices,' were heard simultaneously on every side. The debate waxed fast and furious. In defending his hopeless proposals, Mr. Disraeli gave full scope to his most characteristic gift; he pelted his opponents right and left with sarcasms, taunts, and epigrams, and went as near personal insult as the forms of Parliament permit. He sat down late at night, and Mr. Gladstone rose in a crowded and excited House to deliver an unpremeditated reply which has ever since been celebrated. Even the cold and colorless pages of 'Hansard' show signs of the excitement under which he labored, and of the tumultuous applause and dissent by which his opening sentences were interrupted. 'The speech of the Chancellor of the Exchequer,' he said, 'must be answered on the moment. It must be tried by the laws of decency and propriety.'" He indignantly rebuked his rival's language and demeanor. He reminded him of the discretion and decorum due from every member, but pre-eminently due from the leader of the House. He tore his financial scheme to ribbons. It was the beginning of a duel which lasted till death removed one of the combatants from the political arena. 'Those who had thought it impossible that any impression could be made upon the House after the speech of Mr. Disraeli had to acknowledge that a yet greater impression was produced by the unprepared reply of Mr. Gladstone.' The House divided and the government were left in a minority of nineteen. This happened in the early morning of December 17, 1852. Within an hour of the division Lord Derby wrote to the Queen a letter announcing his defeat and the consequences which it must entail, and that evening at Osborne he placed his formal resignation in her majesty's hands.

It is related as an evidence of the intense excitement, if not frenzy, that prevailed at the time, that Mr. Gladstone met with indignity at his Club. Greville, in his "Memoirs," says that, "twenty ruffians of the Carleton Club" had given a dinner to Major Beresford, who had been charged with bribery at the Derby election and had escaped with only a censure, and that "after dinner, when they were drunk, they went up stairs and finding Mr. Gladstone alone in the drawing-room, some of them proposed to throw him out of the window. This they did not quite dare to do, but contented themselves with giving some insulting message or order to the waiter and then went away." Mr. Gladstone, however, remained a member of the Club until he joined the Whig administration in 1859.

Mr. Gladstone's crushing *exposé* of the blunders of Mr. Disraeli's budget was almost ludicrous in its completeness, and it was universally felt that the scheme could not survive his brilliant attack. The effect that the merciless criticism of Disraeli's budget was not only the discomfiture of Mr. Disraeli and the overthrow of the Russell administration, but the elevation of Mr. Gladstone to the place vacated by Chancellor Disraeli.

The Earl of Aberdeen became Prime Minister. The new government was a coalition of Whigs and Peelites, with a representative of the Radicals in the person of Sir William Molesworth. Mr. Gladstone, the Duke of Newcastle, Sir James Graham and Mr. Sidney Herbert were the Peelites in the Cabinet. Mr. Gladstone was chosen Chancellor of the Exchequer.

We may refer here to a letter of Mr. Gladstone, written Christmas, 1851, in order to show his growing Liberalism. The letter was to Dr. Skinner, Bishop of Aberdeen and Primus, on the positions and functions of the laity in the Church. This letter is remarkable, because, as Dr. Charles Wordsworth, Bishop of St. Andrew's, said at the time, "it contained the germ of liberation and the political equality of all religions." The Bishop published a controversial rejoinder, which drew from Dr. Gaisford, Dean of Christ Church, these emphatic words: "You have proved to my satisfaction that this gentleman is unfit to represent the University," meaning the representation for Oxford in Parliament.

This feeling was growing, for when the Russell Ministry fell and it became necessary for Mr. Gladstone, because he accepted a place in the Cabinet, to appeal for re-election to his constituents at Oxford, he met with much opposition, because of his Liberalism. Appealing to his university to return him, and endorse his acceptance of office in the new Ministry of the Earl of Aberdeen, Mr. Gladstone soon discovered that he had made many enemies by his manifest tendencies toward Liberal-Conservatism. He had given unmistakable evidence that he held less firmly the old traditions of that unbending Toryism of which he was once the most promising representative. Lord

Richard B. Cook

Derby, whom he had deposed, had been elected Chancellor of the University to succeed the Duke of Wellington, deceased. Consequently his return to the House was ardently contested. His opponents looked around for a candidate of strong Conservative principles. The Marquis of Chandos, who was first elected, declined to run in opposition to Mr. Gladstone; but at length a suitable opponent was found in Mr. Dudley Perceval, of Christ Church, son of the Right Hon. Spencer Perceval, who was nominated January 4th.

Dr. Hawkins, Provost of Oriel, one of the twenty colleges of Oxford, proposed Mr. Gladstone, and Archdeacon Denison, leader of the High Church party, proposed Mr. Dudley Perceval. According to the custom at university elections, neither candidate was present. It was objected to Mr. Gladstone that he had voted improperly on ecclesiastical questions, and had accepted office in "a hybrid ministry." The "Times" described Mr. Perceval as "a very near relative of our old friend Mrs. Harris. To remove any doubt on this point, let him be exhibited at Exeter Hall with the documentary evidence of his name, existence and history; his first-class, his defeat at Finsbury, his talents, his principles. If we must go to Oxford to record our votes it would at least be something to know that we were voting against a real man and not a mere name." The "Morning Chronicle," on the other hand, affirmed that a section of the Carleton Club were "making a tool of the Oxford Convocation for the purpose of the meanest and smallest political rancor against Mr. Gladstone."

Mr. Gladstone, who fought the battle on ecclesiastical lines, wrote, after the nomination, to the chairman of his election committee, as follows:

"Unless I had a full and clear conviction that the interests of the Church, whether as relates to the legislative functions of Parliament, or the impartial and wise recommendation of fit persons to her majesty for high ecclesiastical offices, were at least as safe in the hands of Lord Aberdeen as in those of Lord Derby (though I would on no account disparage Lord Derby's personal sentiments towards the Church), I should not have accepted office under Lord Aberdeen. As regards the second, if it be thought that during twenty years of public life, or that during the latter part of them, I have failed to give guarantees of attachment to the interests of the Church—to such as so think I can offer neither apology nor pledge. To those who think otherwise, I tender the assurance that I have not by my recent assumption of office made any change whatever in that particular, or in any principles relating to it."

Mr. Gladstone was again elected by a fair majority and returned to Parliament. Seventy-four of the professors voted for Mr. Gladstone and fifteen for Mr. Perceval.

When Parliament assembled the Earl of Aberdeen announced in the House of Lords that the measures of the Government would be both Conservative and Liberal,—at home to maintain Free Trade principles and to pursue the commercial and financial system of the late Sir Robert Peel, and abroad to secure the general peace of Europe without relaxing defensive measures.

Mr. Gladstone had already proved himself to have a wonderful mastery of figures, and the confused technicalities of finance. He did not disappoint the hopes of his friends in regard to his fiscal abilities. On the contrary, he speedily inaugurated a new and brilliant era in finance. Previous to presenting his first budget, in 1853, Mr. Gladstone brought forward a scheme for the reduction of the national debt, which was approved by Radicals as well as Conservatives, and adopted by the House. The scheme worked most successfully until the breaking out of the Crimean war. During this very short period of two years the public debt was reduced by more than $57,500,000.

In consequence of his general reputation and also of this brilliant financial scheme, the first budget of Mr. Gladstone was waited for with intense interest. His first budget was introduced April 18, 1853. It was one of his greatest budgets, and for statesmanlike breadth of conception it has never been surpassed. In bringing it forward Mr. Gladstone spoke five hours, and during that length of time held the House spellbound. The speech was delivered with the greatest ease, and was perspicuity itself throughout. Even when dealing with the most abstruse financial detail his language flowed on without interruption, and he never paused for a word. "Here was an orator who could apply all the resources of a burnished rhetoric to the elucidation of figures; who could make pippins and cheese interesting and tea serious; who could sweep the widest horizon of the financial future and yet stoop to bestow the minutest attention on the microcosm of penny stamps and post-horses. The members on the floor and ladies in the gallery of the House listened attentively and showed no signs of weariness throughout." A contemporary awarded to him the palm for unsurpassed fluency and choice of diction, and says:

"The impression produced upon the minds of the crowded and brilliant assembly by Mr. Gladstone's evident mastery and grasp of the subject, was, that England had at length found a skillful financier, upon whom the mantle of Peel had descended. The cheering when the right honorable gentleman sat down was of the most enthusiastic and prolonged character, and his friends and colleagues hastened to tender him their warm congratulations upon the distinguished success he had achieved in his first budget."

The budget provided for the gradual reduction of the income tax to expire in 1860; for an increase in the duty on spirits; for the abolition of the soap duties; the reduction of the tax on cabs and hackney coaches; the introduction of the penny receipt stamp and the equalization of the assessed taxes on property. By these provisions it was proposed to make life easier and cheaper for large and numerous classes. The duty on 123 articles was abolished and the duty on 133 others reduced, the total relief amounting to $25,000,000. Mr. Gladstone gave a clear exposition of the income tax, which he declared was never intended to be permanent. It had been the last resort in times of national danger, and he could not consent to retain it as a part of the permanent and ordinary finances of the country. It was objectionable on account of its unequal incidence, of the harassing investigation into private affairs which it entailed and of the frauds to which it inevitably led.

The value of the reduction in the necessities of life proposed by Mr. Gladstone is seen from the following from a contemporary writer:

"The present budget, more than any other budget within our recollection, is a cupboard budget; otherwise, a poor man's budget. With certain very ugly features, the thing has altogether a good, hopeful aspect, together with very fair proportions. It is not given to any Chancellor of the Exchequer to make a budget fascinating as a fairy tale. Nevertheless, there are visions of wealth and comfort in the present budget that mightily recommend it to us. It seems to add color and fatness to the poor man's beef; to give flavor and richness to the poor man's plum-pudding. The budget is essentially a cupboard budget; and let the name of Gladstone be, for the time at least, musical at the poor man's fireside."

It unquestionably established Gladstone as the foremost financier of his day. Greville, in his "Memoirs," says of him: "He spoke for five hours; and by universal consent it was one of the grandest displays and most able financial statements that ever was heard in the House of Commons; a great scheme, boldly and skillfully and honestly devised, disdaining popular clamor and pressure from without, and the execution of its absolute perfection."

We reproduce some extracts from this important speech: "Depend upon it, when you come to close quarters with this subject, when you come to measure and test the respective relations of intelligence and labor and property in all their myriad and complex forms, and when you come to represent those relations in arithmetical results, you are undertaking an operation of which I should say it was beyond the power of man to conduct it with satisfaction, but which, at any rate, is an operation to which you ought not constantly to recur; for

Richard B. Cook

if, as my noble friend once said with universal applause, this country could not bear a revolution once a year, I will venture to say that it cannot bear a reconstruction of the income tax once a year.

"Whatever you do in regard to the income tax, you must be bold, you must be intelligible, you must be decisive. You must not palter with it. If you do, I have striven at least to point out as well as my feeble powers will permit, the almost desecration I would say, certainly the gross breach of duty to your country, of which you will be found guilty, in thus putting to hazard one of the most potent and effective among all its material resources. I believe it to be of vital importance, whether you keep this tax or whether you part with it, that you should either keep it or should leave it in a state in which it will be fit for service on an emergency, and that it will be impossible to do if you break up the basis of your income tax.

"If the Committee have followed me, they will understand that we found ourselves on the principle that the income-tax ought to be marked as a temporary measure; that the public feeling that relief should be given to intelligence and skill as compared with property ought to be met, and may be met with justice and with safety, in the manner we have pointed out; that the income tax in its operation ought to be mitigated by every rational means, compatible with its integrity; and, above all, that it should be associated in the last term of its existence, as it was in the first, with those remissions of indirect taxation which have so greatly redoubled to the profit of this country and have set so admirable an example—an example that has already in some quarters proved contagious to the other nations of the earth, These are the principles on which we stand, and these the figures. I have shown you that if you grant us the taxes which we ask, to the moderate amount of £2,500,000 in the whole, much less than that sum for the present year, you, or the Parliament which may be in existence in 1860, will be in the condition, if it shall so think fit, to part with the income tax."

Sir, I scarcely dare to look at the clock, shamefully reminding me, as it must, how long, how shamelessly, I have trespassed on the time of the committee. All I can say in apology is that I have endeavored to keep closely to the topics which I had before me—

—immensum spatiis confecimus aequor,
Et jam tempus equum fumantia solvere colla.

"These are the proposals of the Government. They may be approved or they may be condemned, but I have at least this full and undoubting confidence, that it will on all hands be admitted that we have not sought to evade the difficulties of our position; that we have not concealed those difficulties, either from ourselves or from others; that we have not attempted to counteract them by narrow or flimsy expedients; that we have prepared plans which, if you will adopt them, will go some way to close up many vexed financial questions— questions such as, if not now settled, may be attended with public inconvenience, and even with public danger, in future years and under less favorable circumstances; that we have endeavored, in the plans we have now submitted to you, to make the path of our successors in future years not more arduous but more easy; and I may be permitted to add that, while we have sought to do justice, by the changes we propose in taxation, to intelligence and skill as compared with property—while we have sought to do justice to the great laboring community of England by furthering their relief from indirect taxation, we have not been guided by any desire to put one class against another. We have felt we should best maintain our own honor, that we should best meet the views of Parliament, and best promote the interests of the country, by declining to draw any invidious distinctions between class and class, by adapting it to ourselves as a sacred aim to differ and distribute—burden if we must, benefit if we may—with equal and impartial hand; and we have the consolation of believing that by proposals such as these we contribute, as far as in us lies, not only to develop the material resources of the country, but to knit the hearts of the various classes of this great nation yet more closely than heretofore to that throne and to those institutions under which it is their happiness to live."

It is seldom that a venture of such magnitude as Mr. Gladstone's first budget meets with universal success. But from the outset the plan was received with universal favor. Besides the plaudits with which the orator was greeted at the conclusion of his speech, his proposals were received favorably by the whole nation. Being constructed upon Free Trade principles, it was welcomed by the press and the country. It added greatly, not only to the growing reputation of the new Chancellor of the Exchequer as a financier, but also to his popularity.

The following anecdote of Mr. Gladstone is told by Walter Jerrold and is appropriate as well as timely here:

"During Mr. Gladstone's first tenure of office as Chancellor of the Exchequer, a curious adventure occurred to him in the London offices of the late Mr. W. Lindsay, merchant, shipowner and M.P. There one day entered a brusque and wealthy shipowner of Sunderland, inquiring for Mr. Lindsay. As Mr. Lindsay was out, the visitor was requested to wait in an adjacent room, where he found a person busily engaged in copying some figures. The Sunderland shipowner paced the room several times and took careful note of the writer's doings, and at length said to him, 'Thou writes a bonny hand, thou dost.'

"'I am glad you think so,' was the reply."

"'Ah, thou dost. Thou makes thy figures weel. Thou'rt just the chap I want."

"'Indeed!' said the Londoner."

"'Yes, indeed,' said the Sunderland man. 'I'm a man of few words. Noo, if thou'lt come over to canny ould Sunderland thou seest I'll give thee a hundred and twenty pounds a year, and that's a plum thou dost not meet with every day in thy life, I reckon. Noo then.'"

"The Londoner replied that he was much obliged for the offer, and would wait till Mr. Lindsay returned, whom he would consult upon the subject. Accordingly, on the return of the latter, he was informed of the shipowner's tempting offer.

"'Very well,' said Mr. Lindsay, 'I should be sorry to stand in your way. One hundred and twenty pounds is more than I can afford to pay you in the department in which you are at present placed. You will find my friend a good and kind master, and, under the circumstances, the sooner you know each other the better. Allow me, therefore, Mr.—, to introduce you to the Right Hon. W. E. Gladstone, Chancellor of the Exchequer.' The Sunderland shipowner was a little taken aback at first, but he soon recovered his self-possession, and enjoyed the joke quite as much as Mr. Gladstone did."

CHAPTER X

THE CRIMEAN WAR

The Crimean War, the great event with which the Aberdeen Cabinet was associated, was a contest between Russia and Turkey, England and France. A dispute which arose between Russia and Turkey as to the possession of the Holy Places of Jerusalem was the precipitating cause. For a long time the Greek and the Latin Churches had contended for the possession of the Holy Land. Russia supported the claim of the Greek Church, and France that of the Papal Church. The Czar claimed a Protectorate over all the Greek subjects of the Porte. Russia sought to extend her conquests south and to seize upon Turkey. France and England sustained Turkey. Sardinia afterwards joined the Anglo-French alliance.

The people of England generally favored the war, and evinced much enthusiasm at the prospect of it. Lord Aberdeen and Mr. Gladstone wished England to stand aloof. The Peelite members of the cabinet were generally less inclined to war than the Whigs. Lord Palmerston and Lord John Russell favored England's support of Turkey. Some thought that England could have averted the war by pursuing persistently either of two courses: to inform Turkey that England would give her no aid; or to warn Russia that if she went to war, England would fight for Turkey. But with a ministry halting between two opinions, and the people demanding it, England "drifted into war" with Russia.

July 2, 1853, the Russian troops crossed the Pruth and occupied the Danubian Principalities which had been by treaty, in 1849, evacuated by Turkey and Russia, and declared by both powers neutral territory between them. London was startled, October 4, 1853, by a telegram announcing that the Sultan had declared war against Russia. England and France jointly sent an *ultimatum* to the Czar, to which no answer was returned. March 28, 1854, England declared war.

On the 12th of March, while great excitement prevailed and public meetings were held throughout England, declaring for and against war, Mr. Gladstone made an address on the occasion of the inauguration of the statue of Sir Robert Peel, at Manchester. He spoke of the designs of Russia, and described her as a power which threatened to override all other powers, and as a source of danger to the peace of the world. Against such designs, seen in Russia's attempt to overthrow the Ottoman Empire, England had determined to set herself at whatever cost. War was a calamity that the government did not desire to bring upon the country, "a calamity which stained the face of nature with human gore, gave loose rein to crime, and took bread from the people. No doubt negotiation is repugnant to the national impatience at the sight of injustice and oppression; it is beset with delay, intrigue, and chicane; but these are not so horrible as war, if negotiation can be made to result in saving this country from a calamity which deprives the nation of subsistence and arrests the operations of industry. To attain that result ... Her Majesty's Ministers have persevered in exercising that self-command and that self-restraint which impatience may mistake for indifference, feebleness or cowardice, but which are truly the crowning greatness of a great people, and which do not evince the want of readiness to vindicate, when the time comes, the honor of this country."

In November a conference of some of the European powers was held at Vienna to avert the war by mediating between Russia and Turkey, but was unsuccessful. Mr. Gladstone said: "Austria urged the two leading states, England and France, to send in their *ultimatum* to Russia, and promised it her decided support.... Prussia at the critical moment, to speak in homely language, bolted.... In fact, she broke up the European concert, by which France and England had hoped to pull down the stubbornness of the Czar."

Mr. Gladstone had opposed the war, not only on humanitarian and Christian grounds, but also because the preparation of a war budget overthrew all his financial schemes and hopes; a new budget was necessary, and he as Chancellor of the Exchequer must prepare it. Knowing that the struggle was inevitable, he therefore bent his energies to the task and conceived a scheme for discharging the expenses of the war out of the current revenue, provided it required no more than ten million pounds extra, so that the country should not be permanently burdened. It would require to do this the imposition of fresh taxes.

"It thus fell to the lot of the most pacific of Ministers, the devotee of retrenchment, and the anxious cultivator of all industrial arts, to prepare a war budget, and to meet as well as he might the exigencies of a conflict which had so cruelly dislocated all the ingenious devices of financial optimism."

Mr. Gladstone afterwards moved for over six and a half millions of pounds more than already granted, and proposed a further increase in the taxes. Mr. Disraeli opposed Mr. Gladstone's budget. He devised a scheme to borrow and thus increase the debt. He opposed the imposition of new taxes. Mr. Gladstone said: "Every good motive and every bad motive, combated only by the desire of the approval of honorable men and by conscientious rectitude—every motive of ease, comfort, and of certainty spring forward to induce a Chancellor of the Exchequer to become the first man to recommend a loan." Mr. Gladstone was sustained.

The war had begun in earnest. The Duke of Newcastle received a telegram on the 21st of September announcing that 25,000 English troops, 25,000 French and 8000 Turks had landed safely at Eupatoria "without meeting with any resistance, and had already begun to march upon Sebastopol."

The war was popular with the English people, but the ministry of Lord Aberdeen, which inaugurated it, was becoming unpopular. This became apparent in the autumn of 1854. There were not actual dissensions in the Cabinet, but there was great want of harmony as to the conduct of the war. The Queen knew with what reluctance Lord Aberdeen had entered upon the war, but she had the utmost confidence in him as a man and a statesman. She was most desirous that the war be prosecuted with vigor, and trusted the Premier for the realization of her hopes and those of the nation, but unity in the Cabinet was necessary for the successful prosecution of the war.

Parliament assembled December 12, 1854, "under circumstances more stirring and momentous than any which had occurred since the year of Waterloo." The management of the war was the main subject under discussion. The English troops had covered themselves with glory in the battles of Alma, Balaclava and Inkermann. But the sacrifice was great. Thousands were slain and homes made desolate, while the British army was suffering greatly, and the sick and wounded were needing attention. Half a million pounds were subscribed in three months, and Miss Florence Nightingale with thirty-seven lady nurses, soon to be reinforced by fifty more, set out at once for the seat of war to nurse the sick and wounded soldiers. It is recorded that "they reached Scutari on the 5th of November, in time to receive the soldiers who had been wounded at the battle of Balaclava. On the arrival of Miss Nightingale the great hospital at Scutari, in which up to this time all had been chaos and discomfort, was reduced to order, and those tender lenitives which only woman's thought and woman's sympathy can bring to the sick man's couch, were applied to solace and alleviate the agonies of pain or the torture of fever and prostration."

It was natural to attribute the want of proper management to the ministry, and hence the Government found itself under fire. In the House of Lords the Earl of Derby condemned the inefficient manner in which the war had been carried on, the whole conduct of the ministry in the war, and the insufficiency of the number of troops sent out to check the power of Russia. The Duke of Newcastle replied, and while not defending all the actions of the ministry during the war, yet contended that the government were prepared to prosecute it with resolve and unflinching firmness. While not standing ready to reject overtures of peace, they would not accept any but an honorable termination of the war. The ministry relied upon the army, the people, and upon their allies with the full confidence of ultimate success.

Mr. Disraeli, in the House of Commons, attacked the policy of the ministry from beginning to end. Everything was a blunder or a mishap of some description or other; the government had invaded Russia with 25,000 troops without providing any provision for their support.

When the House of Commons assembled, in January, 1855, it became apparent that there was a determination to sift to the bottom the charges that had been made against the ministry regarding their manner of carrying on the war. The Queen expressed her sympathy for Lord Aberdeen, who was in a most unenviable position. Motions hostile to the government were introduced in the House of Lords, while in the House of Commons Mr. Roebuck moved for a select committee "to inquire into the condition of the army before Sebastopol, and into the conduct of those departments of the government whose duty it has been to minister to the wants of the army."

Lord John Russell resigned his office and left his colleagues to face the vote. He could not see how Mr. Roebuck's motion could be resisted. This seemed to portend the downfall of the ministry. The Duke of Newcastle, Secretary of War, offered to retire to save the government. Lord Palmerston believed that the breaking up of the ministry would be a calamity to the country, but he doubted the expediency of the retirement of the Duke of Newcastle, and his own fitness for the place of Minister of War, if vacated. Finally the Cabinet resolved to hold together, except Lord John Russell.

In the debate it was declared that the condition of things at the seat of war was exaggerated; but the speech of Mr. Stafford caused a great sensation. He described the sufferings which he declared he had himself witnessed. He summed up by quoting the language of a French officer, who said: "You seem, sir, to carry on war according to the system of the Middle Ages." The situation of the ministry was critical before, but this speech seemed to make sure the passage of the resolutions.

It was under all these depressing circumstances that Mr. Gladstone rose to defend himself and his colleagues. In a fine passage he thus described what the position of the Cabinet would have been if they had shrunk from their duty: "What sort of epitaph would have been written over their remains? He himself would have written it thus: Here lie the dishonored ashes of a ministry which found England at peace and left it in war, which was content to enjoy the emoluments of office and to wield the sceptre of power so long as no man had the courage to question their existence. They saw the storm gathering over the country; they heard the agonizing accounts which were almost daily received of the state of the sick and wounded in the East. These things did not move them. But as soon as the Honorable Member for Sheffield raised his hand to point the thunderbolt, they became conscience-stricken with a sense of guilt, and, hoping to escape punishment, they ran away from duty."

This eloquent passage was received with tumultuous cheers. Mr. Gladstone claimed that there had been many exaggerations as to the state of the army and there were then more than 30,000 British troops under arms before Sebastopol. The administration of the War Department at home was no doubt defective, but he declined to admit that it had not improved, or that it was as bad as to deserve formal censure, and the Duke of Newcastle did not merit the condemnation sought to be cast on him as the head of the War Department.

Mr. Disraeli was eagerly heard when he rose to speak. He said that the government admitted that they needed reconstruction, and that now the House was called upon to vote confidence in the administration. It was not the Duke of Newcastle nor the military system, but the policy of the whole Cabinet which he characterized as a "deplorable administration."

The result of the vote was a strange surprise to all parties, and one of the greatest ever experienced in Parliamentary history. The vote for Mr. Roebuck's committee was 205; and against it, 148; a majority against the ministry of 157. "The scene was a peculiar and probably an unparalleled one. The cheers which are usually heard from one side or the other of the House on the numbers of a division being announced, were not forthcoming. The members were for a moment spellbound with astonishment, then there came a murmur of amazement and finally a burst of general laughter." The resignation of the Aberdeen ministry was announced February 1st, the Duke of Newcastle stating that it had been his intention to give up the office of Secretary of War whether Mr. Roebuck's resolution had passed or not.

Thus was overthrown the famous coalition Cabinet of Lord Aberdeen—one of the most brilliant ever seen—a Cabinet distinguished for its oratorical strength, and for the conspicuous abilities of its chief members. Mr. Gladstone, who was the most distinguished Peelite in the Cabinet, certainly could not, up to this period, be suspected of lukewarmness in the prosecution of the war. Lord Palmerston formed a reconstructed rather than a new Cabinet. Mr. Gladstone and his friends at first declined to serve in the new Cabinet, out of regard for the Duke of Newcastle and Lord Aberdeen, the real victims of the adverse vote. But these noblemen besought Mr. Gladstone not to let his personal feelings stand in the way of his own interests, and not to deprive the country of his great services, so he resumed office as Chancellor of the Exchequer. Lord Palmerston had been regarded as the coming man, and his name carried weight upon the Continent and at home. But the new ministry was surrounded by serious difficulties, and did not pull together very long. The War Minister, Lord Panmure, entered upon his duties with energy, and proposed, February 16th, his remedy for existing evils; but on the 19th of February Mr. Layard in the House of Commons said, "the country stood on the brink of ruin—it had fallen into the abyss of disgrace and become the laughing-stock of Europe." He declared that the new ministry differed little from the last.

Lord Palmerston, in answer to inquiries, lamented the sufferings of the army and confessed that mishaps had been made, but the present ministry had come forward in an emergency and from a sense of public duty, and he believed would obtain the confidence of the country. But another strange turn in events was at hand. Mr. Roebuck gave notice of the appointment of his committee. Hostility to the ministry was disclaimed, but Mr. Gladstone, Sir James Graham and Mr. Sidney Herbert took the same view of the question they had previously taken. They were opposed to the investigation as a dangerous breach of a great constitutional principle, and if the committee was granted, it would be a precedent from whose repetition the Executive could never again escape, however unreasonable might be the nature of the demand. They therefore retired from office.

The report of the committee, when presented, practically advised a vote of censure upon the Aberdeen Cabinet for the sufferings of the British army, hence the house declined to entertain it by a large majority of 107. As the appointment of the committee, however, was the only way to allay the popular excitement, there were many who thought that the Peelites would have done well to recognize the urgency of the crisis and not to have abandoned the Government.

The resignation of Mr. Gladstone made him very unpopular. However, "the wave of unpopularity lasted perhaps for a couple of years, and was afterwards replaced by a long-sustained popularity, which has not been exceeded by any statesman of the country. Greville referred to Gladstone about this time as 'the most unpopular man in the country.'"

March 2d the Emperor Nicholas died suddenly, and there were momentary hopes of peace; but his successor, Alexander, resolved to prosecute the struggle rather than yield the positions taken by the late Czar. He issued a warlike proclamation, and though he agreed to take part in the Vienna Conference of European powers, to be held March 15th, there were no signs that he intended to recede from the Russian claims.

Lord John Russell was sent to Vienna as English Plenipotentiary. The English aimed to secure the limitation of the preponderance of Russia in the Black Sea, and the acknowledgment of Turkey as one of the great European powers. To gain these points would, it was thought, end the war. Russia "would not consent to limit the number of her ships—if she did so she forfeited her honor, she would be no longer Russia. They did not want Turkey, they would be glad to maintain the Sultan, but they knew it was impossible; he must perish; they were resolved not to let any other power have Constantinople—they must not have that door to their dominions in the Black Sea shut against them." The Conference failed, and Lord John Russell was held responsible for its failure, and was eventually forced out of the Cabinet on that account. The failure of the Vienna negotiations produced great excitement, and the ministry were attacked and defeated in both Houses of Parliament. Mr. Disraeli offered a resolution of dissatisfaction in the House of Commons. Mr. Gladstone spoke during the debate on the failure of the Vienna Conference, and defended the war of the Crimea. He did not consider it a failure, for Russia now agreed to most of the points raised by the allies, and the only matter to be adjusted, was the proposition to limit the power of Russia in the Black Sea. Personally, he had formerly favored the curtailment of Russia's power there, but he now thought that such a proposal implied a great indignity to Russia. He believed that the proposal of Russia to give to Turkey the power of opening and shutting the straits was one calculated to bring about a peaceful settlement. The time was favorable to make peace. Lord John Russell replied vigorously to Mr. Gladstone. The House decided by a majority of 100 to support the ministry in the further prosecution of the war until a safe and honorable peace could be secured.

But on the 10th of July Sir E. Bulwer Lytton offered the following resolution: "That the conduct of our Ministry, in the recent negotiations at Vienna, has, in the opinion of this House, shaken the confidence of this country in those to whom its affairs are entrusted." Lord John Russell again declined to face discussion and resigned. During the debate on the motion Mr. Disraeli bitterly attacked Lord John Russell and the Premier, Lord Palmerston. But Mr. Gladstone said that so far from blaming the Ministry for hesitating about the offers of peace at Vienna, he blamed them for not giving the propositions that consideration which their gravity demanded, and for abruptly terminating the Conference and closing the hope of an honorable peace.

Mr. Gladstone, on the 3d of August, made another powerful appeal for the cessation of the war. He held that there was now no definite object for continuing the struggle; defended the Austrian proposals; defied the Western powers to control the future destinies of Russia, save for a moment; and he placed "the individual responsibility of the continuance of the war on the head of the Ministry."

But while Sebastopol held out there was no prospect of peace with Russia. Finally, in September, that fortress was taken and destroyed, and the Peace of Paris was concluded, March, 1856.

Richard B. Cook

CHAPTER XI

IN OPPOSITION TO THE GOVERNMENT

It was in February, 1855, that Mr. Gladstone resigned his seat in the Cabinet. After the Treaty of Paris, March, 1856, which put an end to the Crimean War, Mr. Gladstone found himself in opposition to the Ministry of Lord Palmerston. He had assumed a position of independence, associating politically with neither party. The political parties dreaded criticism and attack from him, for he was not properly constructed for the defense of either. He had himself declared his "sympathies" were "with the Conservatives, and his opinions with the Liberals," and that he and his Peelite colleagues, during this period of political isolation, were like roving icebergs on which men could not land with safety, but with which ships might come into perilous collision. Their weight was too great not to count, but it counted first this way and then that. Mr. Gladstone was conscientious in his opposition. He said: "I greatly felt being turned out of office. I saw great things to do. I longed to do them. I am losing the best years of my life out of my natural service. Yet I have never ceased to rejoice that I am not in office with Palmerston, when I have seen the tricks, the shufflings, the frauds he daily has recourse to as to his business. I rejoice not to sit on the Treasury Bench with him."

In August, 1855, Lord Aberdeen said; "Gladstone intends to be Prime Minister. He has great qualifications, but some serious defects. He is supreme in the House of Commons. He is too obstinate; if a man can be too honest, he is too honest. I have told Gladstone that when he is Prime Minister, I will have a seat in his Cabinet, if he desires it, without an office."

During 1856, several measures came before Parliament which Mr. Gladstone opposed. He vindicated the freedom of the Belgian press, whose liberty some of the powers would curtail, and opposed resolutions to consider the state of education in England and Wales, as tending to create a central controlling power, involving secular instruction and endless religious quarrels. He also opposed the budget of Sir G.C. Lewis, which imposed more duties upon the tea and sugar of the working-man, and was said to be generally at variance with the policy pursued by every enlightened minister of finance. Besides, he condemned the continuance of the war duties in times of peace. "He was a particularly acute thorn in the side of the Chancellor of the Exchequer, and criticised the budget with unsparing vigor. 'Gladstone seems bent on leading Sir George Lewis a weary life,' wrote Mr. Greville. But finance was by no means the only subject of this terrible free-lance."

A resolution was offered in the House of Commons expressing disapprobation with the English Cabinet for sanctioning, in 1855 and '56, the violation of international law, by secretly enlisting the subjects of the United States as recruits for the British army, by the intervention of the English Ambassador. Mr. Gladstone said: "It appears to me that the two cardinal aims that we ought to keep in view in the discussion of this question are peace and a thoroughly cordial understanding with America for one, the honor and fame of England for the other. I am bound to say that in regard to neither of these points am I satisfied with the existing state of things, or with the conduct of Her Majesty's Government. A cordial understanding with America has not been preserved, and the honor of this country has been compromised."

Lord Palmerston, though very popular with the people, had greatly offended a large portion of the House of Commons by his interference in China. A lorcha, called the *Arrow*, flying the British flag, had been seized by the Chinese, and the question arose as to the right of the vessel to the protection of England. The opponents of the government contended that the vessel was built in China, was captured by pirates, and recaptured by the Chinese, and hence had no claim to British protection. To bring the matter to an issue Mr. Cobden introduced a resolution of inquiry and censure. For five nights the debate was protracted, and many able speeches were made on both sides, but Mr. Gladstone made one of the most effective speeches, against the ministry. He said: "Every man, I trust, will give his vote with the consciousness that it may depend upon his single vote whether the miseries, the crimes, the atrocities that I fear are now proceeding in China are to be discountenanced or not. We have now come to the crisis of the case. England is not yet committed. With you, then, with us, with every one of us, it rests to show that this House, which is the first, the most ancient, and the noblest temple of freedom in the world, is also the temple of that everlasting justice without which freedom itself would only be a name or only a curse to mankind."

The Premier ably defended himself, but the resolution of Mr. Cobden was passed. Parliament was dissolved March 21, 1857, and Lord Palmerston appealed to the country. He was victorious at the polls. Among the prominent Liberals who lost their seats were Cobden, Bright, and Milner Gibson. The Peelites suffered loss too, but Mr. Gladstone was again elected for Oxford University. However, Mr. Greville writes, under date of June 3d: "Gladstone hardly ever goes near the House of Commons, and never opens his lips." But his indifference and silence were not to last long.

When the Divorce Bill, which originated in the Lords, came up in the Commons, Mr. Gladstone made an impassioned speech against the measure, contending for the equality of woman with man in all the rights pertaining to marriage. He dealt with the question on theological, legal and social grounds. He contended that marriage was not only or chiefly a civil contract, but a "mystery" of the Christian religion. By the law of God it could not be so annulled as to permit of the remarriage of the parties. "Our Lord," he says, "has emphatically told us that, at and from the beginning, marriage was perpetual, and was on both sides single." He dwelt with pathetic force on the injustice between man and woman of the proposed legislation, which would entitle the husband to divorce from an unfaithful wife, but would give no corresponding protection to the woman; and predicted the gloomiest consequences to the conjugal morality of the country from the erection of this new and odious tribunal. Nevertheless the bill became a law.

In 1858 a bill was introduced in the House of Commons by Lord Palmerston, to make conspiracy to murder a felony. It grew out of the attempt of Orsini upon the life of Napoleon III. The bill at first was carried by an immense majority, but the conviction spread that the measure was introduced solely at the dictation of the French Emperor, and hence the proposal was strongly opposed. Mr. Gladstone said: "These times are grave for liberty. We live in the nineteenth century; we talk of progress; we believe we are advancing, but can any man of observation who has watched the events of the last few years in Europe have failed to perceive that there is a movement indeed, but a downward and backward movement? There are few spots in which institutions that claim our sympathy still exist and flourish.... But in these times more than ever does responsibility centre upon the institutions of England, and if it does centre upon England, upon her principles, upon her laws and upon her governors, then I say that a measure passed by this House of Commons—the chief hope of freedom—which attempts to establish a moral complicity between us and those who seek safety in repressive measures, will be a blow and a discouragement to that sacred cause in every country in the world."

The bill was defeated by a majority of nineteen, and Lord Palmerston again resigned. He was succeeded by Lord Derby, who once more came into power. Mr. Disraeli again became Chancellor of the Exchequer, and leader of the House of Commons. The new ministry, which existed largely on sufferance, passed some good measures.

The one hundredth anniversary of the battle of Plassey was celebrated in England June 23, 1857, to obtain funds for a monument to Lord Clive, who secured India to England. The English then felt secure in the government of that land, yet at that very time one of the most wide-spread, destructive and cruel rebellions was raging, and shaking to its very foundations the English rule in Hindostan. Suddenly the news came of the terrible Indian mutiny and of the indiscriminate slaughter of men, women and children, filling all hearts with horror, and then of the crushing out of the rebellion. Lord Canning, Governor-General, issued a proclamation to the chiefs of Oudh, looking to the confiscation of the possessions of mutineers who failed to return to the allegiance of England. It was meant as clemency. But Lord Ellenborough, the officer in charge of affairs in India, dispatched "a rattling condemnation of the whole proceeding." Says Justin McCarthy: "It was absurd language for a man like Lord Ellenborough to address to a statesman like Lord Canning, who had just succeeded in keeping the fabric of English government in India together during the most terrible trial ever imposed on it by fate." The matter was taken up by Parliament. Lord Shaftesbury moved that the Lords disprove the sending of the dispatch. In the Commons the ministry were arraigned. But Lord Ellenborough took upon himself the sole responsibility of the dispatch, and resigned. Mr. Gladstone was invited to the vacant place, but declined.

The most important among the bills passed by Parliament was the India Bill, by which the government of India was transferred from the East India Company to the Crown and the Home government. Mr. Gladstone, who opposed the bill, proposed a clause providing that the Indian troops should not be employed in military operations beyond the frontiers of India.

In November, 1858, Mr. Gladstone accepted from the Premier the post of Lord High Commissioner Extraordinary to the

Ionian Islands. The people of the Ionian Islands, which in 1800 was formed into the Republic of the Seven Islands, and was under the protection of Great Britain from 1815, were desirous of adding themselves to Greece. But the British government objected to the separation and their union with Greece. Mr. Gladstone was to repair to Corfu for the purpose of reconciling the people to the British protectorate. The Ionians regarded his appointment as a virtual abandonment of the protectorate of Great Britain. Mr. Gladstone, December 3d, addressed the Senate at Corfu in Italian. He had the reputation of being a Greek student, and the inhabitants of the Islands persisted in regarding him not as a Commissioner of a Conservative English Government, but as "Gladstone the Phil-Hellene!" He made a tour of the Islands, holding levees, receiving deputations and delivering harangues, and was received wherever he went with the honors due to a liberator. His path everywhere was made to seem like a triumphal progress. It was in vain he repeated his assurance that he came to reconcile them to the protectorate and not to deliver them from it. But the popular instinct insisted upon regarding him as at least the precursor of their union with the Kingdom of Greece. The legislative assembly met January 27, 1859, and proposed annexation to Greece. Finding that this was their firm wish and determination, Mr. Gladstone despatched to the Queen a copy of the vote, in which the representatives declared that "the single and unanimous will of the Ionian people has been and is for their union with the Kingdom of Greece." Mr. Gladstone returned home in February, 1859. The Ionians continued their agitation, and in 1864 were formally given over to the government of Greece.

Parliament was opened February 3, 1859, by the Queen, who in her speech from the throne said that the attention of Parliament would be called to the state of the law regulating the representation of the people. The plan of the government was presented by Mr. Disraeli. "It was a fanciful performance," says an English writer. The ministry proposed not to alter the limits of the franchise, but to introduce into boroughs a new kind of franchise founded on personal property. Mr. Disraeli

Richard B. Cook

characterized the government measure as "wise, prudent, adequate, conservative, and framed by men who reverence the past, are proud of the present, and confident of the future." Two members of the Cabinet promptly resigned rather than be parties to these proposals. Mr. Bright objected because the working classes were excluded. An amendment was moved by Lord John Russell condemning interference with the franchise which enabled freeholders in boroughs to vote in counties, and demanding a wider extension of the suffrage in boroughs.

Mr. Gladstone, though agreeing with these views, declined to support the amendment, because, if carried, it would upset the government and bring in a weaker administration. He did not propose to support the government, but he desired to see a settlement of the question of reform, and he thought the present opportunity advantageous for such settlement. He pleaded eloquently for the retention of the small boroughs.

The bill was lost by a majority of thirty-nine. Lord Derby having advised the Queen to dissolve Parliament, this was done April 3d. The general elections which resulted from the defeat of the Conservatives in the House of Commons on the Reform Bill, resulted in returning the Liberals with a considerable majority. Mr. Gladstone was again returned unopposed for the University of Oxford. The Queen opened the new Parliament June 7th. In reply to the speech from the throne an amendment to the address was moved by Lord Hartington, proposing a vote of want of confidence in the ministers. After three nights debate it was carried on June 10th, by a majority of thirteen, Mr. Gladstone voting with the government. Lord Derby and his colleagues immediately resigned. The Queen being averse to choosing between Lord John Russell and Lord Palmerston, turned to Lord Granville, leader of the Liberal party in the House of Lords. He failed to form a Cabinet, and Lord Palmerston again became Prime Minister.

The revolution of the political wheel once more brought Mr. Gladstone into office as Chancellor of the Exchequer. It became necessary in accepting a Cabinet position to again appeal to his constituents at Oxford for re-election. He voted as he did to sustain Lord Derby's administration and to settle the Reform question, yet he was misunderstood and some of his constituents alienated. He was strongly opposed by the Conservative Marquis of Chandos. The Conservatives claimed that he should not be returned, because, as Professor Mansel said, by his "acceptance of office he must now be considered as giving his definite adhesion to the Liberal party, as at present reconstructed, and as approving of the policy of those who overthrew Lord Derby's government." It was found on the conclusion of the poll, which continued for five days, that Mr. Gladstone was returned with a majority of nearly two hundred over his opponent. It is worthy of note that this same year Cambridge conferred upon Mr. Gladstone the honorary degree of D.C.L.

CHAPTER XII

HOMERIC STUDIES

"The plenitude and variety of Mr. Gladstone's intellectual powers," says G. Barnett Smith, "have been the subject of such frequent comment that it would be superfluous to insist upon them here. On the political side of his career his life has been as unresting and active as that of any other great party leader, and if we regard him in the literary aspect we are equally astonished at his energy and versatility. Putting out of view his various works upon Homer, his miscellaneous writings of themselves, with the reading they involve, would entitle their author to take high rank on the score of industry.... We stand amazed at the infinity of topics which have received Mr. Gladstone's attention."

To solve the problems associated with Homer has been the chief intellectual recreation, the close and earnest study of Mr. Gladstone's literary life. "The blind old man of Scio's rocky isle" possessed for him an irresistible and a perennial charm. Nor can this occasion surprise, for all who have given themselves up to the consideration and attempted solution of the Homeric poems have found the fascination of the occupation gather in intensity. It is not alone from the poetic point of view that the first great epic of the world attracts students of all ages and of all countries. Homer presents, in addition, and beyond every other writer, a vast field for ethnological, geographical, and historical speculation and research. The ancient world stands revealed in the Homeric poems. Besides, almost numberless volumes have been written based upon the equally debatable questions of the Homeric text and the Homeric unity.

Some literary works of Mr. Gladstone have been already noticed. "Studies on Homer and Homeric Age" shows Mr. Gladstone's classic tastes and knowledge as well as his great industry and ability. This work was published in three volumes, in 1858. It is his *magnum opus* in literature, and exhibits wide and laborious research. "It discusses the Homeric controversy in its broad aspects, the relation of Homer to the Sacred Writings, his place in education, his historic aims, the probable period of the poet's life, the Homeric text, the ethnology of the Greek races, and the politics and poetry of Homer. Among subsequent Greek studies by Mr. Gladstone were his 'Juventus Mundi' and the 'Homeric Synchronism.' There is probably no greater living authority on the text of Homer than Mr. Gladstone, and the Ancient Greek race and literature have exercised over him a perennial fascination."

Mr. Gladstone dwells much on the relation of Homer to Christianity. "The standard of humanity of the Greek poet is different, yet many of his ideas almost carry us back to the early morning of our race; the hours of its greater simplicity and purity, and more free intercourse with God.... How is it possible to overvalue this primitive representation of the human race in a form complete, distinct and separate, with its own religion, stories, policy, history, arts, manners, fresh and true to the standard of its nature, like the form of an infant from the hand of the Creator, yet mature, full, and finished, in its own sense, after its own laws, like some masterpiece of the sculptor's art?" The Homeric scene of action is not Paradise, but it is just as far removed from the vices of a later heathenism.

Mr. Gladstone compares the "Iliad" and the "Odyssey," which he believed to be the poems of one poet, Homer, with the Old Testament writings, and observes that "Homer can never be put into competition with the Scriptures as touching the great fundamental, invaluable code of truth and hope;" but he shows how one may in a sense be supplementary to the other. As regards the history of the Greek race, it is Homer that furnishes "the point of origin from which all distances are to be measured." He says: "The Mosaic books, and the other historical books of the Old Testament, are not intended to present, and do not present, a picture of human society or of our nature drawn at large. The poems of Homer may be viewed as the complement of the earliest portion of the sacred records."

Again: "The Holy Scriptures are like a thin stream, beginning from the very fountain-head of our race, and gradually, but continuously, finding their way through an extended solitude into times otherwise known, and into the general current of the fortunes of mankind. The Homeric poems are like a broad lake, outstretched in the distance, which provides us with a mirror of one particular age and people, alike full and marvelous, but which is entirely disassociated by a period of many generations from any other records, except such as are of the most partial and fragmentary kind. In respect of the influence which they have respectively exercised upon mankind, it might appear almost profane to compare them. In this point of view the Scriptures stand so far apart from every other production, on account of their great offices in relation to the coming of the Redeemer and to the spiritual training of mankind, that there can be nothing either like or second to them."

Mr. Gladstone thinks that "the poems of Homer possess extrinsic worth as a faithful and vivid picture of early Grecian life and measures; they have also an intrinsic value which has given their author the first place in that marvelous trinity of genius—Homer, Dante, and Shakespeare."

As to the historic aims of Homer, Mr. Gladstone says: "Where other poets sketch, Homer draws; and where they draw he carves. He alone of all the now famous epic writers, moves (in the 'Iliad' especially) subject to the stricter laws of time and place; he alone, while producing an unsurpassed work of the imagination, is also the greatest chronicler that ever lived, and presents to us, from his own single hand, a representation of life, manners, history, of morals, theology, and politics, so vivid and comprehensive, that it may be hard to say whether any of the more refined ages of Greece or Rome, with their clouds of authors and their multiplied forms of historical record, are either more faithfully or more completely conveyed to us."

Mr. Gladstone fixes the probable date of Homer within a generation or two of the Trojan war, assigning as his principal reason for so doing the poet's visible identity with the age, the altering but not yet vanishing age of which he sings, and the broad interval in tone and feeling between himself and the very nearest of all that follow him. He presents several arguments to prove the trustworthiness of the text of Homer.

In 1877, Mr. Gladstone wrote an article on the "Dominions of the Odysseus," and also wrote a preface to Dr. Henry Schliemann's "Mycenae."

One of his most remarkable productions bore the title of, "The Vatican Decrees in their Bearing on Civil Allegiance; a Political Expostulation." This book was an amplification of an article from his own pen, which appeared October, 1874, in the *Contemporary Review*. It created great public excitement and many replies. One hundred and twenty thousand copies were sold. Mr. Higginson says: "The vigor of the style, the learning exhibited, and the source whence it came, all contributed to give it an extraordinary influence.... It was boldly proclaimed in this pamphlet that, since 1870, Rome has substituted for the proud boast of *semper eadem*, a policy of violence and change of faith;... 'that she had equally repudiated modern thought and ancient history;' ... 'that she has reburnished and paraded anew every rusty tool she was thought to have disused,' and 'that Rome requires a convert who now joins her to forfeit his moral and mental freedom, and to place his loyalty and civil duty at the mercy of another.'"

Mr. Gladstone issued another pamphlet, entitled "Vaticanism; and Answers to Reproofs and Replies," He reiterated his original charges, saying: "The Vatican decrees do, in the strictest sense, establish for the Pope a supreme command over loyalty and civil duty.... Even in those parts of Christendom where the decrees and the present attitude of the Papal See do not produce or aggravate open broils with the civil power, by undermining moral liberty, they impair moral responsibility, and silently, in the succession of generations, if not in the lifetime of individuals, tend to emasculate the vigor of the mind."

Mr. Gladstone published in seven volumes, in 1879, "Gleanings of Past Years." The essay entitled "Kin Beyond the Sea" at first created much excitement. "The Kin Beyond the Sea" was America, of which he says: "She will probably become what we are now, the head servant in the great household of the world, the employer of all employed; because her services will be the most and ablest." Again: "The England and the America of the present are probably the two strongest nations in the world. But there can hardly be a doubt, as between the America and the England of the future, that the daughter, at some no very distant time, will, whether fairer or less fair, be unquestionably yet stronger than the mother." Mr. Gladstone argues in support of this position from the concentrated continuous empire which America possesses, and the enormous progress she has made within a century.

In an address at the opening of the Art Loan Exhibition of Chester, August 11, 1879, Mr. Gladstone said: "With the English those two things are quite distinct; but in the oldest times of human industry—that is to say amongst the Greeks— there was no separation whatever, no gap at all, between the idea of beauty and the idea of utility. Whatever the ancient Greek produced he made as useful as he could; and at the same time, reward for work with him was to make it as beautiful as he could. In the industrial productions of America there is very little idea of beauty; for example, an American's axe is not intended to cut away a tree neatly, but quickly. We want a workman to understand that if he can learn to appreciate beauty in industrial productions, he is thereby doing good to himself, first of all in the improvement of his mind, and in the pleasure he derives from his work, and likewise that literally he is increasing his own capital, which is his labor."

In his articles on "Ecce Homo" he expresses the hope "that the present tendency to treat the old belief of man with a precipitate, shallow, and unexamining disparagement, is simply a distemper, that inflicts for a time the moral atmosphere, that is due, like plagues and fevers, to our own previous folly and neglect; and that when it has served its work of admonition and reform, will be allowed to pass away."

The "Impregnable Rock of Holy Scripture" is the title of a book by Mr. Gladstone, the articles of which were originally published in *The Sunday School Times*, Philadelphia.

CHAPTER XIII

GREAT BUDGETS

The year 1860 marked the beginning of the second half of Mr. Gladstone's life as a statesman, in which he stood prominently forward as a Reformer. July 18, 1859, as Chancellor in the Liberal government of Lord Palmerston, he brought forward his budget. The budget of 1860 was the greatest of all his financial measures, for a new departure was taken in British commerce and manufactures. Mr. Cobden, in behalf of the English Government, had negotiated with France a treaty based on free trade principles—"a treaty which gave an impetus to the trade of this country, whose far-reaching effects are felt even to our day."

The Chancellor explained the various propositions of his financial statements. Speaking of discontent with the income tax he observed: "I speak on general terms. Indeed, I now remember that I myself had, about a fortnight ago, a letter addressed to me complaining of the monstrous injustice and iniquity of the income tax, and proposing that, in consideration thereof, the Chancellor of the Exchequer should be publicly hanged."

Mr. Gladstone said that the total reduction of duties would be over £1,000,000, requiring a slight extension of taxation; that by this means nearly £1,000,000 would be returned to the general revenue; that the loss to the revenue by the French Treaty, which was based upon free trade principles, and the reduction of duties, would be half made up by the imposts specified; that the abolition of the paper duty would produce the happiest results from the spread of cheap literature. The reductions proposed would give a total relief to the consumer of nearly £4,000,000, and cause a net loss of the revenue of over £2,000,000, a sum about equivalent to the amount coming in from the cessation of government annuities that year. The total revenue was £70,564,000, and as the total expenses of government was £70,000,000, there remained an estimated surplus of £464,000.

Mr. Gladstone concluded; "There were times, now long by, when sovereigns made progress through the land, and when at the proclamation of their heralds, they caused to be scattered whole showers of coin among the people who thronged upon their steps.... Our Sovereign is enabled, through the wisdom of her great council, assembled in Parliament around her, again to scatter blessings among her subjects by means of wise and prudent laws; of laws which do not sap in any respect the foundations of duty or of manhood, but which strike away the shackles from the arm of industry."

"It was one of the peculiarities of Mr. Gladstone's budget addresses that they roused curiosity in the outset, and, being delivered in a musical, sonorous, and perfectly modulated voice, kept the listeners interested to the very close. This financial statement of 1860 was admirably arranged for the purpose of awakening and keeping attention, piquing and teasing curiosity, and sustaining desire to hear from the first sentence to the last. It was not a speech, it was an oration, in the form of a great State paper, made eloquent, in which there was a proper restraint over the crowding ideas, the most exact accuracy in the sentences, and even in the very words chosen; the most perfect balancing of parts, and, more than all, there were no errors or omissions; nothing was put wrongly and nothing was overlooked. With a House crowded in every corner, with the strain upon his own mental faculties, and the great physical tax implied in the management of his voice, and the necessity for remaining upon his feet during this long period, 'the observed of all observers,' Mr. Gladstone took all as quietly, we are told, as if he had just risen to address a few observations to Mr. Speaker. Indeed, it was laughingly said that he could address a House for a whole week, and on the Friday evening have taken a new departure, beginning with the observation, 'After these preliminary remarks, I will now proceed to deal with the subject matter of my financial plan.'"

The ministry was supported by large majorities, and carried their measures, but when the bill for the repeal of the duty on paper at home, as well as coming into the country, came before the House of Lords, it was rejected. Mr. Gladstone appeared to be confronted by the greatest constitutional crisis of his life. He gave vent to his indignation, and declared that the action of the Lords was a gigantic innovation, and that the House of Commons had the undoubted right of selecting the manner in which the people should be taxed. This speech was pronounced by Lord John Russell "magnificently mad," and Lord Granville said that "it was a toss-up whether Gladstone resigned or not, and that if he did it would break up the Liberal party." Quiet was finally restored, and the following year Mr. Gladstone adroitly brought the same feature before the Lords in a way that compelled acceptance.

The budget of 1861 showed a surplus of £2,000,000 over the estimated surplus, and proposed to remit the penny on the income tax, and to repeal the paper duty. Instead of being divided into several bills as in the previous year, the budget was presented as a whole—all included in one. By this device the Lords were forced to acquiesce in the repeal of the paper duty, or take the responsibility of rejecting the whole bill. The Peers grumbled, and some of them were enraged. Lord Robert Cecil, now Marquis of Salisbury, rudely declared that Mr. Gladstone's conduct was only worthy of an attorney. He begged to apologize to the attorneys. They were honorable men and would have scorned the course pursued by the ministers. Another member of the House of Lords protested that the budget gave a mortal stab to the Constitution. Mr. Gladstone retorted: "I want to know, to what Constitution does it give a mortal stab? In my opinion it gives no mortal stab, and no stab at all, to any Constitution that we are bound to care for. But, on the contrary, so far as it alters anything in the most recent course of practice, it alters in the direction of restoring that good old Constitution which took its root in Saxon times, which grew from the Plantagenets, which endured the iron repression of the Tudors, which resisted the aggressions of the Stuarts, and which has come to its full maturity under the House of Brunswick. I think that is the Constitution, if I may presume to say so, which it is our duty to guard, and which—if, indeed, the proceedings of this year can be said to affect it at all—will be all the better for the operation. But the Constitution which my right honorable friend worships is a very different affair."

In 1860, Mr. Gladstone was elected Lord Rector of Edinburgh University, and the degree of LL.D. was conferred upon him.

Mr. Gladstone, in 1861, introduced one of his most beneficial measures—a bill creating the Post Office Savings Bank. The success of the scheme has gone beyond all expectation. At the close of 1891, the amount deposited was £71,608,002, and growing at the average rate of over £4,000,000 annually.

Mr. Gladstone's financial measures for 1862, while not involving such momentous issues as those of the preceding year, nevertheless encountered considerable opposition. The budget was a stationary one, with no surplus, no new taxes, no remission of taxes, no heavier burdens.

In October, 1862, Mr. and Mrs. Gladstone made a journey down the Tyne, which is thus described: "It was not possible to show to royal visitors more demonstrations of honor than were showered on the illustrious Commoner and his wife.... At every point, at every bank and hill and factory, in every opening where people could stand or climb, expectant crowds awaited Mr. Gladstone's arrival. Women and children, in all costumes and of all conditions, lined the shores ... as Mr. and Mrs. Gladstone passed. Cannon boomed from every point;...

such a succession of cannonading never before greeted a triumphant conqueror on the march."

It was during this journey that Mr. Gladstone made the memorable speech, at New Castle, upon the American Civil War, which had broken out the same year. There had been much speculation as to whether the English government would recognize the Confederacy as a separate and independent power, and the utterance of a member of the Cabinet under the circumstances was regarded as entirely unwarranted. Mr. Gladstone himself frankly acknowledged his error in 1867: "I must confess that I was wrong; that I took too much upon myself in expressing such an opinion. Yet the motive was not bad. My sympathies were then—where they had long before been, where they are now—with the whole American people."

The session of 1863 was barren of important subjects of debate, and hence unusual interest was centered in the Chancellor's statement, which was another masterly financial presentation, and its leading propositions were cordially received. The whole reduction of taxation for the year was £3,340,000, or counting the total reductions, present and prospective, of £4,601,000. This still left a surplus of £400,000.

In four years £8,000,000 had been paid for war with China out of the ordinary revenues. A proposition to subject charities to the income tax, although endorsed by the whole cabinet, led to such powerful opposition throughout the country that it was finally withdrawn. The arguments of the Chancellor were endorsed by many who were opposed to the indiscriminate and mistaken beneficence which was so prevalent on death-beds.

A bill was introduced at this session by Sir Morton Peto, entitled the "Dissenters' Burial Bill," the object of which was to enable Nonconformists to have their own religious rites and services, and by their own ministers, in the graveyards of the Established Church. The bill was strongly opposed by Lord

Robert Cecil and Mr. Disraeli. Mr. Gladstone favored the measure. The bill was rejected, and Mr. Gladstone at a later period discovered that his progress in ecclesiastical and political opinions was creating a breach between himself and his constituents at Oxford.

Mr. Gladstone's financial scheme for 1864 was received with undiminished interest. It was characterized as "a policy of which peace, progress and retrenchment were the watch-words." An available surplus of £2,260,000 enabled him to propose reductions.

The subject of reform, which had been coming up in the House of Commons in one way or another and agitating the House and the country since 1859, when the Conservative party was beaten on the question, reappeared in 1864. The question of lowering the borough franchise came up, and Mr. Gladstone startled the House and the country by his declaration upon the subject of reform, which showed the rapid development of his views upon the subject. The Conservative party was filled with alarm, and the hopes of the Reform party correspondingly elated. "The eyes of all Radical Reformers turned to Mr. Gladstone as the future Minister of Reform in Church and State. He became from the same moment an object of distrust, and something approaching to detestation in the eyes of all steady-going Conservatives."

Mr. Gladstone said: "I say that every man who is not presentably incapacitated by some consideration of personal unfitness or political danger, is morally entitled to come within the pale of the constitution." This declaration was the first note sounded in a conflict which, twelve months later, was to cost Mr. Gladstone his seat for Oxford University, and finally to culminate in the disruption of the Liberal Government. The general feeling in regard to this speech was that if the Liberal party had failed in its duty on the subject of reform in the existing Parliament after Mr. Gladstone's utterances, that the condition of things must undergo a change, so great was the effect of his speech in the country. The bill, which was presented by a private member and lost, was made memorable by the speech of the Chancellor. The eyes of careful political leaders were again turned towards Mr. Gladstone, and strong predictions made of his coming exaltation to the Premiership. Mr. Speaker Denison said, in October, 1864: "I now anticipate that Mr. Gladstone will be Premier. Neither party has any leader. I hope Mr. Gladstone may get support from the Conservatives who now support Palmerston." And these expectations were known to Mr. Gladstone himself, for Bishop Wilberforce had a conversation with him and writes: "Long talk with Gladstone as to Premiership: he is for acting under John Russell." Again to Mr. Gladstone: "Anything which breaks up, or tends to break up, Palmerston's supremacy, must bring you nearer to the post in which I long to see you, and, if I live, shall see you." Lord Palmerston himself said: "Gladstone will soon have it all his own way; and whenever he gets my place we shall have strange things."

The hostile feeling towards the Palmerston government, which had been growing in intensity, chiefly on the ground of its foreign policy, reached its full height in a fierce battle between the Ministry and the Opposition. July 4, 1864, Mr. Disraeli brought forward his motion of "no confidence." Mr. Gladstone replied for the government, and sought to rebut the accusations made by the leader of the Opposition. He said that it was the very first time in which the House of Commons had been called upon to record the degradation of the country, simply for the sake of displacing a ministry.

An amusing episode which occurred during this debate is worthy of record here; Mr. Bernard Osborne "grew amusingly sarcastic at the expense of the government, though he paid at the same time a great compliment to Mr. Gladstone. He likened the Cabinet to a museum of curiosities, in which there were some birds of rare and noble plumage, both alive and stuffed. There had been a difficulty, unfortunately, in keeping up the breed, and it was found necessary to cross it with the famous Peelites. 'I will do them the justice to say that they have a very great and noble Minister among them in the

Chancellor of the Exchequer, and it is to his measures alone that they owe the little popularity and the little support they get from this Liberal party.' Describing Mr. Milner Gibson, the honorable gentleman said he was like some 'fly in amber,' and the wonder was 'how the devil he got there.' Mr. Cobden and Mr. Bright must have been disappointed in this 'young man from the country.' He had become insolent and almost quarrelsome under the guidance of the noble lord. Should that Parliament decide on terminating its own and their existence, they would find consolation that the funeral oration would be pronounced by Mr. Newdegate, and that some friendly hand would inscribe on their mausoleum, 'Rest and be thankful.'" Mr. Disraeli's motion was lost, and the ministry was sustained.

The budget of 1865 represented the country as in a prosperous financial condition. The total reduction was over £5,000,000. Such a financial showing gained the warm approval of the people, and excited but little opposition in the House. It was evident that a master-hand was guiding the national finances, and fortunately the Chancellor's calculations were verified by the continued prosperity of the country. At a later period, in commenting upon the policy of the two parties—Conservative and Liberal—Mr. Gladstone said: "From thence it follows that the policy of the Liberal party has been to reduce the public charges and to keep the expenditure within the estimates, and, as a result, to diminish the taxation of the country and the national debt; that the policy of the Tory government, since they took office in 1866, has been to increase the public charges, and to allow the departments to spend more than their estimates, and, as a result, to create deficits and to render the reduction of taxation impossible. Which policy will the country prefer?"

CHAPTER XIV

LIBERAL REFORMER AND PRIME MINISTER

July, 1865, Parliament having run its allotted course, according to the constitution, was dissolved, and a general election took place, which resulted in the Liberal party being returned again with a majority. Mr. Gladstone's relations with many of his constituents were not harmonious, owing to his pronounced Liberal views, and his seat for Oxford was seriously imperilled. Mr. Gathorne Hardy was nominated to run against him. The High Tory party resolved to defeat him, and he was defeated by a majority of 180. "The electors preferred the uncompromising defender of the Church and Toryism to the brilliant statesman and financier." Almost all of the distinguished residents of Oxford and three-fourths of the tutors and lecturers of the University voted for Mr. Gladstone, and his rejection was entirely owing to the opposing vote of non-residents and the bigotry of the hostile country clergymen of the Church of England. From the Bishop of Oxford Mr. Gladstone received the following indignant protest:

"I cannot forbear expressing to you my grief and indignation at the result. It is needless for me to say that everything I could with propriety do I did heartily to save our University this great loss and dishonor, as well from a loving honor of you. You were too great for them."

"The enemies of the University," observed the *Times*, "will make the most of her disgrace. It has hitherto been supposed that a learned constituency was to some extent exempt from the vulgar motives of party spirit, and capable of forming a higher estimate of statesmanship than common tradesmen or tenant-farmers."

His valedictory address to his former constituents was short: "After an arduous connection of eighteen years, I bid you, respectfully, farewell.... It is one imperative duty, and one alone, which induces me to trouble you with these few parting words, the duty of expressing my profound and lasting gratitude for indulgence as generous, and for support as warm and enthusiastic in itself, and as honorable from the character and distinctions of those who have given it, as has, in my belief, ever been accorded by any constituency to any representative."

One event in Parliament, in 1865, contributed much to Mr. Gladstone's defeat: In March, 1865, Mr. Dillwyn, the Radical member for Swansea, moved "that the present position of the Irish Church Establishment is unsatisfactory, and calls for the early attention of her Majesty's Government."

Sir Stafford Northcote wrote: "Gladstone made a terribly long stride in his downward progress last night, and denounced the Irish Church in a way which shows how, by and by, he will deal not only with it, but with the Church of England too.... He laid down the doctrines that the tithe was national property, and ought to be dealt with by the State in a manner most advantageous to the people; and that the Church of England was only national because the majority of the people still belong to her."

"It was now felt that henceforth Mr. Gladstone must belong to the country, and not to the University." He realized this himself, for driven from Oxford, he went down to South Lancashire, seeking to be returned from there to Parliament, and in the Free Trade Hall, Manchester, said: "At last, my friends, I am come among you, and I am come among you unmuzzled." These words were greeted with loud and prolonged applause. The advanced Liberals seemed to take the same view, and regarded Mr. Gladstone's defeat at Oxford by the Conservatives as his political enfranchisement. His defeat was not wholly unexpected to himself. In 1860 he said: "Without having to complain, I am entirely sick and weary of the terms upon which I hold the seat."

Mr. Gladstone felt keenly the separation, for he wrote to the Bishop of Oxford: "There have been two great deaths, or transmigrations of spirit, in my political existence—one, very slow, the breaking of ties with my original party, the other, very short and sharp, the breaking of the tie with Oxford. There will probably be a third, and no more." And in a speech at Liverpool, there was something of pathos in his reference to Oxford, when he said that if he had clung to the representation of the University with desperate fondness, it was because he would not desert a post to which he seemed to have been called. But he had now been dismissed from it, not by academical, but by political agencies.

Mr. Gladstone was elected to represent his native district in Parliament, and he was at the head of the poll in Manchester, Liverpool, and all the large towns. The result of the general elections was a considerable gain to the Liberal party, but that party sustained a severe loss by the death of Lord Palmerston, October 18, 1865.

A new cabinet was constructed, with Earl Russell as Premier, and Mr. Gladstone as the Chancellor of the Exchequer. Mr. Gladstone became for the first time the recognized leader in the House of Commons, which then meant virtually Prime Minister, for with the aged Premier in the House of Lords, and the youthful Chancellor in the Commons, it meant nothing else. But Earl Russell and his younger colleague were calculated to work in harmonious action, for they were both Reformers. The ardent temperament and the severe conscientiousness of the leader was the cause of much speculation and anxiety as to his management. His first appearance as leader of the House was therefore waited for with much curiosity. The new

Parliament was opened February 6, 1866, by the Queen in person, for the first time since the death of Prince Albert. In the speech from the throne it was announced that Parliament would be directed to consider such improvements in the laws which regulate the right of voting in the election of the members of the House of Commons as may tend to strengthen our free institutions, and conduce to the public welfare. Bishop Wilberforce wrote: "Gladstone has risen entirely to his position, and done all his most sanguine friends hoped for as leader.... There is a general feeling of insecurity of the ministry, and the Reform Bill to be launched to-night is thought a bad rock."

May 3, 1866, Mr. Gladstone brought forward what was destined to be his last budget for some years. There was a surplus of over a million and a quarter of pounds, which allowed a further and considerable reduction of taxation.

The condition of Ireland was very grave at this time, and as apprehensions were felt in regard to the Fenians, a bill suspending the Habeas Corpus Act in Ireland was passed. Mr. Gladstone, in explaining the necessity for the measure, said that the government were ready at any time to consider any measure for the benefit of Ireland, but it was the single duty of the House at the moment to strengthen the hands of the Executive in the preservation of law and order. The bill was renewed by the Derby government, and passed as before, as the result of an anticipated great Fenian uprising under "Head-Centre" Stephens.

During a debate on the bill for the abolition of Church rates, Mr. Gladstone said that the law requiring Church rates was *prima facie* open to great objection, but he could not vote for total abolition. He offered a compromise and proposed that Dissenters be exempted from paying Church rates, and at the same time be disqualified from interfering with funds to which they had not contributed. The compromise was accepted, but failed to become a law.

On the subject of reform, mentioned in the address, there were great debates, during the session of 1866. The new Cabinet, known as the Russell-Gladstone Ministry, set themselves to work in earnest upon a question that had baffled all the skill of various administrations. As a part of the reform scheme, Mr. Gladstone brought forward a Franchise Bill in the House of Commons, March 12th.

The bill satisfied most of the Liberal party. Mr. Robert Lowe, a Liberal, became one of its most powerful assailants. His enmity to the working classes made him extremely unpopular. Mr. Horseman also joined the Conservatives in opposing the bill. Mr. Bright, in a crushing retort, fastened upon the small party of Liberals, led by these two members in opposition to the bill, the epithet of "Adullamites." Mr. Horseman, Mr. Bright said, had "retired into what may be called his political Cave of Adullam, to which he invited every one who was in distress, and every one who was discontented. He had long been anxious to found a party in this house, and there is scarcely a member at this end of the House who is able to address us with effect or to take much part, whom he has not tried to bring over to his party and his cabal. At last he has succeeded in hooking ... Mr. Lowe. I know it was the opinion many years ago of a member of the Cabinet that two men could make a party. When a party is formed of two men so amiable and so disinterested as the two gentlemen, we may hope to see for the first time in Parliament a party perfectly harmonious and distinguished by mutual and unbroken trust. But there is one difficulty which it is impossible to remove. This party of two is like the Scotch terrier that is so covered with hair that you could not tell which was the head and which was the tail." This sally, which excited immoderate laughter, remains one of the happiest examples of Parliamentary retort and badinage.

During this session the Conservative party met at the residence of the Marquis of Salisbury, and decided upon strongly opposing the measure proposed by the Liberal government. Mr. Bright characterized it as "a dirty conspiracy." On the other hand, the country supported the bill, and great meetings were held in its interest. Mr. Gladstone spoke at a great meeting at Liverpool. He said: "Having produced this measure, founded in a spirit of moderation, we hope to support it with decision.... We have passed the Rubicon, we have broken the bridge and burned the boats behind us. We have advisedly cut off the means of retreat, and having done this, we hope that, as far as time is yet permitted, we have done our duty to the Crown and to the nation." This was regarded as the bugle-call to the Liberal party for the coming battle.

The debate began April 12th, and continued for eight nights. "On no occasion since, and seldom before, has such a flow of eloquence been heard within the walls of the House of Commons." Mr. Disraeli spoke for three hours against the bill, and in his speech accused Mr. Gladstone of introducing American ideas of Government, and of having once assailed the very principles he now advocated, when in the Oxford Union he spoke against the Reform Bill of 1832. Mr. Gladstone's reply was one of the most noteworthy parts of this famous debate. He rose at one o'clock in the morning to conclude a legislative battle which had begun two weeks before. "At last," Mr. Gladstone said, "we have obtained a declaration from an authoritative source that a bill which, in a country with five millions of adult males, proposes to add to a limited constituency 200,000 of the middle class and 200,000 of the working class, is, in the judgment of the leader of the Tory party, a bill to reconstruct the constitution upon American principles.

"The right honorable gentleman, secure in the recollection of his own consistency, has taunted me with the errors of my boyhood. When he addressed the honorable member of Westminster, he showed his magnanimity by declaring that he would not take the philosopher to task for what he wrote twenty-five years ago; but when he caught one who, thirty-six years ago, just emerged from boyhood, and still an undergraduate at Oxford, had expressed an opinion adverse to the Reform Bill of 1832, of which he had so long and bitterly repented, then the right honorable gentleman could not resist

Richard B. Cook

the temptation."

The bill was put upon its passage. The greatest excitement prevailed. "The house seemed charged with electricity, like a vast thunder-cloud; and now a spark was about to be applied. Strangers rose in their seats, the crowd at the bar pushed half-way up the House, the Royal Princes leaned forward in their standing places, and all was confusion." Presently order was restored, and breathless excitement prevailed while the tellers announced that the bill had been carried by a majority of only five.

"Hardly had the words left the teller's lips than there arose a wild, raging, mad-brained shout from floor and gallery, such as has never been heard in the present House of Commons. Dozens of half-frantic Tories stood up in their seats, madly waved their hats and hurrahed at the top of their voices. Strangers in both galleries clapped their hands. The Adullamites on the Ministerial benches, carried away by the delirium of the moment, waved their hats in sympathy with the Opposition, and cheered as loudly as any. Mr. Lowe, the leader, instigator, and prime mover of the conspiracy, stood up in the excitement of the moment—flushed, triumphant, and avenged.... He took off his hat, waved it in wide and triumphant circles over the heads of the very men who had just gone into the lobby against him.... But see, the Chancellor of the Exchequer lifts up his hand to bespeak silence, as if he had something to say in regard to the result of the division. But the more the great orator lifts his hand beseechingly, the more the cheers are renewed and the hats waved. At length the noise comes to an end by the process of exhaustion, and the Chancellor of the Exchequer rises. Then there is a universal hush, and you might hear a pin drop."

"Few, if any, could anticipate at this time, that in the course of one short year a Conservative Government would find itself compelled to take up that very question of Reform, whose virtual defeat its opponents now hailed with such intoxicating expressions of delight." However, the bill was unexpectedly wrecked June 18th, by an amendment substituting a ratal instead of a rental basis for the borough franchise. The ministry regarding this as a vital point, could not agree to it, and consequently threw up their measure and resigned office. The Queen was unwilling to accept their resignation. But the ministry felt that they had lost the confidence of the House, so their resignation was announced June 26th.

The apathy of the people about reform that Earl Russell thought he perceived, as far as London was concerned, at once disappeared. A great demonstration was made at Trafalgar Square, where some ten thousand people assembled and passed resolutions in favor of reform. A serious riot occurred at Hyde Park in consequence of the prohibition by the Government of the meeting of the Reform League. The Reformers then marched to Carleton House Terrace, the residence of Mr. Gladstone, singing songs in his honor. He was away from home, but Mrs. Gladstone and her family came out on the balcony to acknowledge the tribute paid by the people. It is said that Mr. Gladstone, now for the first time, became a popular hero. Great meetings were held in the interest of reform in the large towns of the North and the Midlands, where his name was received with tumultuous applause. Mr. Gladstone was hailed everywhere as the leader of the Liberal party. Reform demonstrations continued during the whole of the recess. A meeting was held at Brookfields, near Birmingham, which was attended by nearly 250,000 people. The language of some of the ardent friends of reform was not always discreet, but Mr. Gladstone appears to have preserved a calm and dignified attitude.

In the summer of 1866, Lord Derby had announced his acceptance of office as Premier, and the formation of a Conservative Cabinet. The demonstrations of the people compelled the Conservatives to introduce measures in Liberal Reform. Accordingly, in 1867, Mr. Disraeli and his colleagues passed a Reform Bill, which, after various modifications, was far more extreme than that presented by the Liberals and defeated. Owing to a division in the ranks of the Liberal members on the pending bill, Mr. Gladstone withdrew from the active leadership of the House, but soon resumed it. Mr. Bright said, at Birmingham, that since 1832, there had been no man of Mr. Gladstone's rank as a statesman who had imported into the Reform question so much of conviction, of earnestness, and of zeal.

Not long after this deputations from various parts of the country, accompanied by their representatives in Parliament, called on Mr. Gladstone to present addresses expressive of confidence in him as Liberal leader.

Lord Cranborne expressed his astonishment at hearing the bill described as a Conservative triumph. It was right that its real parentage should be established. The bill had been modified by Mr. Gladstone. All his points were conceded. If the adoption on the principles of Mr. Bright could be described as a triumph, then indeed the Conservative party, in the whole history of its previous annals, had won no triumphs so simple as this. In the House of Lords the Duke of Buccleuch declared that the only word in the bill that remained unaltered was the first word, "whereas."

"The work of reform was completed in the session of 1868, by the passing of the Scotch and Irish Reform Bills, a Boundary Bill for England and Wales, an Election Petitions and Corrupt Practices Prevention Bill, and the Registration of Voters Bill. The object of the last-named measure was to accelerate the elections, and to enable Parliament to meet before the end of 1868."

In the autumn of 1866, Mr. Gladstone and his family again visited Italy, and at Rome had an audience with Pope Pio Nono. It became necessary two years later, owing to this interview, for Mr. Gladstone formally to explain his visit.

In February, 1868, Lord Derby, owing to failing health, resigned. The Derby Ministry retired from office, and Mr. Disraeli became Prime Minister. An English author writes:

"There was, of course, but one possible Conservative Premier —Mr. Disraeli—he who had served the Conservative party for more than thirty years, who had led it to victory, and who had long been the ruling spirit of the Cabinet."

The elevation of Mr. Disraeli to the Premiership before Mr. Gladstone, produced, in some quarters, profound regret and even indignation. But Mr. Disraeli, though in office, was not in power. He was nominally the leader of a House that contained a large majority of his political opponents, now united among themselves. The schism in the Liberal party had been healed by the question of Reform, and they could now defeat the government whenever they chose to do so; consequently Mr. Gladstone took the initiative. His compulsory Church Rates Abolition Bill was introduced and accepted. By this measure all legal proceedings for the recovery of church rates were abolished. The question that overshadowed all others, however, was that of the Irish Church.

On the 16th of March Mr. Gladstone struck the first blow in the struggle that was to end in the disestablishment of the Irish Church. Mr. Maguire moved that the House consider the condition of Ireland. Mr. Gladstone said that Ireland had a controversy with England and a long account against England. It was a debt of justice, and he enumerated six particulars, one of which was the Established Episcopal Church. Religious Equality, he contended, must be conceded. He said, in referring to his speech made on the motion of Mr. Dillwyn in 1865: "The opinion I held then and hold now—namely, that in order to the settlement of this question of the Irish Church, that Church, as a State Church must cease to exist."

This speech excited feelings of consternation amongst the Ministerialists. Mr. Disraeli bewailed his own unhappy fate at the commencement of his career as Prime Minister, at finding himself face to face with the necessity of settling an account of seven centuries old. He complained that all the elements of the Irish crisis had existed while Mr. Gladstone was in office, but no attempt had been made to deal with them.

March 23d Mr. Gladstone proposed resolutions affirming that the Irish Episcopal Church should cease to exist as an establishment, and asking the Queen to place at the disposal of Parliament her interest in the temporalities of the Irish Church.

Mr. Gladstone's resolution was carried by a majority of 65, and the Queen replied that she would not suffer her interests to stand in the way of any measures contemplated by Parliament. Consequently Mr. Gladstone brought in his Irish Church Suspensory Bill, which was adopted by the Commons, but rejected by the Lords. During the discussion, ministerial explanations followed; Mr. Disraeli described, in his most pompous vein, his audiences with the Queen. His statement amounted to this—that, in spite of adverse votes, the Ministers intended to hold on till the autumn, and then to appeal to the new electorate created by the Reform Act.

Lord Houghton wrote: "Gladstone is the great triumph, but as he owns that he has to drive a four-in-hand, consisting of English Liberals, English Dissenters, Scotch Presbyterians, and Irish Catholics, he requires all his courage to look the difficulties in the face and trust to surmount them."

An appeal was now made to the country. The general election that followed, in November, was fought out mainly upon this question. A great Liberal majority was returned to Parliament, which was placed at 115. But there were several individual defeats, among them Mr. Gladstone himself, who was rejected by South Lancaster. This was in part owing to the readjustment of seats according to the Reform Bill. But Mr. Gladstone received an invitation from Greenwich, in the southwestern division, where he was warmly received by the electors. "He spoke everywhere, with all his fiery eloquence, on the monstrous foolishness of a religious establishment which ministered only to a handful of the people." Is the Irish Church to be or not to be? was the question. He was returned for that borough by a large majority over his Conservative opponents.

Archbishop Wilberforce wrote in November: "The returns to the House of Commons leave no doubt of the answer of the country to Gladstone's appeal. In a few weeks he will be in office at the head of a majority of something like a hundred, elected on the distinct issue of Gladstone and the Irish Church."

The feeling was so enormously great in its preponderance for Mr. Gladstone's policy of Liberal Reform, especially for the disestablishment of the Irish Church, that Mr. Disraeli did not adopt the usual course of waiting for the endorsement of the new Parliament, which he felt sure would be given to Mr. Gladstone, but resigned, and the first Disraeli Cabinet went out of office, December 2d.

December 4, 1868, the Queen summoned Mr. Gladstone to Windsor to form a Cabinet. He had now attained the summit of political ambition. He was the first Commoner in the land—the uncrowned king of the British Empire—for such is the English Premier. "All the industry and self-denial of a laborious life, all the anxieties and burdens and battles of five and thirty years of Parliamentary struggle were crowned by this supreme and adequate reward. He was Prime Minister of England—had attained to that goal of the Eton boy's ambition; and, what perhaps was to him of greater consideration, he was looked up to by vast numbers of the people as their great leader."

December 9th the new government was completed and the ministers received their seals from the Queen. Mr. Bright, contrary to all expectation, became President of the Board of Trade. In offering themselves for re-election, the members of the new Cabinet found no trouble—all were returned. Mr. Gladstone was returned by Greenwich.

With the year 1869 Mr. Gladstone entered upon a great period of Reform. The new Parliament was opened December 10th. On the 11th Mr. and Mrs. Gladstone paid a visit to Lord and Lady Salisbury, at Hatfield. Bishop Wilberforce was there and had opportunity to observe his old and honored friend in the first flush of his new dignity. Here are his comments: "Gladstone, as ever, great, earnest, and honest; as unlike the tricky Disraeli as possible." To Dr. Trench the Bishop wrote: "The nation has decided against our establishment, and we bow to its decision, and on what tenure and conditions it is to be held, remains confessedly open." "But his sagacious and statesmanlike counsel was disregarded. The Irish Bishops ranged themselves in bitter but futile hostility to the change. A frantic outbreak of Protestant violence began in Ireland and spread to England." Bishop Wilberforce notes this conversation at Windsor Castle: "The Queen very affable. 'So sorry Mr. Gladstone started this about the Irish Church, and he is a great friend of yours.'"

On the 15th of February Parliament assembled. March 1st Mr. Gladstone introduced his momentous bill in a speech of three hours, his first speech as Prime Minister, which was characterized as "calm, moderate and kindly." It was proposed that on January 1, 1871, the Irish Church should cease to exist as an establishment and should become a free Church.

Mr. Disraeli, in the Commons, moved the rejection of the bill. In opposing the measure he objected to disestablishment, because he was in favor of the union of Church and State.

Mr. Gladstone eloquently concluded as follows: "As the clock points rapidly towards the dawn, so as rapidly flow out the years, the months, the days, that remain to the existence of the Irish Established Church.... Not now are we opening this great question. Opened, perhaps, it was when the Parliament which expired last year pronounced upon it that emphatic judgment which can never be recalled. Opened it was, further, when in the months of autumn the discussions were held in every quarter of the Irish Church. Prosecuted another stage it was, when the completed elections discovered to us a manifestation of the national verdict more emphatic than, with the rarest exceptions, has been witnessed during the whole of our Parliamentary history. The good cause was further advanced towards its triumphant issue when the silent acknowledgment of the late government, that they declined to contest the question, was given by their retirement from office, and their choosing a less responsible position from which to carry on a more desultory warfare against the policy which they had in the previous session unsuccessfully attempted to resist. Another blow will soon be struck in the same good cause, and I will not intercept it one single moment more."

The bill passed by an overwhelming vote—368 against 250—and went up to the Lords, where stirring debates occurred. But there, as well as in the House, the Irish Establishment was doomed. The bill, substantially unaltered, received the Royal assent July 26, 1869.

The Annual Register for 1869 declared that the bill "was carried through in the face of a united and powerful opposition, mainly by the resolute will and unflinching energy of the Prime Minister.... Upon the whole, whatever may be thought of its merits or demerits, it can hardly be disputed that the Act of the Disestablishment of the Irish Church, introduced and carried into a law within somewhat less than five months, was the most remarkable legislative achievement of modern times."

The parliamentary session of 1870 was rendered memorable by the passing of a scarcely less popular and important measure—the Irish Land Bill. Mr. Gladstone, in speaking of Ireland, had referred to three branches of an Upas tree, to the growth of which her present sad condition was largely owing—the Irish Church, the Irish Land Laws, and the Irish Universities. The first branch had fallen with the disestablishment of the Irish Church, and Mr. Gladstone, pressing on in his reform, now proposed to lop off the second branch by his Irish Land Bill, which was in itself a revolution. It was claimed for Mr. Gladstone's new bill, or Land Scheme, that while it insured for the tenant security of holding, it did not confiscate a single valuable right of the Irish land-owner. Mr. Gladstone remarked that he believed there was a great fund of national wealth in the soil of Ireland as yet undeveloped, and said he trusted that both tenant and landlord would accept the bill because it was just. The bill passed, and received the approval of the Queen, August 1, 1870.

CHAPTER XV

THE GOLDEN AGE OF LIBERALISM

In what has been denominated the "Golden Age of Liberalism" the Liberal party was united, enthusiastic, victorious, full of energy, confidence and hope. "I have not any misgivings about Gladstone personally," says an English writer, "but as leader of the party to which the folly of the Conservatives and the selfish treachery of Disraeli, bit by bit, allied him, he cannot do what he would, and, with all his vast powers, there is a want of sharp-sighted clearness as to others. But God rules. I do not see how we are, after Disraeli's Reform Bill, long to avoid fundamental changes, both in Church and State."

Justin McCarthy has well summed up the aims of Mr. Gladstone and his party on their accession to power: "Nothing in modern English history is like the rush of the extraordinary years of reforming energy on which the new administration had now entered. Mr. Gladstone's government had to grapple with five or six great questions, any one of which might have seemed enough to engage the whole attention of an ordinary administration. The new Prime Minister had pledged himself to abolish the State Church in Ireland, and to reform the Irish Land Tenure system. He had made up his mind to put an end to the purchase of commissions in the army. Recent events and experiences had convinced him that it was necessary to introduce the system of voting by ballot. He accepted for his government the responsibility of originating a complete system of national education."

Richard B. Cook

The first great measure of the new administration had been successfully pushed through, and, flushed with triumph, the Liberal leaders were now ready to introduce other important legislation. In 1870, the Elementary Education Act, providing for the establishment of school boards, and securing the benefits of education for the poor in England and Wales was introduced. By it a national and compulsory system of education was established for the first time. "It is important to note that the concessions made during its course to the convictions of Tories and Churchmen, in the matter of religious education, stirred the bitter and abiding wrath of the political Dissenters." The measure was passed, while the half-penny postage for newspapers, and the half-penny post cards were among the benefits secured.

In April, 1870, a party of English travelers in Greece were seized by brigands. The ladies were released and also Lord Muncaster, who was sent to Athens to arrange for ransom and a free pardon. But the Greek Government sending soldiers to release the captives and capture the captors, the English were murdered. The English Minister at Athens was in treaty for the release of his countrymen, but the great difficulty was to procure pardon from the Greek government. This terrible affair created a profound sensation in England, and it was brought before Parliament. Mr. Gladstone pleaded for further information before taking decided steps. But for the arrest and execution of most of the brigands, and the extirpation of the band, the diabolical deed went unavenged.

In July, war broke out suddenly between France and Germany, which resulted in the dethronement of Napoleon III. England preserved neutrality. However, Mr. Gladstone had his opinion regarding the war and thus represented it: "It is not for me to distribute praise and blame; but I think the war as a whole, and the state of things out of which it has grown, deserve a severer condemnation than any which the nineteenth century has exhibited since the peace of 1815." And later, in an anonymous article, the only one he ever wrote, and which contained the famous phrase, "the streak of silver sea," he "distributed blame with great impartiality between both belligerent powers."

Among the business transacted in the session of 1870 was the following: All appointments to situations in all Civil Departments of the State, except the Foreign Office and posts requiring professional knowledge, should be filled by open competition; and the royal prerogative that claimed the General Commanding-in-Chief as the agent of the Crown be abolished, and that distinguished personage was formally declared to be subordinate to the Minister of War. Mr. Gladstone announced the intention of the government to release the Fenian prisoners then undergoing sentences for treason or treason-felony, on condition of their not remaining in or returning to the United Kingdom. The Premier, alluding to the enormity of their offenses, said that the same principles of justice which dictated their sentences would amply sanction the prolongation of their imprisonment if the public security demanded it. The press and country generally approved this decision of the Premier, but some condemned him for the condition he imposed in the amnesty. The religious test imposed upon all students entering at the universities was abolished, and all students of all creeds could now enter the universities on an equal footing. Heretofore special privileges were accorded to members of the Established Episcopal Church, and all others were cut off from the full enjoyment of the universities.

A bill to establish secret voting was rejected by the Lords, but was passed the next session. The House of Lords, emboldened by their success in throwing out the voting bill, defeated a bill to abolish the purchase of commissions in the army, but Mr. Gladstone was not to be turned from his purpose, and startled the peers by a new departure—he dispensed with their consent, and accomplished his purpose without the decision of Parliament. Finding that purchase in the army existed only by royal sanction, he, with prompt decision, advised the Queen to issue a royal warrant declaring that on and after November 1, 1871, all regulations attending the purchase of commissions should be cancelled. The purchase of official positions in the army was thus abolished. It was regarded as a high-handed act on the part of the Prime Minister, and a stretch of executive authority, and was denounced by Lords and Commons, friends and foes. Tories and Peers especially were enraged, and regarded themselves as baffled.

The condition of affairs in Ireland was alarming. The spread of an agrarian conspiracy at Westmeath compelled the government to move for a committee to inquire into the unlawful combination and confederacy existing. "Mr. Disraeli was severely sarcastic at the expense of the government."

The grant proposed by the government to the Princess Louise on her marriage aroused the opposition of some members of the House, who claimed to represent the sentiments of a considerable number of people. It was proposed to grant £30,000 and an annuity of £6,000. The Premier stated that the Queen in marrying her daughter to one of her own subjects, had followed her womanly and motherly instincts. He dwelt upon the political importance of supporting the dignity of the crown in a suitable manner; upon the value of a stable dynasty; and the unwisdom of making minute pecuniary calculations upon such occasions. It was carried by a remarkable majority of 350 votes against 1.

In 1871 the treaty of Washington was concluded. But the Geneva awards for the damage done to American shipping by the "Alabama," did much to undermine Mr. Gladstone's popularity with the warlike portion of the British public and there were various indications that the Ministry were becoming unpopular. There were other causes tributary to this effect. His plans of retrenchment had deprived Greenwich of much of its trade, hence his seat was threatened. Mr. Gladstone resolved to face the difficulty boldly, and to meet the murmurers on their own ground, October 28, 1871, he addressed his Greenwich constituents. The air was heavy with murmurs and threats. Twenty thousand people were gathered at Blackheath. It was a cold afternoon when he appeared bare-headed, and defended the whole policy of the administration. "His speech was as long, as methodical, as argumentative, and in parts as eloquent, as if he had been speaking at his ease under the friendly and commodious shelter of the House of Commons." The growing unpopularity of the Government was evidenced in the first reception given to the Premier by his constituents. Groans and cheers were mingled, and his voice at first was drowned by the din. Finally he was heard, and won the day, the people enthusiastically applauding and waving a forest of hats. One cause of unpopularity was what is called "the Ewelme Scandal," and another the elevation of Sir Robert Collin to the Judicial Committee of the Privy Council.

Mr. Gladstone said: "I have a shrewd suspicion in my mind that a very large proportion of the people of England have a sneaking kindness for the hereditary principle. My observation has not been of a very brief period, and what I have observed is this, that wherever there is anything to be, done, or to be given, and there are two candidates for it who are exactly alike—alike in opinions, alike in character, alike in possessions, the one being a commoner and the other a lord—the Englishman is very apt indeed to prefer the lord." He detailed the great advantage which had accrued from the legislation of the past generation, including free-trade, the removal of twenty millions of taxation, a cheap press, and an education bill, Mr. Gladstone thus restored himself to the confidence of his constituents, but the ministry did not wholly regain the popularity they once enjoyed. The Gladstone period had passed its zenith and its decadence had already begun.

During the autumn Mr. Gladstone received the freedom of the city of Aberdeen, and made a speech, in which occurred a remarkable reference to "the newly-invented cry of Home Rule." He spoke of the political illusions to which Ireland was periodically subject, the extremes to which England had gone in satisfying her demands, and the removal of all her grievances, except that which related to higher education. He said that any inequalities resting between England and Ireland were in favor of Ireland, and as to Home Rule, if Ireland was entitled to it, Scotland was better entitled, and even more so Wales.

Ireland had proved the glory of Mr. Gladstone's administration. Its name had been associated with the most brilliant legislative triumphs of government. But Ireland was also destined to be the government's most serious stumbling-block, and fated to be the immediate measure of its overthrow. In the session of 1873 Mr. Gladstone endeavored to further his plans for Reform, and consequently vigorously attacked the third branch of the "upas tree," to which he had referred. He labored to put the universities on a proper basis, that they might be truly educational centres for the whole of Ireland, and not for a small section of its inhabitants alone. This step followed legitimately after the disestablishment of the Irish Church. He introduced to this end a large and comprehensive measure, but although it was favorably received at the outset, a hostile feeling soon began and manifested itself. Mr. Gladstone pleaded powerfully for the measure, and said: "To mete out justice to Ireland, according to the best view that with human infirmity we could form, has been the work—I will almost say the sacred work—of this Parliament. Having put our hands to the plough, let us not turn back. Let not what we think the fault or perverseness of those whom we are attempting to assist have the slightest effect in turning us, even by a hair's-breadth, from the path on which we have entered. As we begun so let us persevere, even to the end, and with firm and resolute hand let us efface from the law and practice of the country the last—for I believe it is the last—of the religious and social grievances of Ireland." Mr. Disraeli made fun of the bill, stalwart Liberals condemned it, and the Irish members voted against it, hence the bill was defeated by a small majority of three votes. Mr. Gladstone consequently resigned, but Mr. Disraeli positively declined to take office with a majority of the House of Commons against him, and refused to appeal to the country. Mr. Gladstone read an extract from a letter he had addressed to the Queen, in which he contended that Mr. Disraeli's refusal to accept office was contrary to all precedent. But under the extraordinary circumstances he and his colleagues consented to resume office, and they would endeavor to proceed, both with regard to legislation and administration upon the same principle as those which had heretofore regulated their conduct. Mr. Lowe, the Chancellor of the Exchequer, having resigned, Mr. Gladstone assumed the duties of the office himself, thus serving in the double offices of Premier and Chancellor. During the recess various speeches were made in defence of the Ministerial policy, but the government failed to recover its once overwhelming popularity.

On the 19th of July, 1873, Mr. Gladstone lost by sudden death one of his oldest and most highly esteemed friends—Samuel Wilberforce, Bishop of Winchester. He was riding to Holmbury with Earl Granville, when he was thrown from his horse and killed instantly.

The end of Mr. Gladstone's first ministry was now drawing near. The people no longer desired to keep up with the reforming zeal of the administration. Mr. Disraeli's strongly exaggerated description of the Premier's policy had the effect of forming the popular discontent; Liberal members were deserting him. The Bible was in danger of being left out of the schools, and beer was threatened with taxation. The flag of "Beer and the Bible"—strange combination—having been hoisted by clergy and publicans, the cry against the ministry became irresistible. Deserted by the people and by many of his own party, what was to be done unless to appeal to the country and decide by a general election what was wanted and who would be sustained.

January, 1874, Mr. Gladstone issued a manifesto dissolving Parliament. In this document, entitled to be called a State paper for its political and historical importance, Mr. Gladstone stated his reasons for what was regarded by many as a *coup d' tat*. It is impossible to describe the public excitement and confusion which attended the general election thus unexpectedly decreed. Mr. Gladstone, recovering from a cold, appealed with great energy to Greenwich for re-election. The general election resulted in the defeat of the Liberals, and gave to the

Conservatives a majority of forty-six in the House. Mr. Gladstone was elected, but Greenwich which returned two members, placed the Premier second on the poll—below a local distiller. Following the example of his predecessor, in 1868, Mr. Gladstone resigned. "Thus was overthrown one of the greatest administrations of the century; indeed, it may be doubted whether any other English Ministry was ever able to show such a splendid record of great legislative acts within so short a period. There was not one measure, but a dozen, which would have shed lustre upon any government; and the six years of Mr. Gladstone's first Premiership are well entitled to the epithet which has been accorded to them of 'the Golden Age of Liberalism.'"

Before the next Parliament met Mr. Gladstone was to give the country another surprise. He was now sixty-four years old, had been forty years in active parliamentary labors, and thought himself justified in seeking rest from the arduous duties of public life, at least the pressing cares as leader of one of the great political parties. When his contemplated retirement had before become known to his friends, they induced him for a while longer to act as leader, but in February, 1875, he finally retired from the leadership and indeed appeared but rarely in the House of Commons during that session.

"The retirement of Mr. Gladstone from active leadership naturally filled his party with dismay. According to the general law of human life, they only realized their blessings when they had lost them. They had grumbled at their chief and mutinied against him and helped to depose him. But, now that this commanding genius was suddenly withdrawn from their councils they found that they had nothing to put in its place. Their indignation waxed fast and furious, and was not the less keen because they had to some extent, brought their trouble on themselves. They complained with almost a ludicrous pathos that Mr. Gladstone had led them into a wilderness of opposition and left them there to perish. They were as sheep without a shepherd and the ravening wolves of Toryism seemed to have it all their own way."

Between the time of Mr. Gladstone's retirement from the Premiership and his resignation of leadership in the House, he had quickly reappeared in the House of Commons and vigorously opposed the Public Worship Regulation Bill. Mr. Gladstone attacked the bill with a power and vehemence which astonished the House. The great objection to it was its interference with liberty, and with the variety of customs which had grown up in different parts of the country. To enforce strict uniformity would be oppressive and inconvenient. The bill became law, however, though it has largely proved inoperative, Mr. Gladstone also opposed the Endowed Schools Act Amendment Bill, which practically gave to the Church of England the control of schools that were thrown open to the whole nation by the policy of the last Parliament. So great a storm was raised over this reactionary bill that Mr. Disraeli was obliged to modify its provisions considerably before it could become a law. Mr. Gladstone was also active at this time in delivering addresses at Liverpool College, the Buckley Institute and the well-known Nonconformist College at Mill Hill.

CHAPTER XVI

THE EASTERN QUESTION

During his retirement from the leadership of the Liberal Party, Mr. Gladstone employed his great abilities in theological controversy and literary productions. It was during this period that he collected his miscellaneous writings, entitled "Gleanings from Past Years." A little more than a year had elapsed when he again entered the political arena. "He threw aside polemics and criticisms, he forgot for awhile Homer and the Pope," and "rushed from his library at Hawarden, forgetting alike ancient Greece and modern Rome," as he flung himself with impassioned energy and youthful vigor into a new crusade against Turkey. A quarter of a century before he had aroused all Europe with the story of the Neapolitan barbarities, and now again his keen sense of justice and strong, humanitarian sympathies impel him with righteous indignation to the eloquent defence of another oppressed people, and the denunciation of their wrongs. It was the Eastern Question that at once brought back the Liberal leader into the domain of politics. "The spirit of the war-horse could not be quenched, and the country thrilled with his fiery condemnation of the Bulgarian massacres." His activity was phenomenal. "He made the most impassioned speeches, often in the open air; he published pamphlets which rushed into incredible circulations; he poured letter after letter into the newspapers; he darkened the sky with controversial postcards, and, as soon as Parliament met in February, 1877, he was ready with all his unequalled resources of eloquence, argumentation and inconvenient enquiry, to drive home his great indictment against the Turkish government and its champion, Mr. Disraeli, who had now become Lord Beaconsfield."

"The reason of all this passion is not difficult to discover. Mr. Gladstone is a Christian; and in the Túrk he saw the great anti-Christian power where it ought not, in the fairest provinces of Christendom, and stained with the record of odious cruelty practised through long centuries on its defenceless subjects who were worshippers of Jesus Christ."

Turkish oppression, which had for a long time existed in its worst forms, resulted in an insurrection against Turkey and Herzegovina, July 1, 1875. This, however, was only the beginning, for others suffering under Ottoman oppression rebelled, and all Europe was involved.

In January, 1876, the Herzegovinians gained a victory over the Turkish troops. The European powers then suggested a settlement favorable to the insurgents, which was accepted by the Sultan. But early in May another insurrection broke out in several Bulgarian villages, which was quickly followed by the most horrible atrocities. A conference on the Eastern question was held at Berlin in May, and soon afterward the English ministers announced in Parliament that they were unable to assent to the terms agreed upon at the Berlin Conference. This announcement caused much surprise and comment in England. Public feeling already aroused, was not allayed when it became known that the British fleet in the Mediterranean had been ordered to Besiki Bay, seemingly for the protection of the Turkish Empire.

June 28th the Bulgarian insurrection was suppressed. On the 10th of July the Sultan, Abdul Aziz, was deposed and was succeeded by Murad V, who declared that he desired to guarantee liberty to all. Mr. Disraeli stated, in the House of Commons, that the steps taken by the Ministry would lead to permanent peace. But within two weeks the *Daily News* published a letter from Constantinople detailing the massacre in Bulgaria by the Turks, which moved all England with indignation. Innocent men, women and children had been slaughtered by the thousands; at least sixty villages had been utterly destroyed; the most revolting scenes of violence had been enacted; and a district once the most fertile in the Empire had been laid waste and completely ruined. Forty girls were shut up in a straw loft and burnt, and outrages of the most fearful description were committed upon hundreds of defenceless captives.

Mr. Disraeli, in the House of Commons, grew "jocular upon the cruelties and sufferings almost unparalleled in the world's history," and expressed his belief that the outrages committed by the Turkish troops had been exaggerated, and sneered at the rumor as "coffee-house babble;" while as to the torture of the impalement, which had caused universal anger and disgust, that an Oriental people have their way of executing malefactors, and generally terminated their connection with culprits in an expeditious manner.

In the official report presented to Parliament by Mr. W. Baring, the reported outrages in Bulgaria were corroborated. No fewer than 12,000 persons had perished in the sandjak of Philippopolis! The most fearful tragedy, however, was at Batak, where over 1000 people took refuge in the church and churchyard. The Bashi-Bazouks fired through the windows, and, getting upon the roof, tore off the tiles and threw burning pieces of wood and rags dipped in petroleum among the mass of unhappy human beings inside. At last the door was forced in and the massacre was completed. The inside of the church was then burnt, and hardly one escaped. "The massacre at Batak was the most heinous crime which stained the history of the present century;" and for this exploit the Turkish Commander, Achmet Agha, had bestowed on him the order of the Medjidie. Sir Henry Elliot, the English Ambassador at Constantinople, was directed to lay these facts before the Sultan and to demand the punishment of the offenders. The demand, however, was never enforced.

Prince Milan issued a proclamation to his people, declaring that, while professing neutrality, the Sultan had continued to send military forces of savage hordes to the Servian frontier. In June, Prince Milan left Belgrade and joined his army on the frontier. The Montenegrins declared war on Turkey and joined forces with Servia. July 6th the Servians were defeated. Thus was Turkey plunged into war with her Christian provinces, and all through her own misrule in peace and her barbarities in war.

Mr. Disraeli in a speech made in the House of Commons, August 11th, explained that he had not denied the existence of the "Bulgarian. Atrocities," but he had no official knowledge of them. He affirmed that Great Britain was not responsible for what occurred in Turkey, nor were the Turks the special *protégés* of England. He announced that the special duty of the Government at that moment was to preserve the British Empire, and that they would never consent to any step that would hazard the existence of that empire, This speech, which was distinguished by much of his old brilliancy and power, was his last speech in the House. On the morning after this speech it was publicly announced that Mr. Disraeli would immediately be elevated to the peerage under the title of the Earl of Beaconsfield.

In September, 1876, deeming it high time that the indignant voice of England should be heard in demonstration of the infamous deeds practiced by the Turk, Mr. Gladstone issued his pamphlet, entitled "Bulgarian Horrors and the Question of the East." It had an enormous circulation. He called for a stop to be put to the anarchy, the misrule and the bloodshed in Bulgaria, and demanded that the Ottoman rule should be excluded, not only from Bosnia and Herzegovina, but also from Bulgaria. The Turks must clear out, "bag and baggage," from the provinces they have desolated and profaned. The pamphlet, and the latter expression especially, produced a great sensation.

The pamphlet "brought home to the English people the idea

that for these horrors which were going on, they too, as non-interfering allies of Turkey, were in part responsible." Soon after this Mr. Gladstone addressed a large concourse of his constituents at Blackheath, in which he severely arraigned the Government. This address was one of the most impassioned and eloquent of Mr. Gladstone's political orations, and at some points the people were literally carried away with their feelings.

November 1st, Turkey was forced by Russia to agree to an armistice of eight weeks. On the 2d the Russian Emperor pledged his word to the English Ambassador that he had no intention of acquiring Constantinople; that if compelled to occupy Bulgaria, it would be only until the safety of the Christian inhabitants be secured; and urged the Ambassador to remove the distrust of Russia prevailing in England. Yet, in the face of all these assurances, Lord Beaconsfield delivered a war-like speech, at the banquet at Guildhall, November 9th. Informed of this speech the Czar declared that if the Porte did not accede to his demands, Russia would then act independently.

On the 8th of December there was a great conference at St. James' Hall, London, to discuss the Eastern question. The Duke of Westminster presided at the afternoon meeting. At the evening gathering Lord Shaftesbury occupied the chair. Mr. E. Freeman said: "Perish the interests of England, perish our dominion in India, sooner than we should strike one blow or speak one word on behalf of the wrong against the right." The chief interest of the occasion centered in the speech of Mr. Gladstone who was received with unbounded applause. He declared that there had been no change in public sentiment in England on the question; that the promoters of that meeting had no desire to embarrass the Government; that the power and influence of England had been employed to effect results at variance with the convictions of the country; that Lord Beaconsfield had only recently appeared anxious; and that England had duties towards the Christian subjects of Turkey. Mr. Gladstone continued that he hoped that the instructions given to Lord Salisbury, who had been sent for conference to Constantinople, were not in accordance with the speech at Guildhall, but that he would be left to his own clear insight and generous impulses; that the conference would insist upon the independence of the provinces, or at least would insure them against arbitrary injustice and oppression, and that the work indicated was not merely a worthy deed but an absolute duty.

Mr. Gladstone, during the recess of Parliament, delivered speeches upon the burning question of the day all over England. At Hawarden he pleaded that it was the wretched Turkish system that was at fault, and not the Turks themselves, and hoped for a remedy. To the electors of Frome he spoke of the tremendous responsibility of the Ministers. In a speech at the Taunton Railway Station, he said, in reference to the injunction for himself and friends to mind their own business, that the Eastern question was their own business. And when the Constantinople Conference failed he spoke of this "great transaction and woeful failure," and laid all the blame of failure on the Ministry. As to the treaties of 1856 being in force, his opinion was, that Turkey had entirely broken those treaties and trampled them under foot.

January 20, 1877, the conference closed. Parliament met February 8, 1877, and the conflict was transferred from the country to that narrower arena. In the House of Lords the Duke of Argyle delivered a powerful speech, to which the Premier, Disraeli, replied, that he believed that any interference directed to the alleviation of the sufferings of the Turkish Christians would only make their sufferings worse. He asked for calm, sagacious and statesmanlike consideration of the whole subject, never forgetting the great interests of England, if it was to have any solution at all.

Mr. Gladstone, upon his appearance in the House, was greeted as a Daniel come to judgment. He was taken to task by Mr. Chaplin, who complained that Mr. Gladstone and others of the Liberal party "had endeavored to regulate the foreign policy of the country by pamphlets, by speeches at public meetings, and by a so-called National Conference, instead of leaving it in the hands of the Executive Government," and intimated that Mr. Gladstone was afraid to meet the House in debate upon the question. Mr. Gladstone, rebuking Mr. Chaplain, said that it was the first time in a public career extending over nearly half a century, he had been accused of a disinclination to meet his opponents in a fair fight, and promised him that neither he nor his friends would have reason to complain of his reticence. Tories and Liberals knew he had not shrunk from meeting the public on this question. He was glad that there was a tremendous feeling abroad upon this Eastern question. He had been told that by the pamphlet he wrote and the speech he delivered, he had done all this mischief, and agitated Europe and the world; but if that were the case why did not the honorable gentleman, by writing another pamphlet, and delivering another speech, put the whole thing right? If he (the speaker) had done anything, it was only in the same way that a man applies a match to an enormous mass of fuel already prepared. Mr. Gladstone closed with the following words: "We have, I think, the most solemn and the greatest question to determine that has come before Parliament in my time.... In the original entrance of the Turks into Europe, it may be said to have been a turning point in human history. To a great extent it continues to be the cardinal question, the question which casts into the shade every other question."

April 24, 1877, war was declared by Russia against Turkey. The Czar issued a manifesto, assigning as reasons for this war the refusal of guarantee by the Porte for the proposed reforms, the failure of the Conference and the rejection of the Proteol signed on the previous 31st of March. England, France and Italy proclaimed their neutrality. Mr. Gladstone initiated a great debate in the House of Commons, May 7th, which lasted five days. He presented a series of resolutions expressing grave dissatisfaction with the policy of Turkey, and declared that she had forfeited all claim to support, moral and material. Mr. Gladstone asked whether, with regard to the great battle of freedom against oppression then going on, "we in England could lay our hands upon our hearts, and in the face of God and man, say, 'We have well and sufficiently performed our part?'"

These resolutions were of course hostile to the Government, and many Liberals refused to vote for them, because they pledged England to a policy of force in connection with Russia. Besides the Government gave assurances to avail themselves of any opportunity of interposing their good offices. The resolutions consequently were lost. Mr. Gladstone was not quite the leader of his party again.

Shortly after this debate, and before the close of the session, Mr. Gladstone addressed a large meeting at Birmingham on the Eastern question and the present condition of the Liberal party. Later on he visited Ireland. On his return he addressed, by their request, the people gathered to receive him. He expressed his belief that Turkey would have yielded to the concerted action of Europe; noticed the change in the tone of the ministry from the omission in the Premier's speech of the phrase, "the independence of Turkey;" protested strongly against England being dragged into war, and warmly eulogized the non-conformists for the consistency and unanimity with which they had insisted on justice to the Eastern Christians. Political feeling entered into everything at this time, but as an evidence of the hold Mr. Gladstone retained in the Scottish heart, he was in November elected Lord Rector of Glasgow University by a large majority. Lord Beaconsfield was the retiring Lord Rector, and the Conservatives nominated Sir S. Northcote, the Chancellor of the Exchequer, as Mr. Gladstone's opponent.

The war in the East went disastrously for the Ottoman arms. January 23, 1878, the Porte agreed to accept the terms of peace submitted by the Grand Duke Nicholas.

Mr. Gladstone was invited January 30, 1878, to attend a meeting of undergraduates at Oxford, held to celebrate the formation of a Liberal Palmerston Club. He strongly condemned the sending of the British fleet into the Dardanelles as a breach of European law; and confessed that he had been an agitator for the past eighteen months, day and night, to counteract what he believed to be the evil purposes of Lord Beaconsfield.

In February the House of Commons passed a vote of credit, but on the 3d of March a treaty of peace was signed between Turkey and Russia, at Sanstefano, the terms of which in part were: Turkey to pay a large war indemnity; Servia and Montenegro to be independent and to receive accessions of territory; Bulgaria to be formed into a principality with greatly extended boundaries, and to be governed by a prince elected by the inhabitants; the navigation of the Straits was declared free for merchant vessels, both in times of peace and war; Russian troops to occupy Bulgaria for two years; Batoum, Ardahan, Kars and Bayazid, with their territories, to be ceded to Russia, and Turkey to pay an indemnity to Roumania. The terms of the treaty were regarded oppressive to Turkey by the Beaconsfield Ministry, who proposed that the whole treaty be submitted to a congress at Berlin, to meet in June, 1878. The treaty was approved after some modifications. The English Plenipotentiaries were the Earl of Beaconsfield and Marquis of Salisbury, who, for their share in the treaty, received a popular ovation and rewards from the Queen. Thus was Turkey humiliated and Russia benefited, having obtained her demands. To the people assembled Lord Beaconsfield said from the window of the Foreign Office: "Lord Salisbury and myself have brought you back peace, but a peace, I hope with honor, which may satisfy our Sovereign and tend to the welfare of the country." But at this very time the envoy of Russia, whom the ministry thought to be circumvented, was entering the Afghan capital; so that, although there was peace on the Bosphorus, as a direct result of the Eastern policy, there was war in Afghanistan. The Conservatives were very ready for awhile to use as a watchword the phrase, "Peace and Honor," but before long it became the occasion of ridicule.

Parliament was called upon to appropriate £8,000,000 to defray the cost of the Afghan and Zulu wars. When Mr. Gladstone's government retired from office, there was a surplus of over £3,000,000, but the budgets of 1878 and 1879 both showed large deficits. The people had applauded the "imperial policy," "the jingoism" of Lord Beaconsfield's administration during the past two or three years, but they were not so appreciative when they found it so costly a policy to themselves. The depression in business also had its effect upon the country. The unpopularity of the Liberal government, which culminated in its defeat in 1873, was now, in 1879, being shifted to their Conservative opponents, whose term of office was fast drawing to a close.

"Mr. Gladstone's resolute and splendid hostility to Lord Beaconsfield's whole system of foreign policy restored him to his paramount place among English politicians. For four years—from 1876 to 1880—he sustained the high and holy strife with an enthusiasm, a versatility, a courage and a resourcefulness which raised the enthusiasm of his followers to the highest pitch, and filled his guilty and baffled antagonists with a rage which went near to frenzy. By frustrating Lord Beaconsfield's design of going to war on behalf of Turkey, he saved England from the indelible disgrace of a second and more gratuitous Crimea. But it was not only in Eastern Europe that his saving influence was felt. In Africa and India, and wherever British honor was involved, he was the resolute and unsparing enemy of that odious system of bluster and swagger and might against right, on which Lord Beaconsfield and his colleagues bestowed the tawdry nickname of Imperialism."

CHAPTER XVII

MIDLOTHIAN AND THE SECOND PREMIERSHIP

The leadership of the Liberal party had, upon the retirement of Mr. Gladstone, been turned over to Lord Hartington. His sympathies were upon the right side on the Eastern question, but he was a calm, slow-moving man. At the proper time he would have taken the right measures in Parliament, but the temper of the Liberal party and of the people demanded present action and emphatic speech, then Mr. Gladstone came to the rescue, and Lord Hartington found himself pushed aside. Mr. Gladstone was again in fact the leader of the Liberal party, whose standard he had carried aloft during those stirring times when the Eastern question was the all-absorbing topic of debate in Parliament and among the people of the land. The foreign policy of Lord Beaconsfield in 1878 and 1879 found a sleepless critic in Mr. Gladstone.

The day after the Parliament of 1878 had adjourned for the Easter recess, it was announced that the Ministry had ordered the Indian Government to dispatch 7000 native troops to the Island of Malta. The order occasioned much discussion— political, legal, and constitutional. It was warmly debated. It was thought that Lord Beaconsfield had transcended his powers and done what could be done only by a vote of Parliament. In the House of Commons Mr. Gladstone condemned the proceedings as unconstitutional, and pointed out the dangers of the Ministerial policy. Lord Beaconsfield received what he calculated upon—the support of the House.

For a member to differ from his policy was almost to incur the imputation of disloyalty to Crown and country. Indeed, Mr. Gladstone was seriously accused of treason by a member of the House for an article in the *Nineteenth Century*.

Mr. Gladstone undauntedly continued the contest. He addressed a meeting of Liberals in the Drill Hall, Bermondsey, July 20th, in which he said that the Dissolution of Parliament could not long be postponed, and urged the union and organization of all Liberals, and prompt measures to secure such representation as the Liberals deserved in the coming Parliament. Speaking of the Anglo-Turkish treaty, he pointed out the serious obligations which devolved upon England under it. He added, regarding the Turkish Convention, that, possibly it was necessary to sustain the credit of the country, but whether that credit should be sustained at such a price remained for the people to determine at the polls. He rejoiced that these most unwise, extravagant, unwarrantable, unconstitutional and dangerous proceedings had not been the work of the Liberal party, but he was grieved to think that any party should be found in England to perform such transactions.

A great debate arose in the House of Commons, extending over the whole range of the Eastern question: The Treaty of Berlin, the Anglo-Turkish Convention, the acquisition of Cyprus, the claims of Greece, etc. It was begun by the Marquis of Hartington, who offered a resolution regretting the grave responsibilities the Ministry had assumed for England with no means of securing their fulfillment, and without the previous knowledge of Parliament. Mr. Gladstone's speech during this debate is described as "a long and eloquent address, unsurpassable for its comprehensive grasp of the subject, its lucidity, point, and the high tone which animated it throughout." Mr. Gladstone denied that his strictures upon the Government in a speech made out of Parliament could be construed as Lord Beaconsfield had taken them as a personal attack and provocation. If criticism of this kind is prohibited the doors of the House might as well be shut. He observed that, "Liberty of speech is the liberty which secures all other liberties, and the abridgment of which would render all other liberties vain and useless possessions." In discussing the Congress at Berlin, Mr. Gladstone said, that he could not shut his eyes to the fact that the Sclavs, looking to Russia had been freed, while the Greeks, looking to England, remained with all their aspirations unsatisfied; that Russia had secured much territory and large indemnity, with the sanction of Europe; that the English Plenipotentiaries at the Congress, Lord Salisbury and Lord Beaconsfield, as a general rule, took the side of servitude, and that opposed to freedom.

With regard to the English responsibilities in Asiatic Turkey put upon England at the Convention, he called them an "unheard of," and "mad-undertaking," accomplished "in the dark," by the present Ministry. Dealing with the treaty-making power of the country, he claimed that it rested with Parliament in conjunction with the Executive. The strength and the eloquence were on the side of the opposition, but the votes were for the Government. The resolutions of Lord Hartington were defeated, and the "imperial policy" of the Ministry was sustained. The *Spectator* said, that, "Reason, prudence, and patriotism have hardly ever in our times been voted down with so little show of argument, and even of plausible suggestion."

The next step taken by the Ministry was to undertake war with Afghanistan, in hopes of checking the advances of Russia in that direction and of redressing grievances. England accomplished her purpose in part, but greatly suffered for her exploit. Mr. Gladstone could not remain quiet under the "adventurous policy" of the Premier. He condemned the ministerial policy which had made the Queen an Empress, then manipulated the prerogative in a manner wholly unexampled in this age, and employed it in inaugurating policies about which neither the nation nor the Parliament had ever been consulted. But arguments were of no avail. The Conservative majority in Parliament had imbibed the idea that the honor of England had to be protected. Some thought it had never been assailed, but Lord Beaconsfield declared it was in peril, and men and money were voted to defend it. "So the order was given for distant peoples to be attacked, English blood to be spilled, the burdens of the people, already too heavy, to be swollen, and the future liabilities of this country to be enormously increased."

In November, at the Lord Mayor's banquet, Lord Beaconsfield, speaking of Eastern affairs, said that the Government was not afraid of any invasion of India by its northwestern frontier; but the frontier was "haphazard and not a scientific one," and the Government wanted a satisfactory frontier. Mr. Gladstone, in a letter to the Bedford Liberal Association, asked: "What right have we to annex by war, or to menace the territory of our neighbors, in order to make 'scientific' a frontier which is already safe?"

In the autumn of 1879 Mr. Gladstone, having resolved to retire from the representation of Greenwich at the next election, paid a farewell visit to his constituents. At a luncheon given by the Liberal Association he dwelt upon the necessity of a Liberal union. The Liberals had, owing to their dissensions, given twenty-six votes to their opponents in 1874, while the Government had been carried on for years by a Conservative majority of less than twenty-six, showing the importance of organization. At night Mr. Gladstone attended a great public meeting in the Plumstead Skating Rink. On his entrance the whole audience rose and cheered for several minutes. An address was presented, expressing regret at his retirement, and the pride they would ever feel at having been associated with his name and fame. Mr. Gladstone alluded to Lord Beaconsfield's phrase respecting "harassed interests," and said he knew of only one harassed interest, and that was the British nation. He protested against the words "personal government" being taken to imply that the Sovereign desired to depart from the traditions of the constitution, yet he charged the advisers of the Crown with having invidiously begun a system intended to narrow the liberties of the people of England and to reduce Parliament to the condition of the French Parliaments before the great Revolution.

Mr. Gladstone threw the whole responsibility of the Afghan war on the Ministry, and maintaining that England had departed from the customs of the forefathers, concluded as follows: "It is written in the eternal laws of the universe of God that sin shall be followed by suffering. An unjust war is a tremendous sin. The question which you have to consider is whether this war is just or unjust. So far as I am able to collect the evidence, it is unjust."

In December, 1878, the following resolution was offered in the House of Commons: "That this House disapproves the conduct of her Majesty's Government, which has resulted in the war with Afghanistan." Mr. Gladstone strongly condemned the war with Afghanistan and the irritating policy towards the Ameer, and concluded his address with the following eloquent responses to the historical and moral aspects of the Afghan difficulty: "You have made this war in concealment from Parliament, in reversal of the policy of every Indian and Home Government that has existed for the last twenty-five years, in contempt of the supplication of the Ameer and in defiance of the advice of your own agent, and all for the sake of obtaining a scientific frontier." This powerful speech greatly impressed, for the moment, both parties in the House, but the vote of censure was defeated, and the policy of the administration was endorsed. During the debate Mr. Latham made a witty comparison. He said that the Cabinet reminded him of the gentleman, who seeing his horses run away, and being assured by the coachman that they must drive into something, replied, "Then smash into something cheap!"

The Ministry presented a motion that the revenues of India should be applied for the purposes of the war. Mr. Gladstone observed that it was the people of England who had had all the glory and all the advantage which resulted from the destruction of the late administration, and the accession of the present Cabinet; and hence it was the people who must measure the *pros* and the *cons*, and who must be content, after having reaped such innumerable benefits, to encounter the disadvantage of meeting charges which undoubtedly the existing government would leave behind it as a legacy to posterity. England gained her end in the humiliation of Russia, but there were those who felt that the result of the English policy would further the advance of Russia in Europe, and that force would never make friends of the Afghans.

In the sessions of 1879 the Greek question came up in the House of Commons on a motion, "That, in the opinion of this House, tranquillity in the East demands that satisfaction be given to the just claims of Greece, and no satisfaction can be considered adequate that does not ensure execution of the recommendations embodied in Protocol 13 of the Berlin Congress." Mr. Gladstone hoped that even in the present House there would be found those who would encourage the first legitimate aspirations of the Hellenic races after freedom. The government had given pledges to advance the claims of Greece that had not been redeemed at Berlin. Not one of the European powers was now averse to the claims of the Greek kingdom, whose successful pleadings depended wholly upon England for favorable answer. But the government objected, and the motion was rejected. In July, Sir Charles Dilke called the attention of the House to the obligations of Turkey under the Treaty of Berlin, when Mr. Gladstone again earnestly enforced the claims of "Greece, weak as she may be, is yet strong in the principles in which she rests."

December 29, 1879, Mr. Gladstone attained the seventieth year of his age. His friends in Liverpool, and the Greenwich Liberal Association presented him with congratulatory addresses. The journals paid him warm tributes for his long and eminent public services. But few thought that the veteran that had so successfully gone through one electoral campaign was destined in a few months to pass through another, still more remarkable, and yet be fresh for new triumphs. In the autumn of 1879 Mr. Gladstone resolved upon a very important, and as his enemies thought, a hopeless step. He had retired from the representation of Greenwich, and he now boldly decided to contest the election for Midlothian, the county of Edinburgh. He consequently proceeded to Scotland, in November, where such an ovation was given him as has never been accorded to any man in modern times. During the period of three weeks he addressed meetings numbering seventy-five thousand people, while a quarter of a million of people, with every exhibition of good-will and admiration, took part in some way in the demonstration in his honor. In this canvass of delivering political speeches he performed an oratorical and intellectual feat unparalleled in the history of any statesman who had attained his seventieth year. Mr. Gladstone addressed large concourses of people. When he reached Edinburgh, "his progress was as the progress of a nation's guest, or a king returning to his own again."

Midlothian, the scene of Mr. Gladstone's astonishing exertions, was one of the Conservative strongholds, under the dominent influence of the Duke of Buccleuch, whose son, Lord Dalkeith, Mr. Gladstone opposed in contesting for the representation in Parliament. Mr. Gladstone said: "Being a man of Scotch blood, I am very much attached to Scotland, and like even the Scottish accent," and he afterwards said, "and Scotland showed herself equally proud of her son." He spoke at Edinburgh, November 26th, and on the following day at Dalkeith, in the very heart of the Duke of Buccleuch's own property to an audience of three thousand people, mostly agriculturists. At Edinburgh he met nearly five thousand persons at the Corn Exchange, representing more than one hundred Scottish Liberal Associations. In the Waverley Market Mr. Gladstone addressed more than twenty thousand people, one of the largest congregations ever assembled in-doors in Scotland, and met with a reception which for enthusiasm was in keeping with the vastness of the audience. December 5th, at Glasgow, he delivered his address as Lord Rector to the students of the University, and in the evening addressed an immense audience of nearly six thousand in St. Andrew's Hall. He was most enthusiastically received, and he dwelt chiefly on Cyprus, the Suez Canal, India, and Afghanistan. "We had Afghanistan ruined," he urged, "India not advanced, but thrown back in government, subjected to heavy and unjust charges, subjected to what might well be termed, in comparison with the mild government of former years, a system of oppression; and with all this we had at home the law broken and the rights of Parliament invaded."

On the 8th of March, 1880, the immediate dissolution of Parliament was announced in both Houses of Parliament, and the news created intense political excitement and activity throughout the land. In his manifesto, in the shape of a letter to the Duke of Marlborough, the Prime Minister referred to the attempt made to sever the constitutional tie between Great Britain and Ireland, and said: "It is to be hoped that all men of light and leading will resist this destructive doctrine. There are some who challenge the expediency of the Imperial character of this realm. Having attempted and failed to enfeeble our colonies by their policy of decomposition, they may now perhaps recognize in the disintegration of the United Kingdom a mode which will not only accomplish, but precipitate, that purpose. Peace rests on the presence, not to say the ascendency, of England in the councils of Europe."

Mr. Gladstone and Lord Hartington issued their counter-manifestoes. Mr. Gladstone repudiated Lord Beaconsfield's dark allusion to the repeal of the union and the abandonment of the colonies, characterizing them as base insinuations, the real purpose of which was to hide from view the policy pursued by the Ministry, and its effect upon the condition of the country; and said that public distress had been aggravated by continual shocks from neglected legislation at home, "while abroad they had strained the prerogative by gross misuse, had weakened the Empire by needless wars, and dishonored it in the eyes of Europe by their clandestine acquisition of the Island of Cyprus."

Mr. Gladstone began the electoral campaign with a speech at Marylebone on the 10th of March, in which he announced Lord Derby's secession from the Conservative to the Liberal party; and then he left London to enter upon his second Midlothian campaign. At various points on the journey Mr. Gladstone stopped and addressed the people from the cars, and

Richard B. Cook

it is a remarkable fact that wherever he delivered an address the Liberals gained a seat.

The first address made by Mr. Gladstone on his own account, was delivered on the 17th of March, in the Music Hall, Edinburgh. After dwelling at great length upon various questions of foreign policy, he concluded with the following references personal to his opponents and himself: "I give them credit for patriotic motives; I give them credit for those patriotic motives which are incessantly and gratuitously denied to us. I believe that we are all united, gentlemen—indeed it would be most unnatural if we were not—in a fond attachment, perhaps in something of a proud attachment, to the great country to which we belong."

In his final speech at West Calder Mr. Gladstone drew a powerful indictment against the administration, and placed the issue before the country in a strong light. Throughout all the campaign, as the time for the general election was approaching, only one question was submitted to the electors, "Do you approve or condemn Lord Beaconsfield's system of foreign policy?" And the answer was given at Easter, 1880, when the Prime Minister and his colleagues received the most empathic condemnation which had ever been bestowed upon an English Government, and the Liberals were returned in an overwhelming majority of fifty over Tories and Home Rulers combined. Mr. Gladstone succeeded in ousting Lord Dalkeith from the representation of Midlothian by a respectable majority. He was also elected at Leeds, but this seat was afterwards given to his son, Herbert Gladstone. At the conclusion of the election all the journals joined in admiring the indomitable energy and vigor of the orator, who could carry out this great enterprise when he had already passed the age of three-score years and ten. Edinburgh was illuminated in the evening, and everywhere were to be witnessed signs of rejoicing at Mr. Gladstone's victory. The result of the elections throughout the country exceeded the most sanguine expectations of the Liberals. So large a proportion of Liberal members had not been returned to the House of Commons since the days of the first Reform Bill.

Lord Beaconsfield, as soon as the result of the election was known, and without waiting for the meeting of Parliament, resigned. The Queen, in conformity with the constitutional custom, summoned Lord Hartington, the titular leader of the Liberal party in the House of Commons, to form a cabinet. But he could do nothing. Then the Queen sent for Lord Granville, who with Lord Hartington, went to Windsor April 23d. They both assured the Queen that the victory was Mr. Gladstone's; that the people had designated him for office, and that the Liberal party would be satisfied with no other, and that he was the inevitable Prime Minister. They returned to London in the afternoon, sought Mr. Gladstone at Harley Street, where he was awaiting the message they brought from the Queen—to repair to Windsor. That evening, without an hour's delay, he went to Windsor, kissed hands, and returned to London Prime Minister for the second time.

Mr. Gladstone again filled the double office of Premier and Chancellor of the Exchequer in the new cabinet, which for general ability and debating power was one of the strongest of the century. While some of the cabinet officers were like Mr. Gladstone himself, without title, others were representatives of the oldest nobility of the land. At the very beginning the new administration were confronted by perplexing questions. The Eastern question, chiefly by Mr. Gladstone's influence, had been settled in accordance with the dictates of humanity and religion. But there were other difficulties to be overcome. "At home, his administration did good and useful work, including the extension of the suffrage to the agricultural laborers; but it was seriously, and at length fatally, embarrassed by two controversies which sprang up with little warning, and found the Liberal party and its leaders totally unprepared to deal with them."

The first embarrassing question which arose when the new Parliament met was the great deficit of nine million pounds instead of an expected surplus in the Indian Budget, owing to the Afghan war.

Foremost among the difficulties encountered was the case of Mr. Charles Bradlaugh, elected a member of Parliament for Northampton. He demanded to be permitted to make a solemn affirmation or declaration of allegiance, instead of taking the usual oath. The question created much discussion and great feeling, and Mr. Bradlaugh's persistence was met by violence. Mr. Bright contended for liberty of conscience. Mr. Gladstone favored permitting Mr. Bradlaugh to affirm on his own responsibility which was finally done, but Mr. Bradlaugh was prosecuted in the courts. The great difficulty arose from Mr. Bradlaugh's atheism.

A considerable share of the session of 1880 was occupied in the consideration of the Irish Compensation for Disturbance Bill and other Irish measures. In consequence of the rapid increase of evictions by landlords, this protective measure had become absolutely necessary in the interests of the Irish tenants. After prolonged debate—very prolonged for so short a bill—thirty-five lines only—the bill was passed by the Commons, but defeated by the Lords. The result was "seen in a ghastly record of outrage and murder which stained the following winter."

Home Rule for Ireland, which movement was started in the "seventies," was gaining ground, and every election returned to the House more members pledged to its support. Those who were bent upon obtaining Home Rule at any cost used obstructive means against other legislation to gain their object, but as yet the movement was confined to the members who had been elected by Irish constituents.

About the close of the session of 1880 the heavy burdens and responsibilities of public service borne by Mr. Gladstone began to tell upon him. At the end of July, while returning from home for the House of Commons, Mr. Gladstone was taken ill. He was prostrated by fever and great fears for his recovery were entertained by his family, his party and a host of admirers throughout the country. A great outburst of popular sympathy was manifested and frequent messages were received from the Queen and many foreign potentates and celebrities. Distinguished callers and telegrams continued to arrive at Downing Street for ten days while the patient was confined to his bed at home. The President of the United States and the King and Queen of the Belgians were among those who sent messages of sympathy. "Rarely indeed, if ever, has there been witnessed such a general and spontaneous expression of the national sympathy towards a distinguished statesman whose life had been imperilled by illness."

Mr. Gladstone's large store of vital energy brought him safely through his dangerous illness and on approaching convalescence he took a sea voyage round the entire coast of England in Sir Donald Currie's steamer, "Grantully Castle."

Three years after this voyage around England the Premier visited the Orkneys on a similar trip, in the "Pembroke Castle," the poet laureate being of the party on this occasion. From the Orkneys he sailed across to Denmark and suddenly appeared at Copenhagen, where Mr. Gladstone entertained the Czar and Czarina, the King of Greece, and the King and Queen of Denmark, and many others of their relatives who happened to be visiting them at that time.

A great meeting was held June 21, 1880, in Her Majesty's opera house, for the purpose of presenting an address from the Liberals of Middlesex to Mr. Herbert Gladstone, who had made a gallant contest in that country at the general election. The entrance of the Premier some time after the meeting began was the signal for an outburst of enthusiasm. Before Mr. Gladstone appeared, the chairman, Mr. Foster, had paid a high tribute to the Premier for his great abilities and his self-denial in the public service. After his son had received the address, the Premier arose to speak, when the whole audience arose to their feet and welcomed him with immense cheering.

Mr. Gladstone referred at length to the Midlothian campaign, and paid a tribute to the spirit and energy of the Liberals of the whole country. The sound which went forth from Midlothian reverberated through the land and was felt to be among the powerful operative causes which led to the great triumph of the Liberal party.

At the Lord Mayor's banquet, November 9, 1880, Mr. Gladstone's speech was looked forward to with much anxiety, owing to the singularly disturbed condition of Ireland. Referring to the "party of disorder" in Ireland, he said that as anxious as the government was to pass laws for the improvement of the land laws, their prior duty was to so enforce the laws as to secure order. If an increase of power was needed to secure this, they would not fail to ask it.

In 1881, at the Lord Mayor's banquet, Mr. Gladstone said that he was glad to discern signs of improvement in Ireland during the last twelve months; but the struggle between the representatives of law and the representatives of lawlessness had rendered necessary an augmentation of the executive power.

In August, 1881, at Greenwich, the Liberals of the borough presented Mr. Gladstone with an illustrated address and a carved oak chair as a token of their esteem and a souvenir of his former representation of their borough. On the cushion back of the chair were embossed in gold the arms of Mr. and Mrs. Gladstone, with a motto "Fide et Virtute," and above, in the midst of some wood-carving representing the rose, the thistle, the shamrock, and the leek, was a silver plate, bearing a suitable inscription.

The Parliamentary session of 1881 was almost exclusively devoted to Irish affairs. Instead of the contemplated Land Act, the ministry were compelled, on account of the disturbed condition of Ireland, to bring in first a Coercion Act, although the measure was naturally distasteful to such friends of Ireland in the Cabinet as Mr. Gladstone and Mr. Bright. Property and life had become very insecure, and there was a startling increase of agrarian crime that such a measure was deemed necessary. But while passing the Coercion Act, Mr. Gladstone accompanied it by a great and beneficial measure—a second Irish Land Bill, which instituted a court for the purpose of dealing with the differences between landlord and tenant.

This bill—one of Mr. Gladstone's greatest measures—became a law August 23, 1881. Mr. Gladstone in his speech remarked that the complaint was made that the bill was an infringement of liberty in Ireland and was aimed at the Land League, but no person or body could be touched by the bill unless they violated the law, and then could only be arrested upon reasonable suspicion of crime committed or of inciting to crime or of interfering with law or order. There would be the fullest freedom of discussion allowed. Dealing with the Land League he said it had been attempted to compare it with the Corn Laws, but Mr. Bright had completely demolished that miserable argument. It was compared also to the trade unions, but they made an onward step in the intelligence and in the love of law and order among the working classes. They had never tainted themselves by word or deed which would bring them into suspicion in connection with the maintenance of law. The leaders of the Land League were now put forward as martyrs on the same platform as O'Connell; but on every occasion of his life-long agitation O'Connell set himself to avoid whatever might tend to a breach of law and order. Then Mr. Gladstone showed the necessity of the Coercion Act from the condition of Ireland, where during the past year there had been a great increase of crime, and the outrages were agrarian, and not connected with the distress. It was a significant fact that the agrarian outrages had risen and fallen with the meetings of the Land League. Nothing could be more idle than to confound the agrarian crime of Ireland with the ordinary crime of England, or even of Ireland. In regard to general crime, Ireland held a high and honorable place, but how different was the case with agrarian crime! He referred to the miscarriage of justice in Ireland, and said that the bill, if passed, would restore to Ireland the first conditions of Christian and civilized existence. But it "only irritated while it failed to terrify."

Mr. Gladstone's was a great speech and showed his mastery of details, and his power of expounding and illustrating broad and general principles. He began his exposition by confessing that it was the most difficult question with which he had ever been called upon to deal. He concluded with an eloquent invocation to justice.

On the 19th of April, 1881, Lord Beaconsfield died. For many years he and Mr. Gladstone had been at the head of their respective parties. "Their opposition, as one critic has well and tersely put it, like that of Pitt and Fox, was one of temperament and character as well as of genius, position and political opinions." The Premier paid an eloquent tribute to him and proposed a public funeral, which was declined. Mr. Gladstone then moved for a monument in Westminster Abbey to the memory of the deceased Earl.

In October, 1881, Mr. Gladstone made a visit to Leeds, for which borough he was returned in 1880, but for which his son Herbert sat. He delivered several important addresses on subjects which then absorbed the public attention, especially dealing with the land question local government, and Free Trade *versus* Fair Trade. Mr. Gladstone said:

"My boyhood was spent at the mouth of the Mersey, and in those days I used to see those beautiful American liners, the packets between New York and Liverpool, which then conducted the bulk and the pick of the trade between the two countries. The Americans were then deemed to be so entirely superior to us in shipbuilding and navigation that they had four-fifths of the whole trade between the two countries in their hands, and that four-fifths was the best of the trade. What is the case now, when free trade has operated and has applied its stimulus to the intelligence of England, and when, on the other hand, the action of the Americans has been restrained by the enactment, the enhancement and the tightening of the protective system? The scales are exactly reversed, and instead of America doing four-fifths and that the best, we do four-fifths of the business, and the Americans pick up the leavings of the British and transact the residue of the trade. Not because they are inferior to us in anything; it would be a fatal error to suppose it; not because they have less intelligence or less perseverance. They are your descendants; they are your kinsmen; and they are fully equal to you in all that goes to make human energy and power; but they are laboring under the delusion from which you yourselves have but recently escaped, and in which some misguided fellow-citizens seek again to entangle you.

"I am reminded that I was guilty on a certain occasion of stating in an article—not a political article—that, in my opinion, it was far from improbable that as the volume of the future was unrolled, America, with its vast population and its wonderful resources, and not less with that severe education which, from the high price of labor, America is receiving in the strong necessity of resorting to every description of labor-saving contrivances, and consequent development, not only on a large scale, but down to the smallest scale of mechanical genius of the country—on that account the day may come when that country may claim to possess the commercial primacy of the world, I gave sad offence to many. I at present will say this, that as long as America adheres to the protective system your commercial primacy is secure. Nothing in the world can wrest it from you while America continues to fetter her own strong hands and arms, and with these fettered arms is content to compete with you, who are free, in neutral markets. And as long as America follows the doctrine of protection, or the doctrines now known as those of 'fair trade,' you are perfectly safe, and you need not allow, any of you, even your slightest slumbers to be disturbed by the fear that America will take from you your commercial primacy."

After his return to London Mr. Gladstone received an address from the Corporation, setting forth the long services he had rendered to the country. Mr. Gladstone, in his reply, touched upon Irish obstruction, and announced, incidentally, the arrest of Mr. Parnell. Mr. Parnell, the leader of the Irish party, having openly defied the law, had been arrested and

Richard B. Cook

imprisoned without trial, under the Coercion Act, passed at the last session.

On the opening night of the Parliament, of 1882, Mr. Gladstone laid before the House the proposed new rules of Parliamentary procedure. The *clôture*, by a bare majority, was to be established, in order to secure the power of closing debate by a vote of the House.

The House of Lords decided upon the appointment of a Select Committee to inquire into the working of the Land Act, including the alleged total collapse of the clauses relating to purchase, emigration, and arrears. The Prime Minister in the House of Commons introduced a resolution condemning the proposed inquiry as tending to defeat the operation of the Land Act and as injurious to the good government of Ireland.

Early in May, 1882, the whole country was startled and terrified by the news of the assassination of Lord Frederick Cavendish, the new chief secretary for Ireland, and Mr. Burke under-secretary, in the Phoenix Park, Dublin. A social revolution was raging in Ireland. Outrages and murders had been fearfully frequent, and such brutal murders as those of Mrs. Smythe and Mr. Herbert had filled England with terror. In the first week of May announcement was made that Earl Cowper had resigned the Viceroyalty. Rather than share the responsibility of releasing Mr. Parnell, Mr. Dillon and Mr. O'Kelly, Mr. Forster left the Cabinet. Lord Spencer was appointed to the Viceroyalty, and Lord Frederick Cavendish succeeded Mr. Forster, and two days thereafter all England was thrilled with sorrow and indignation by the terrible news of the assassination in Phoenix Park. The news shattered the hopes of many concerning Ireland, and fell with special severity upon Mr. Gladstone, because he and Lord Cavendish enjoyed the closest friendship. The government presented a Prevention of Crimes Bill of a very stringent character. In the course of debate warm discussions arose over an "understanding" called, "The Kilmainham Compact," but Mr. Gladstone successfully defended the government in regard to its supposed negotiations with Mr. Parnell. This bill was directed against secret societies and illegal combinations, and it was hoped that as the Land League party had expressed its horror at the Phoenix Park crime, and charged that it was the work of American conspirators, they would allow the measure speedily to become law. Mr. Bright declared that the bill would harm no innocent person, and explained his own doctrine, that "Force is no remedy," was intended to apply not to outrages, but to grievances. For three weeks Mr. Parnell and his followers obstructed legislation in every conceivable way, and were finally suspended for systematic obstruction. The obstructionists removed, the bill was then passed, after a sitting of twenty-eight hours. The measure was passed by the Lords July 7th, and the Queen signed the bill July 12th. A crisis nearly arose between the Lords and the Commons over the Irish Arrears Bill, but the Lords finally yielded.

CHAPTER XVIII

THIRD ADMINISTRATION AND HOME RULE

It is our purpose next to trace the events that led to the overthrow of the Second Administration of Mr. Gladstone, and to the formation of his Third Cabinet. The question that seemed to begin the work of weakening the foundations of his existing government was their policy in regard to Egypt, which began with the occupation of Egypt in 1882.

The budget of the session of 1882 was presented by Mr. Gladstone April 24th. It was not expected that anything novel in the way of legislation would be attempted in it. But its main interest was in this, that it proposed a vote of credit for the Egyptian Expedition, which was to be provided for by addition to the income-tax, making it sixpence half-penny in the pound for the year. The financial proposals were agreed to. In the course of the session Mr. Bright resigned his place in the Cabinet on the ground that the intervention in Egypt was a manifest violation of the moral law, that the Government had interfered by force of arms in Egypt, and directed the bombardment of Alexandria. Mr. Gladstone denied that the Ministry were at war with Egypt, and stated that the measures taken at Alexandria were strictly measures of self-defence. In justifying his resignation Mr. Bright said there had been a manifest violation of the moral law; but the Premier, while agreeing with his late colleague generally on the question of the moral law differed from him as to this particular application of it.

The Prime Minister attended the Lord Mayor's Banquet at the Mansion House, August 9, 1882. In replying to the toast to Her Majesty's Ministers, after some preliminary remarks, Mr. Gladstone alluded to the campaign in Egypt, which had been so much discussed, and said: "Let it be well understood for what we go and for what we do not go to Egypt. We do not go to make war on its people, but to rescue them from the oppression of a military tyranny which at present extinguishes every free voice and chains every man of the people of that country. We do not go to make war on the Mohammedan religion, for it is amongst the proudest distinctions of Christianity to establish tolerance, and we know that wherever the British rule exists, the same respect which we claim for the exercise of our own conscientious convictions is yielded to the professors of every other faith on the surface of the globe. We do not, my Lord Mayor, go to repress the growth of Egyptian liberties. We wish them well; for we have no other interest in Egypt, which cannot in any other way so well and so effectually attain her own prosperity as by the enjoyment of a well regulated, and an expanding freedom."

Mr. Gladstone's confidence respecting the early termination of the war in Egypt was somewhat justified by Sir Garnet Wolseley's victory at Tel-el-Kebir, but the future relations of England with Egypt were still left an open subject of discussion and speculation. Again, November 9th, at the banquet at the Guildhall, to the Cabinet Ministers, Mr. Gladstone spoke. He called attention to the settlement of the troubles in the East of Europe, congratulating his hearers on the removal by the naval and military forces of the Egyptian difficulty, and calling attention to Ireland, compared its condition with that of the previous March and October, 1881, showing a diminution of agrarian crime to the extent of four-fifths. This happy result had been brought about, not by coercive means alone, but by the exercise of remedial measures. "If the people of Ireland were willing to walk in the ways of legality, England was strong, and generous, and free enough to entertain in a friendly and kindly spirit any demand which they might make."

On the 13th of December, 1882, Mr. Gladstone's political jubilee was celebrated. Fifty years before, on that day, he had been returned to Parliament as member for Newark. A large number of congratulatory addresses, letters, and telegrams complimenting him on the completion of his fifty years of parliamentary service were received by him. He had entered the first Reformed Parliament as a conservative, had gone ever forward in the path of reform, and was yet to lead in greater measures of reform.

The excellent prospects regarding domestic measures with which the session of 1883 was opened were dispelled by prolonged and fruitless debates on measures proposed and on the address from the Queen. But Mr. Gladstone was absent, the state of his health requiring him to pass several weeks at Cannes. He returned home in March greatly invigorated, and at once threw himself with wonted ardour into the parliamentary conflict. Mr. Parnell offered a bill to amend the Irish Land Act of 1887, which was opposed by the Premier and lost.

An affirmation bill was introduced at this session by the Government, which provided that members who objected to taking the oath might have the privilege of affirming. The opposition spoke of the measure as a "Bradlaugh Relief Bill." Its rejection was moved, and in its defense Mr. Gladstone made one of his best speeches, which was warmly applauded. He said: "I must painfully record my opinion, that grave injury has been done to religion in many minds—not in instructed minds, but in those which are ill-instructed or partially instructed—in consequence of things which ought never to have occurred. Great mischief has been done in many minds by a resistance offered to the man elected by the constituency of Northampton, which a portion of the people believe to be unjust. When they see the profession of religion and the interests of religion, ostensibly associated with what they are deeply convinced is injustice, it leads to questions about religion itself, which commonly end in impairing those convictions, and that belief, the loss of which I believe to be the most inexpressible calamity which can fall either upon a man or upon a nation." But the measure was lost.

During the session of 1883 the Bankruptcy Bill and the Patents Bill were both passed, and effected reforms which had long been felt to be necessary. The Corrupt Practices Act was designed to remove from British parliamentary and borough elections the stigma which attached to them in so many parts of the country. The Government was checked, however, in its policy in the Transvaal, and Mr. Childers' action in regard to the Suez Canal.

Mr. Gladstone attended, in March, the celebration of the inauguration of the National Liberal party, predicting for it a useful and brilliant future, if it remained faithful to its time-honored principles and traditions.

Sir Stafford Northcote, in the session of 1884, moved a vote of censure, and vigorously attacked the Egyptian policy of the administration. Mr. Gladstone defended the ministerial action with spirit and effect. He declared that the Government had found, and not made, the situation in Egypt and the Soudan. The Prime Minister "traced all the mischief to Lord Salisbury's dual control. Though the motive and object had been to secure a better government for Egypt, a great error had been committed. The British Government had fulfilled all the obligations imposed upon them, and they were acting for the benefit of the civilized world. Reforms had been effected in the judicature, legislature, police, and military organizations of Egypt; and they were resolved to see all the vital points recommended carried out by the Khedive's Government. As to the war in the Soudan, it was hateful to the people of Egypt; and England declined to have anything to do with the reconquest of the Soudan.... General Gordon, whom Mr. Gladstone characterized as a hero and a genius, had been despatched to Khartoum for the purpose of withdrawing, if possible, in safety the 29,000 soldiers of the Khedive scattered over the Soudan. The General's mission was not the reconquest of the Soudan, but its peaceful evacuation, and the reconstruction of the country, by giving back to the Sultan the

Richard B. Cook

ancestral power which had been suspended during the Egyptian occupation. The Government had to consider in any steps which they took the danger of thwarting Gordon's peaceful mission and endangering his life." Mr. Gladstone said that the policy of the Government was to "rescue and retire." Sir S. Northcote's resolution was rejected by 311 to 292 votes, showing the growing strength of the Opposition.

The pacific mission of General Gordon to Khartoum having failed, there was great solicitude felt for that gallant soldier's welfare and safety. Sir M. Hicks-Beach offered another vote of censure, complaining of the dilatory conduct of the Government for not taking steps to secure the safety of General Gordon. Mr. Gladstone, in reply, admitted the obligations of the Government to General Gordon, and stated that on reasonable proof of danger he would be assisted. "The nation would never grudge adequate efforts for the protection of its agents, but it was the duty of the Government to consider the treasure, the blood, and the honor of the country, together with the circumstances of the time, the season, the climate, and the military difficulties. Conscious of what their obligations were, they would continue to use their best endeavours to fulfil them, unmoved by the threats and the captious criticisms of the Opposition." The proposed censure was defeated.

A conference of European powers was held on Egyptian affairs, but was abortive; and Mr. Gladstone while announcing that he wished to get out of Egypt as soon as circumstances would allow, admitted that institutions, however good, were not likely to survive the withdrawal of our troops. Lord Northbrook was next despatched by the government on a mission to Egypt, with the object of rescuing her from her financial embarrassments, and averting the impending dangers of a national bankruptcy.

In February, 1884, Mr. Gladstone introduced the Government Franchise Bill in the House of Commons. It was a great measure and proposed to complete the work of parliamentary reform by conferring the suffrage upon every person in the United Kingdom who was the head of a household. Mr. Gladstone said that the results of the bill would be to add to the English constituency upwards of 1,300,000 voters; to the Scotch constituency over 200,000 voters; and to the Irish constituency over 400,000 voters; which would add to the aggregate constituency of the United Kingdom, which was then 3,000,000 voters, 2,000,000 more, or nearly twice as many as were added in 1832. The Premier appealed for union on this great reform, and observed: "Let us hold firmly together, and success will crown our efforts. You will, as much as any former Parliament that has conferred great legislative benefits on the nation, have your reward, and read your history in a nation's eyes; for you will have deserved all the benefits you will have conferred. You will have made a strong nation stronger still—stronger in union without, and stronger against its foes (if and when it has any foes) within; stronger in union between class and class, and in rallying all classes and portions of the community in one solid compact mass round the ancient Throne which it has loved so well, and round the Constitution, now to be more than ever free and more than ever powerful."

The measure was warmly debated. Besides this opposition there were, outside of the House, ominous utterances threatening the rejection of the scheme. Mr. Gladstone, referring to these hostile murmurings, said that hitherto the attitude of the government had been, in Shakespeare's words, "Beware of entrance to a quarrel; but, being in, bear it, that the opposer may beware of thee." He deprecated a quarrel and declared that the government had done everything to prevent a collision between the two Houses of Parliament on this question, which would open up a prospect more serious than any he remembered since the first Reform Bill.

The House of Lords passed a resolution to the effect that the Lords would not concur in any measure of reform without having the complete bill before them, including the redistribution and registration, as well as an extension of the suffrage. The Premier promised to introduce a Redistribution Bill in the following session, but Lord Salisbury, since the death of Lord Beaconsfield, the leader of the Conservative party, declined to discuss the Redistribution Bill, "with a rope around his neck," by which he meant a franchise act under which his party must appeal to the country. Negotiations followed between the Liberal and Conservative leaders with fruitless results, and the House of Lords finally passed a resolution that it would be desirable for Parliament to have an autumn session, to consider the Representation of the People Bill, in connection with the Redistribution Bill, which the government had brought before Parliament.

Public meetings were held at various places throughout the country, and the question of the enlargement of the franchise discussed. The policy of the Tories was strongly condemned at many large and influential public gatherings. In August Mr. Gladstone visited Midlothian and delivered a powerful address in the Edinburgh Corn Exchange. He explained that the special purpose for which he appeared before his constituents was to promote, by every legitimate means in his power, the speedy passage of the Franchise Bill. "The unfortunate rejection of the measure," he observed, "had already drawn in its train other questions of the gravest kind, and the vast proportion of the people would soon be asking whether an organic change was not required in the House of Lords. He, however, did not believe that the House of Lords had as yet placed itself in a position of irretrievable error. He believed that it was possible for it to go back, and to go back with dignity and honor."

With regard to the foreign policy of the Government, which had been attacked and compared unfavorably with the Midlothian programme of 1879, Mr. Gladstone defended it with spirit. He expressed his satisfaction with the expansion of Germany abroad, and reviewed the policy of the Government in Eastern Europe, Afghanistan, India and South Africa. As to the Transvaal, he contended that "they were strong and could afford to be merciful," and that it was not possible without the grossest and most shameful breach of faith to persist in holding the Boers to annexation, "when we had pledged ourselves beforehand that they should not be annexed except with their own good will." In reply to the oft-repeated question, "What took you to Egypt?" the Premier said: "Honor and plighted faith." The covenants they were keeping were those entered into by their Tory predecessors, and most unfortunate and most unwise he considered them to be. The Government had respected the sovereignty of the Porte and the title of the European Powers to be concerned in all matters territorially affecting the Turkish Empire; they had discouraged the spirit of aggression as well as they could, and had contracted no embarrassing engagements. Great improvements had been introduced in the administration of Egypt, but he regretted the total failure of the late Conference of the Powers to solve the problem of Egyptian finance. With regard to General Gordon the Government were considering the best means to be adopted for fulfilling their obligations.

Parliament met in October, 1884. The Franchise Bill was introduced and sent to the House of Lords, and the Redistribution Bill, upon which a compromise with the Conservatives had been reached, was presented in the House of Commons. The measure, as altered, proposed to disfranchise all boroughs with a population under 15,000, to give only one member to towns with a population between 15,000 and 50,000, and to take one member each from the counties of Rutland and Hereford. By this arrangement one hundred and sixty seats would be "extinguished," which, with the six seats extinguished before, would be revived and distributed as follows: "Eight new boroughs would be created, the representation of London, Liverpool, and other large cities and towns would be greatly increased, while in dealing with the remainder of the seats unappropriated, the Government would apply equal electoral areas throughout the country." The Franchise Bill—a truly democratic bill—-was carried through both Houses, and became a law. The Redistribution Bill was carried, January, 1885, after animated debate. Registration measures were also passed for England, Scotland and Ireland, which received the royal assent May 21st.

January, 1885, Mr. Gladstone wrote a kindly, serious, yet courtly letter of congratulation to Prince Albert Victor, eldest son of the Prince of Wales and heir presumptive to the Crown, on the attainment of his majority.

In the hour of triumph the government was doomed to receive a stunning blow. The news of the fall of Khartoum and the untimely death of General Gordon sent a thrill of horror and indignation throughout England. The government was seriously condemned for its procrastination in not sending timely relief, for the rescue of the imperiled English. But when the facts became fully known it was found that no blame could be attached to Mr. Gladstone, who was himself strongly moved by the death of General Gordon, whose work and character he highly esteemed. The Prime Minister was, however, equal to the emergency, and announced that it was necessary to overthrow the Mahdi at Khartoum, to renew operations against Osman Digna, and to construct a railway from Suakin to Berber with a view to a campaign in the fall. The reserves were called out by royal proclamation.

However, these measures met with opposition. Sir Stafford Northcote brought forward a motion affirming that the risks and sacrifices which the government appeared to be ready to encounter could only be justified by a distinct recognition of England's responsibility for Egypt, and those portions of the Soudan which were necessary to its security. An amendment was proposed by Mr. John Morley, but regretting its decision to continue the conflict with the Mahdi. Mr. Gladstone replied forcibly to both motion and amendment, and appealed to the Liberal party to sustain the administration and its policy by an unmistakable vote of confidence. The government was sustained.

The Great Powers of Europe, in convention for the settlement of the finances of Egypt, had concluded that it would require a loan of £9,000,000 to save Egypt from bankruptcy. This loan was to be issued on an international guarantee, with an international inquiry at the end of two years into the success of the scheme. This plan of adjustment was agreed to by the House. A short time after this settlement Mr. Gladstone announced a vote of credit to provide against any danger from Russian action, stated that no farther operations would be undertaken either on the Nile or near Suakin, and that General Graham's campaign would be abandoned, as well as the construction of the new railway.

Great excitement was created in England by the announcement of the advance of the Russians on the Indian frontier. March 13th Mr. Gladstone stated in the House that as the protests formerly made against the advance of Russia had been allowed to lapse, it had been agreed that pending the delineation of the frontier there should be no further advance on either side. In April, however, a conflict occurred between the Russians and the Afghans, which seemed to indicate that General Komaroff had committed an act of unprovoked aggression on the Ameer. Mr. Gladstone moved a vote of credit on the 27th in a speech, whose eloquence and energy greatly stirred both sides of the House. Happily, the difficulty with Russia was adjusted by conceding Pendjeh to Russia in consideration of the surrender of Zulfiker to the Ameer.

The administration of Mr. Gladstone, which had weathered through many storms, was destined to fall in a wholly unexpected way. When the budget for 1885 was produced there was a deficit of upwards of a million pounds, besides the depressed revenue and an estimated expenditure for the current year of not less than £100,000,000. Mr. Childers, the Chancellor of the Exchequer, proposed to make the taxation upon land proportionate to that on personal property, and to augment the duties on spirits and beer. But various interests were antagonized, and opposition was aroused. The country members demanded that no new taxes be put on the land until the promised relief of local taxation had been granted. The agricultural and liquor interests were discontented, as well as the Scotch and Irish members, with the whisky duty.

Concessions were made, but they failed to reconcile the opposition. A hostile motion was offered by Sir M. Hicks-Beach, and Mr. Gladstone declared that the Cabinet would resign if defeated. Many Liberals were absent when the vote was taken, regarding a majority for the Ministry as certain, but the amendment was carried June 9th by a vote of 264 to 252, and the Premier and his colleagues resigned. The Liberals were desirous of passing a vote of confidence in the administration, but Mr. Gladstone deprecated this, as he felt the situation to be intolerable, and was desirous of being relieved from the responsibility of office. Misfortunes, both in reference to affairs at home and abroad, had fallen heavily upon the Government, for many of which they were not responsible, and the Cabinet had been held together chiefly by the masterly personality of the Premier. Hence it was not without a feeling of personal satisfaction that Mr. Gladstone transferred the seats of office to his successor, Lord Salisbury. On his retirement from office the Queen offered an Earldom to Mr. Gladstone, which he declined. Its acceptance would have meant burial in the House of Lords, and an end to his progressive action.

The events that led to the third administration of Mr. Gladstone will next engage our attention.

The first general election under the New Reform Act was held in November, 1885. Mr. Gladstone again appealed to his constituents, and, although nearly seventy-six years of age, spoke with an energy and force far beyond all his contemporaries. His attitude on the question of Dis-establishment drew back many wavering Scotch votes. He discussed the Scotch question at Edinburgh, and said there was no fear of change so long as England dealt liberally, equitably, and prudently with Ireland, but demands must be subject to the condition that the unity of the empire, and all the powers of the Imperial Parliament for maintaining that authority, must be preserved.

In another address he stated his conviction, that the day had not come when the Dis-establishment of the Church in Scotland should be made a test question. The question pressing for settlement by the next Parliament was land reform, local government, parliamentary procedure, and the imperial relations between Ireland and England; and every sensible man would admit that it was right to direct attention to them rather than to a matter impossible of immediate solution.

At West Calder Mr. Gladstone made an address, in which he "approved Lord Salisbury's action with regard to Servia, complained of the ministerial condemnation of Lord Ripon's Indian administration, ridiculed the idea of benefit resulting from a Royal Commission on trade depression, warned the electors against remedies which were really worse than the disease, and defended Free-Trade principles. He furthur advocated comprehensive land reforms, including free transfer, facility of registration, and the uprooting of mortmain."

Mr. Gladstone was returned again for Midlothian by an overwhelming majority. The elections resulted in the return of 333 Liberals, 249 Conservatives, 86 Parnellites, and 2 Independents. The Liberals thus secured a substantial triumph. The agricultural districts were faithful to the Liberals, but they lost in the boroughs. The clergy and the publicans, and the Parnellites were found "arrayed" in "scandalous alliance" against the Liberal cause. The Liberal party was just short of the numbers required to defeat the combined forces of Tories and Parnellites. Lord Salisbury was retained in office, but the Conservatives were disunited, and the life of his administration hung by a thread. The Liberals were strong, hopeful, and united. In Mr. Chamberlain they had a popular champion of great ability and industry.

December 17, 1885 England was astonished by the appearance of an anonymous paragraph in the *Times*, affirming that, if Mr. Gladstone returned to power, he would deal with a liberal hand with the demands of Home Rule. The author of the paragraph has never been clearly ascertained, but the atmosphere of mystery with which it was surrounded was not regarded as becoming, either to such an important policy or to the personal dignity of the illustrious statesman. A storm of questions, contradictions, explanations, enthusiasms, and jeremiads followed its appearance. Mr. Gladstone would neither affirm nor deny, but held his peace. The question, he said, was one for a responsible Ministry alone to handle. There was great uncertainty. It was, however, plain that if Mr. Gladstone should favor Home Rule, the Parnellites would support him, and the Tories must leave office. But only twelve months before Lord Shaftesbury wrote: "In a year or so we shall have Home Rule disposed of (at all hazards), to save us from daily and hourly bores."

The Parliament of 1886 had scarcely opened before the Salisbury government was defeated upon an amendment to the Queen's address, affirming the necessity for affording facilities to agricultural laborers to obtain allotments and small holdings. Some of the leading Liberals opposed the amendment, but Mr. Gladstone earnestly favored it, as a recognition of the evils arising from the divorce of so large a proportion of the population from the land. The Irish and the Liberals coalesced, and the Government was placed in a minority of seventy-nine, and Lord Salisbury immediately resigned.

Late at night, January 29, 1886, Sir Henry Ponsonby arrived at Mr. Gladstone's residence with a summons from the Queen for him to repair to her at Osborne. On the 1st of February Mr. Gladstone "kissed hands," and became for the third time Prime Minister of England. The new Premier was forced to face unusual difficulties, but he finally came to the conclusion that it was impossible to deal with the Irish question upon the old stereotyped lines. He was resolved to treat this subject upon large and generous principles. Accordingly, on the 8th of April, Mr. Gladstone, in the presence of a crowded House, brought forward his Home Rule Bill—his bill for the government of Ireland. With certain imperial reservations and safeguards the bill gave to Ireland what she had long demanded—the right to make her own laws. The interest in the expected legislation was so great that members began to arrive at half-past five in the morning, while sixty of them were so eager to secure seats that they breakfasted at Westminster.

Mr. Gladstone's new measure was not only opposed by the Conservatives, but it alienated from the Premier some of the most influential of the Liberal party. Among the Liberals who opposed the measure were those who had been the colleagues of Mr. Gladstone only the June before in the Cabinet—Lord Hartington, Lord Shilborne, Lord Northbrook, Lord Derby and Lord Carlingford. Mr. Gladstone's forces, however, were reinforced by Mr. Morley, Lord Herschell and others. May 10th, Mr. Gladstone denied that he had ever declared Home Rule for Ireland incompatible with Imperial unity. It was a remedy for social disorder. The policy of the opposition was coercion, while that of the government was autonomy.

On the 18th of April the Premier presented the Irish Land Purchase Bill, for the buying out of the Irish landlords, which was intended to come into operation on the same day as the Home Rule Bill. The object of this measure was to give to all Irish landowners the option of being bought out on the terms of the Act, and opening towards the exercise of that option where their rent was from agricultural land. The State authority was to be the purchaser, and the occupier was to be the proprietor. The nominal purchase price was fixed at twenty years' purchase of the net rental, ascertained by deducting law charges, bad debts, and cost of management from judicial rent. Where there was no judicial rental the Land Court could, if it chose, make use of Griffiths' valuation for coming to a fair decision. To meet the demand for the means of purchase thus established, Mr. Gladstone proposed to create £50,000,000 three per cents. The repayment of advances would be secured by a Receiver General, appointed by and acting upon British authority.

The Land Purchase Bill was also opposed. It was the final cause which led to the retirement from the government of Mr. Chamberlain, "the able and enterprising exponent of the new Radicalism." He was soon followed by Sir George Trevelyan, "who combined the most dignified traditions, social and literary, of the Whig party with a fervent and stable Liberalism which the vicissitudes of twenty years had constantly tried and never found wanting." Mr. Bright also arrayed himself in opposition to the government, and accused Mr. Gladstone of successfully concealing his thoughts upon the Irish question in November. Mr. Gladstone replied that the position of Ireland had changed since 1881.

The debate extended over many nights, and the opposition to the Irish bills of so many Liberal leaders in every constituency, soon led to disaffection among the people. What was lost in some districts, however, was to some extent made up, says an English writer, by "the support of that very broken reed, the Irish vote, which was destined to pierce the hand of so many a confiding candidate who leaned upon it." While this debate was in progress a bill directed against the carrying of arms in Ireland was introduced and pushed forward rapidly through both Houses, and became a law.

Mr. Gladstone explained the position of the Cabinet on the Home Rule and Land Bills at a meeting of Liberals held at the Foreign Office, May 27th. He stated that the Government at present only asked for an endorsement of the leading principles of the two measures; and in closing the debate afterwards on the second reading of the Home Rule Bill, in the House of Commons, he made an eloquent appeal for Ireland. But all parties were preparing for the conflict, and members of opposite parties were consolidating themselves for opposition. "The Whigs, under Lord Hartington, coalesced with the Radicals, under Mr. Chamberlain, and both together made a working alliance with the Tories. This alliance was admirably organized in London and in the constituencies."

It seems that the Premier was deceived by his official counsellors of the Liberal party as to the real condition of affairs respecting Home Rule and the prospects for the passage of his bills. He did not dream of defeat, but if by some mischance they would suffer defeat, then he could appeal to the country with the certainty of being sustained by the popular vote. This was what Mr. Gladstone hoped, and what he thought he had the assurance of. But hopes of success began to give way to fears of defeat as the time drew near to take the vote. However, some still hopeful prophesied a small majority against the bill—only ten votes at the most. The Cabinet desperately resolved not to resign if beaten by so small a majority, but would have some adherent move a vote of confidence. This they argued would be favored by some opposed to Home Rule, and the question be deferred to another session, leaving the Liberals still in office. But these hopes were doomed to be blasted. Early in the morning of June 8th the momentous division took place, and it was found that the Government, instead of getting a majority, was defeated by thirty votes. It was found that ninety-three Liberals had voted with the majority.

The Premier at once advised the Queen to dissolve Parliament, and though Her Majesty at first demurred at the trouble of another election within seven months of the last, and begged Mr. Gladstone to reconsider his counsel, yet he argued that a general election would cause less trouble than a year of embittered and fanatical agitation against Home Rule. Besides, as he said to a colleague, "If we did not dissolve we would be showing the white feather." Mr. Gladstone finally had his way, the Queen yielded and Parliament was dissolved June 26, 1886. June 14th Mr. Gladstone issued an address to the electors of Midlothian, and later paid a visit to Edinburgh and Glasgow, where he made powerful addresses. He then spoke at Manchester, and, passing on to Liverpool, he advocated the cause of Ireland, calling upon the people to "ring out the old, ring in the new," and to make Ireland not an enemy but a friend.

The result of this appeal to the country was the return of a decided majority of over a hundred against Home Rule, and thus, after a short term of five months in office, the third administration of Mr. Gladstone was brought to a close, and he became again the leader of the Opposition. The dissolution and appeal to the country was a practical blunder, but Mr.

Gladstone's address to the people was skilfully worded. He freely admitted that the Irish bills were dead, and asked the constituencies simply to sanction a principle, and that, too, a very plain and reasonable one in itself. He invited the people to vote aye or no to this question: "Whether you will or will not have regard to the prayer of Ireland for the management by herself of the affairs specifically and exclusively her own?" The separation of the bare principle of self-government from the practical difficulties presented by the bills enabled many Liberals who were opposed to the measures to support Mr. Gladstone, but the majority of voters failed to make this distinction, and hence came defeat. The decision of the people was not regarded as final.

In 1887 the Jubilee of the Queen was celebrated. Fifty years before Queen Victoria had ascended the throne of England. Mr. and Mrs. Gladstone celebrated the Queen's Jubilee by giving a treat to all the inhabitants of the estates of Hawarden, who were of the Queen's age, which was sixty-eight and upwards. The treat took the shape of a dinner and tea, served in a large tent erected in front of the castle, and the guests numbered upwards of two hundred and fifty. The principal toast, proposed by Mr. Gladstone, was the Queen. He contrasted the jubilee then being celebrated all over the English-speaking world, with that of George the Third, which was "a jubilee of the great folks, a jubilee of corporations and of authorities, a jubilee of the upper classes." On the other hand, he continued, the Victorian Jubilee was one when "the population are better fed, better clothed, and better housed— and by a great deal—than they were fifty years ago, and the great mass of these happy and blessed changes is associated with the name and action of the Queen."

In the year of the Queen's Jubilee, 1887, Mr. Gladstone addressed many gatherings, and at Swansea, where he was the guest of Sir Hussey Vivian, he spoke to a vast concourse of people, estimated at one hundred thousand.

CHAPTER XIX

PRIME MINISTER THE FOURTH TIME

When Parliament met in 1887 Mr. Gladstone entered upon "a course of extraordinary physical and intellectual efforts, with voice and pen, in Parliament and on the platform, on behalf of the cause, defeated but not abandoned, of self-government for Ireland." The Tory administration passed a Crimes Prevention Bill for Ireland of great severity. Irish members of Parliament were thrown into prison, but the Act failed of its object—the suppression of the Land League.

In December, 1887, Mr. Gladstone visited Italy and made Naples his headquarters. He was received with joy for the service he had rendered to the Italian people. The University of Bologna, in celebrating the eighth century of its existence, conferred upon him the degree of Doctor of Arts.

In 1888 the House of Commons appointed a Commission to try the "Times" charges against Mr. Parnell. The charges were found to be false.

Mr. Gladstone visited Birmingham in November, 1888. After paying a glowing tribute to John Bright, and expressing an earnest desire for his recovery to health, he condemned the Coercion Act. Mr. Gladstone received many handsome presents from the workingmen, and Mrs. Gladstone received from the ladies a medallion cameo portrait of her husband. A great demonstration was made at Bingley Hall, in which were gathered over 20,000 persons.

A number of Liberals, who had deserted Mr. Gladstone, returned upon the promise of certain imperial guarantees which were granted, among them Sir George Trevelyan. Mr. Chamberlain, who had asked for these safeguards, did not accept them.

July 25, 1889, Mr. and Mrs. Gladstone celebrated their "Golden Wedding." Among the many to offer congratulations were the Queen by telegram, and the Prince of Wales by letter. A pleasant surprise met them at home. A portrait of Mr. Gladstone, by Sir John Millais, was found hanging in the breakfast-room, "A gift from English, Scottish, Welsh and Irish Women."

In 1890 trouble came to the Liberal party through the scandal connecting the names of Mr. Parnell and Mrs. O'Shea. Mr. Gladstone announced that the Irish party must choose between himself and Mr. Parnell. In November, 1890, Mr. Parnell was deposed from the chairmanship of the United Irish National Party. This led to a division. Mr. Justin McCarthy was elected leader by the Anti-Parnellites, and the Parnellites selected Mr. John Redmond.

Parliament would soon terminate by limitation, so Mr. Gladstone devoted himself to preparing the people for the coming general election. Besides, in February, 1891, he made an address, at the opening of St. Martin's Free Public Library, and in March to the boys at Eton College on Homeric Studies. June 28, 1892, Parliament came to an end. Mr. Gladstone's journey to Edinburgh, in July, was all along the route "a triumphal progress." He was re-elected. The question of the day was Home Rule, and wherever the people had the opportunity of declaring themselves, they pronounced condemnation upon the policy of Lord Salisbury's administration, and in favor of Home Rule for Ireland.

The new Parliament met, and, August 12, 1892, a motion was

made of "No Confidence" in the Salisbury government. The division was the largest ever taken in the House of Commons, the vote being 350 for the motion and 310 against it—a majority of 40 for Mr. Gladstone. The scene in the House which attended the overthrow of the Salisbury government was less dramatic than that which accompanied the defeat of the Gladstone ministry in 1885, but it was full of exciting episodes. The House was packed to the doors. The excitement was intense, and the confusion great. When the figures were announced, another wild scene of disorder prevailed and there was prolonged cheering. "Ten minutes later the great forum was empty and the excited assembly had found its way to the quiet outside under the stars."

Monday, August 15, 1892, Mr. Gladstone repaired to Osborne on the Royal Yacht, and became for the fourth time Prime Minister. Since 1868 he had been the undisputed leader of his party. His main supporters in all his reform measures were the Nonconformists, whose claim for "the absolute religious equality of all denominations before the law of the land," must, in time, it was thought, bring about the disestablishment of the Episcopal Church.

In September, 1892, Mr. Gladstone went to Sir E. Watkin's *Chalet* on Mount Snowdon, Wales, where he made his Boulder Stone speech. To commemorate his visit a slab of gray Aberdeen granite was "let into the actual brown rock," on which is the following inscription in Welsh and in English: "September 13, 1892. Upon this rock the Right Honorable W.E. Gladstone, M.P., when Prime Minister for the fourth time, and eighty-three years old, addressed the people of Eryi upon justice to Wales. The multitude sang Cymric hymns and 'The Land of My Fathers.'"

December 29, 1892, Mr. Gladstone celebrated his eighty-third birthday. Mr. and Mrs. Gladstone were at Biarritz. Congratulatory telegrams and messages were received in great numbers, besides many handsome presents. The event was celebrated all over England. The Midlothian Liberals sent congratulations upon the return of the Liberal Party to power under his leadership, and the completion of his sixty years' service in the House. Resolutions were passed deploring the wickedness of the dynamite outrage at Dublin, December 24, and yet avowing the justice of granting to Ireland the right to manage her own affairs.

January 31, 1893, Parliament was opened. In the House of Commons there was a brilliant gathering, and nearly all the members were present, many of them standing. Just before noon the Hon. Arthur Wellesley Peel, Speaker, took his seat, and Archdeacon Farrar, Chaplain, offered prayer. When Mr. Gladstone entered from behind the Speaker's chair, every Liberal and Irish Nationalist stood up and greeted him with prolonged and enthusiastic cheers; and when he took the oath as Prime Minister, he received another ovation. The members were then summoned to the House of Lords to hear the Queen's speech, which was read by the Lord High Chancellor, Baron Herschall. The Prince of Wales and his son, the Duke of York, occupied seats on the "cross bench."

February 13, the excitement in and about the Parliament Houses was as great as that which prevailed two weeks before. Enthusiastic crowds greeted Mr. and Mrs. Gladstone. When the doors of the House of Commons were opened, there was a "disorderly rush" of the members into the House to obtain seats, "the members shouting and struggling, several being thrown to the floor in the excitement." Peers, Commons, and visitors filled the floor and galleries. The Prince of Wales and other members of the royal family were present. When Mr. Gladstone arose he was greeted with applause. He reminded the House that for seven years the voices which used to plead the cause of Irish government in Irish affairs had been mute within the walls of the House. He then asked permission to introduce a "Bill to Amend the Provision for the Government of Ireland," which was the title of the Home Rule Bill. Mr. Balfour led the opposition to the bill. Mr. Chamberlain declared that the bill would not accomplish its purpose, whereupon Mr. Justin McCarthy, for the anti-Parnellities, replied that the Irish would accept it as a message of everlasting peace, and Mr. John Redmond, for the Parnellites, answered that if disturbances followed in Ireland it would be due to the Conservatives.

The Ulster Unionists opposed the bill. The Scotch-Irish Protestants of the north of Ireland declared that they preferred to stand where they did in 1690, when they defeated James II and his Catholic followers, in the battle of the Boyne, and fought for William of Orange for the English throne and liberty and Protestantism. Their opposition to Home Rule for Ireland grew out of their hostility to Roman Catholicism and the fear of its supremacy.

After six months of earnest debate in the House of Commons, the Home Rule Bill for Ireland was passed, with slight amendments, September 1, 1893, by a vote of 301 to 267, a majority of thirty-four, The struggle was perhaps the most heated in the history of Parliament.

The bill was sent to the House of Lords, where it was defeated, midnight, September 8, by the surprising majority of 419 to 41, after only one week's discussion. Members that never attended were drummed up to vote against the bill. The usual working force of the House of Lords is from thirty to forty members. The vote was the largest ever taken in the Lords.

At once the cry, "Down with, the House of Lords!" was heard. The National Liberal Federation issued a circular, in which were the words: "The question of mending or ending the House of Lords ... displaces for awhile all other subjects of reform." Mr. Gladstone was probably aware of the contents of this manifesto before it was issued, and the sentiments were in accord with those uttered by him two years before at New Castle.

September 27th, Mr. Gladstone addressed his constituents at Edinburgh. He was received with an outburst of enthusiasm. He said that the People's Chamber had passed the bill. If the nation was determined it would not be baffled by the Peers. If the Commons should go before the country, then the Lords should go too, and if defeated, should do what the Commons would do—clear out.

The Queen wanted Mr. Gladstone to appeal to the country, and there was an opinion among some that Mr. Gladstone would be defeated at the polls upon the question; but the Premier intimated to the Queen his intention not to appeal, and announced the readiness of the Cabinet to be dismissed by the Queen. However, the Queen would hardly expose the throne to the danger threatening the Peers.

December 29, 1893, Mr. Gladstone attained the eighty-fourth year of his age. When he entered the House of Commons that day his political associates of the Liberal party all rose anta greeted him with cheers. When the applause had subsided, the Conservatives raised their hats and their leader, Mr. Balfour, rose and tendered his congratulations. Mr. Gladstone was much pleased with the demonstrations of his friends, as well as with the graceful compliments of his political opponents. Besides about two hundred congratulatory messages, letters and telegrams were received, those from Queen Victoria, and the Prince and Princess of Wales, being among the first.

July 6, 1893, Prince George of Wales, Duke of York, and Princess Mary of Teck were married. The Prince was by inheritance heir, after the Prince of Wales, to the throne of England. Mr. Gladstone attended the wedding, arrayed in the blue and gold uniform of a brother of the Trinity House, with naval epaulettes, and was conducted to the royal pew reserved for him.

Among the great measures proposed at this time by Mr. Gladstone were the Employers' Liability, and the Parish Councils Bills. The latter was as evolutionary and as revolutionary as the Home Rule Bill. Its object was to take the control of 10,000 rural English parishes out of the hands of the squire and the parson and put it into the hands of the people. With its amendments regarding woman suffrage, to which Mr. Gladstone was opposed, it gave to every man and woman in England one vote—and only one—in local affairs. February 21, 1894, when Mr. Gladstone had returned from Biarritz, where he had gone for his health, there was again a notable assemblage in the House of Commons to hear him speak. It was expected that he would make a bitter attack upon the House of Lords, which had attempted to defeat both these bills by amendments. But he calmly spoke of the lamentable divergence between the two branches of the legislature upon the Employers' Liability Bill, and asked that the amendment be rejected, which was done by a majority of 225 to 6. The bill was therefore withdrawn, and the responsibility of its defeat thrown upon the Lords. The House also rejected all the important amendments of the Parish Councils Bill, but concurred in the unimportant changes made by the Lords. It was sent back then to the lords, and finally passed by them. But Mr. Gladstone greatly disappointed many of his political friends by his mild manner of dealing with the House of Lords. The extreme Radicals were angered and condemned severely the Premier for what they called his "backing down" and his "feeble speech."

Rumors in reference to Mr. Gladstone's resignation, which had been started by the *Pall Mall Gazette*, while he was yet at Biarritz, were now renewed. February 28, 1894, Mr. Gladstone informed the Queen of his contemplated retirement, giving as reasons his failing eyesight, deafness and age. March 1st, he made an important speech in the House of Commons. He displayed so much vigor and earnestness in his speech that it was thought that he had given up the idea of retiring. But this was his last speech as Premier. March 2d, Mr. and Mrs. Gladstone were summoned to Windsor, where they dined with the Queen, and remained over night. Saturday, March 3, 1894, Mr. Gladstone tendered his resignation as Premier to the Queen, who accepted it with many expressions of favor and regret, and offered him again a peerage, which was declined. On the way to Windsor and return to London, Mr. Gladstone was greeted by a large and enthusiastic crowd.

Hundreds of letters and telegrams expressing regret, because of his retirement, were received by the ex-Premier, On Sunday he attended church as usual and was looking well, Mr. Balfour in the Commons, and Lord Salisbury in the Lords, vied with Mr. Gladstone's political friends in speaking his praise, and referring in the highest terms to his character and labors. The press in all parts of the world spoke in glowing terms of his natural endowments, great attainments, invaluable services, pure character and wonderfully vigorous old age. It was quite evident that Mr. Gladstone's retirement was not enforced by mental or physical infirmities, or by his unfitness for the leadership of the House and the Premiership, but that as a wise precaution, and upon the solicitation of his family, he had laid down his power while he was yet able to wield it with astonishing vigor. Thus closed the fourth administration of this remarkable man, the greatest English statesman of his time. In all history there is no parallel case, and no official record such as his.

Lord Rosebery was appointed Premier in the place of Mr. Gladstone, and Sir William V. Harcourt became the leader of the Liberal party in the House of Commons. Mr. Gladstone wrote congratulating Lord Rosebery, and promised to aid him whenever his assistance was required. In assuming office Lord Rosebery eulogized Mr. Gladstone, and announced that there would be no change in the policy of reform of the Liberal party under the new administration, and declared for Home Rule for Ireland, the disestablishment of the church in Wales and Scotland, and the reform of the House of Lords.

CHAPTER XX

IN PRIVATE LIFE

Justin McCarthy, in the closing pages of his Story of Gladstone's Life, says: "The long political struggle was over and done. The heat of the opposition this way and that had gone out forever, and Mr. Gladstone had none left but friends on both sides of the political field. Probably that ceremonial, that installation of the Prince of Wales as Chancellor of the Welsh University, was the last occasion on which Mr. Gladstone would consent to make an appearance on a public platform. It was a graceful close to such a great career."

The occasion referred to was the ceremonial at Aberystwith, Wales, June 26, 1896, when the Prince of Wales was installed as Chancellor of the Welsh University, and when the Prince presented to the Princess of Wales and to Mr. Gladstone honorary degrees conferred upon them by the University. The appearance of Mr. Gladstone was the signal for great applause. The Prince in his remarks was very complimentary to Mr. Gladstone, and spoke of the honor paid the University by the presence of the aged scholar and statesman, and also said it was truly one of the proudest moments of his life, when he found himself in the flattering position of being able to confer an academic honor upon one furnishing the rare instance of occupying the highest position as a statesman and who at the same time had attained such distinction in scholarship.

But Mr. McCarthy was mistaken about this being the closing

public service in the life of Mr. Gladstone. It was very far from his last public appearance. After that event Mr. Gladstone appeared repeatedly. Though his official life had closed, yet he was to emerge from retirement many times, and especially when it became necessary for him to raise his strong voice for humanity. His advocacy of the great causes of Armenian rescue, of Grecian independence, of Arbitration instead of War, and the unity and harmony of the two great English-speaking people, was given with all the old time fire of youth. What Mr. Gladstone did and said with pen and voice since the occasion mentioned, was enough not only for another chapter, but a whole volume, and sufficient alone to immortalize any man.

After the great struggle for Home Rule and during the sultry summer of 1893, Mr. Gladstone repaired to his favorite winter resort, Biarritz, in the south of France, It was while he was there that rumors of his resignation were heard, based on the ground of his failing health. Dr. Granger, of Chester, who was also an oculist, was summoned to examine Mr. Gladstone's eyes. He told Mr. Gladstone that a cataract had obliterated the sight of one eye, and that another cataract had begun to form on the other. In other words Mr. Gladstone was threatened with total blindness. The Prime Minister reflected a moment, and then requested—almost ordered—the physician to operate immediately upon his eye. He said: "I wish you to remove the cataract at once." The physician replied that it was not far enough advanced for an operation. "You do not understand me," answered the patient, "it is the old cataract I wish removed. If that is out of the way, I shall still have one good eye, when the new cataract impairs the sight of the other." As the physician still hesitated, Mr. Gladstone continued: "You still seem not to understand me. I want you to perform the operation here and now while I am sitting in this chair." "But it might not be successful," said Dr. Granger. "That is a risk I accept," was the instant reply. However, the physician dared not then undertake it, and afterwards said that Mr. Gladstone's eyes were as good as they were a year before, and that his general health was also good.

In May, 1894, Mr. Gladstone's eye was successfully operated upon for cataract. He took no anaesthetic, and was conscious during the time. Every precaution was taken to insure success, and the patient was put to bed for rest and quiet and kept on low diet. Mr. Gladstone's eyes were so improved by judicious treatment that before long he could read ten or twelve hours a day. This could be regarded as complete restoration of sight, and enabled him, upon his retirement from public life, to devote himself to the work he so well loved when at home in his study at Hawarden.

Mr. Gladstone's retirement from public life, from the Premiership, the Cabinet, the leadership of the Liberal Party, and from Parliament did not mean his entrance upon a period of inactivity. In the shades of Hawarden and in the quiet of his study he kept up the industry that had characterized his whole life heretofore.

It had been the custom for centuries for English statesmen, upon retiring from official life, to devote themselves to the classics. Mr. Gladstone, who was pre-eminently a statesman-scholar, found it very congenial to his mind and habits to follow this old English custom. He first translated and published "The Odes of Horace." Then he took Butler's "Analogy" as a text book, and prepared and published "Studies Subsidiary to the Works of Bishop Butler." The discussion necessarily takes a wide range, treating, among other matters, of Butler's method, its application to the Scriptures, the future life, miracles and the mediation of Christ. Says W.T. Stead: "No one who reads the strenuous arguments with which Mr. Gladstone summarizes the reasoning of Bishop Butler on the future life is conscious of any weakening in the vigorous dialectic which was so often employed with brilliant success in the House of Commons."

One of Mr. Gladstone's latest productions was his "Personal Recollections of Arthur H. Hallam," which was written for the "Youth's Companion." It is a tribute to the memory and worth of one of his early friends at Eton.

These and other literary works occupied most of his time. But Mr. Gladstone would not content himself with quiet literary work. He had too long and too intensely been active in the world's great movements and on humanity's behalf to stand aloof. Hence it was not long before he was again in the arena, doing valiant service for the Armenian and against the Turk.

In 1892 the Sultan, in the execution of a plan devised in 1890, issued an edict against religious freedom. In 1894, he threw off the mask and began to execute his deliberate and preconcerted plan to force all Christian Armenians to become Mohammedans or to die. Robbery, outrage and murder were the means used by the hands of brutal soldiers.

In a letter to an indignation meeting held in London, December 17th, 1894, Mr. Gladstone wrote denouncing these outrages of the Turks. The reading of the letter was greeted with prolonged applause.

A deputation of Armenian gentlemen, residing in London and in Paris, took occasion on Mr. Gladstone's 85th birthday, December 29th, 1894, to present a silver chalice to Hawarden Church as "a memorial of Mr. Gladstone's sympathy with and assistance to the Armenian people." Mr. Gladstone's address to the deputation was regarded as one of the most peculiar and characteristic acts of his life. He gave himself wholly to the cause of these oppressed people, and was stirred by the outrages and murders perpetrated upon them as he was 18 years before. He said that the Turks should go out as they did go out of Bulgaria "bag and baggage," and he denounced the government of the Sultan as "a disgrace to Mahomet, the prophet whom it professed to follow, a disgrace to civilization at large, and a curse to mankind." He contended that every nation had ever the right and the authority to act "on behalf of humanity and of justice."

There were those who condemned Mr. Gladstone's speech, declaring that it might disrupt the peace of Europe, but there were many others who thought that the sooner peace secured at such a cost was disturbed the better. It was but natural for those who wrongfully claimed the sovereign right to oppress their own subjects, to denounce all interference in the affairs of the Sultan.

It was reported, March 19, 1895, that Francis Seymour Stevenson, M.P., Chairman of the Anglo-Armenian Association, on behalf of the Tiflis Armenians, would present to Mr. Gladstone, on his return to London, the ancient copy of the Armenian Gospels, inscribed upon vellum, which was to accompany the address to the ex-Premier, then being signed by the Armenians there. In a letter Mr. Gladstone had but recently declared that he had abandoned all hope that the condition of affairs in Armenia would change for the better. The Sultan, he declared, was no longer worthy of the courtesies of diplomatic usage, or of Christian tolerance. Mr. Gladstone promised that when these Gospels were formally presented to him he would deliver a "rattling" address on behalf of the Armenians. When a delegation waited on him, he said, after assuring them of his sympathy, that the danger in the Armenian situation now was that useful action might be abandoned, in view of the promises of the Turkish Government to institute reforms.

In June 1895, Mr. and Mrs. Gladstone attended the opening of the Kaiser Wilhelm Canal as guests of Sir Donald Currie, on his steamship Tantallon Castle, returning home on the twenty-fifth. During this trip an effort was made to arrange for an interview between the Ex-Premier and the Prince Bismarck, but the Prince seemed disinclined and the project failed.

It was while Mr. Gladstone was at Kiel, that the Rosebery Ministry fell by an accidental defeat of the Liberal Party in Parliament, and which again brought Mr. Gladstone to the front in the public mind. Lord Rosebery telegraphed Mr. Gladstone full particulars of the situation, and Mr. Gladstone strongly advised against the resignation of the Government and urged that a vote of confidence be taken. Mr. Gladstone wrote that the Liberal Party could well afford to stand on its record. The Ministry with but two exceptions, was the same, as that formed by Mr. Gladstone in August 1892, and had his confidence.

Nevertheless, the cabinet of Lord Rosebery resigned, and the Marquis of Salisbury again became Prime Minister,—on the very day of Mr. Gladstone's arrival home. However Lord Rosebery retained the leadership of the Liberal Party.

There is no doubt that if the wishes of the Liberal Party had been gratified, Mr. Gladstone would have taken the leadership and again become Prime Minister. Subsequent events proved that he would have been equal, at least for a while, to the task of succeeding Lord Rosebery. But Mr. Gladstone was not willing. He refused to re-enter Parliament, and wrote a letter to his old constituents at Midlothian, declining their kind offer to send him to the House and bade them a kind farewell. In his letter he said that the Liberal Party is a party of progress and reform, and urged his constituents to stand by it. He regarded the changes of the century exceedingly beneficial.

August 6, 1895, Mr. Gladstone made a great speech at Chester. A meeting was held in the Town Hall to arouse public sentiment against the slaughter of Armenian Christians within the Empire of the Sultan by Turkish soldiers, and to devise some means of putting an end to such crimes, and of punishing the oppressor. The audience was very large, including many Armenians resident in England, and rose with vociferous cheering when Mr. and Mrs. Gladstone, the Duke of Westminster, the Bishop of Chester, and the Mayor of Chester entered the hall. The Bishop of Ripon was already there. The Duke of Westminster presided, and read a letter from the Marquis of Salisbury, the Premier.

Mr. Gladstone arose amid an outburst of enthusiastic applause, and addressing the vast audience said:

That the massacres in Armenia resulted from intolerable government—perhaps the worst in the world. He offered a resolution pledging the support of the entire nation to the British Government in its efforts to secure for the Armenians such reforms as would guarantee the safety of life, honor, religion and property. Mr. Gladstone said that language failed to describe the horrors of the massacre of Sussoun, which made the blood run cold. The Sultan was responsible, for these barbarities were not the act of the criminal class, such as afflicts every country, the malefactors who usually perpetrate horrible crime, but were perpetrated by the agents of the Sultan—the soldiers and the Kurds, tax-gatherers and police of the Turkish Government. And what had been done, and was daily being done, could be summed up in four awful words—plunder, murder, rape and torture. Plunder and murder were bad enough, but these were almost venial by the side of the work of the ravisher and the torturer. And the victims were defenceless men, women and children—Armenians, one of the oldest Christian civilized races, and one of the most pacific, industrious and intelligent races of the world.

There was no exaggeration in the language used to describe the horrible outrages visited upon whole communities of innocent and helpless people. The truth of these terrible charges in their most hideous form, was established by unbiased American testimony, by Dr, Dillon, an eye witness, and by the representatives of England, France and Russia.

Nothing but a sense of duty, said Mr. Gladstone, had brought him at his age to resign the repose, which was the last of many great earthly blessings remaining to him, to address them.

If the Powers of Europe were to recede before the irrational resistance of the Sultan, they would be disgraced in the eyes of the world, and the Christian population of the Turkish Empire would be doomed to extermination, according to the plan of the Porte. Terrible word, but true in its application.

As to the remedy the cleanest was to make the Turk march out of Armenia, as he did out of Bulgaria, "bag and baggage." He cautioned against trusting the promises of the government at

Constantinople, which he knew from long experience, were worthless; and declared that the Sultan was bound by no treaty obligation. The word "ought" was not heeded at Constantinople, but the word "must" was understood fully there. Coercion was a word perfectly comprehended there—a drastic dose which never failed. If we have the smallest regard for humanity, he concluded, we shall, with the help of God, demand that which is just and necessary. Mr. Gladstone was frequently and loudly applauded during his speech, at the conclusion of which the resolution was adopted.

The most powerful voice in all Britain had been raised with stirring and thrilling power for justice and humanity. The testimony of an eye witness is to the effect, that never did the grand old man seem in finer form. His undimmed eye flashed as he spoke with withering scorn against hypocrisy and with hottest hate against wrong. His natural force was not abated, his health robust, and his conviction unsubdued. His deeply lined and pale face was transfigured with the glow of righteous indignation. The aged statesman was in his old House of Commons vigor. "There was the same facile movement of his body, and the same penetrating look as though he would pierce the very soul of his auditors; the same triumphant march of sentence after sentence to their chosen goal, and yet the same subtle method of introducing qualifying clauses all along the march without loosing the grip of his theme; the same ascent to lofty principles and commanding generalizations, blended with the complete mastery of details; and, above all, the same sublimity of outlook and ringing emphasis of sincerity in every tone." It was an occasion never to be forgotten. A distinguished hearer said: "To read his speech, as thousands will, is much; but to have heard it, to have felt it-oh! that is simply indescribable, and will mark for many, one of the most memorable days of this last decade of this closing century. The sweet cadence of his voice, the fascination of his personality, and, above all, the consecration of his splendid gifts to the cause of plundered men and ravished women, raise the occasion into prominence in the annals of a great people. Chiefly, I feel the triumphs of soul. His utterance of the words 'wives,' 'women,' lifted them into an atmosphere of awe and solemnity, and his tone in speaking of 'rape' and 'torture' gave them an ineffable loathsomeness. It seemed as if so much soul had never been put into a Saxon speech. Keen satire, rasping rebuke, an avalanche of indignation, rapier-like thrusts to the vital fibre of the situation, and withal the invincible cogency of argument against the Turkish Government, gave the oration a primary place amongst the master-pieces of human eloquence."

In the course of this famous speech Mr. Gladstone referred to America; once when welcoming the sympathy of the American people with the suffering Armenians, and again as he described the testimony of the United States as a witness that gained enormously in value because it was entirely free from suspicion.

A large meeting was held in St. James Hall, London, October 19, 1896, in memory of Christian Martyrs in Turkey. The Bishop of Rochester presided. The hall was packed with an audience of 2,600, while nearly 7,000 applied for admission. Many prominent persons were present. The large audience was in sombre funeral attire. About thirty front seats were occupied by Armenians. It was stated that 60,000 Armenians so far had been murdered with tortures and indignities indescribable. To this meeting Mr. Gladstone addressed a letter which was greeted with the wildest enthusiasm. He said that he hoped the meeting would worthily crown the Armenian meetings of the past two months, which were without a parallel during his political life. The great object, he said, was to strengthen Lord Salisbury's hands and to stop the series of massacres, which were probably still unfinished, and to provide against their renewal. As he believed that Lord Salisbury would use his powerful position for the best, personally he objected in the strongest manner to abridging Lord Salisbury's discretion by laying down this or that as things which he ought not to do. It was a wild paradox, without the support of reason or history, to say that the enforcement of treaty rights to stop systematic massacre, together with effective security against Great

Britain's abusing them for selfish ends, would provoke the hostilities of one or more of the powers.

To advertise beforehand in the ears of the Great Assassin that Great Britain's action would cut down—what the most backward of the six Powers think to be sufficient—would be the; abandonment of duty and prudence and would be to doom the national movement to disappointment. The concert of Europe was valuable and important, but such an announcement would be certain to be followed by its failure.

One of the immediate effects of Mr. Gladstone's denunciation of the Sultan for the Armenian massacres was the resignation by Lord Rosebery of the leadership of the Liberal Party. Mr. Gladstone's return to politics, the agitation of the Turkish question and the differences between these two leaders of the Liberal movement as to the best way of dealing with the Sultan, were assigned as reasons by Lord Rosebery for his resignation.

It was then again suggested that Mr. Gladstone assume the leadership of the Liberal Party and accept a peerage and a seat in the House of Lords, so often tendered him by the Queen. Then Sir William Vernon-Harcourt could lead in the House of Commons and bear the burden, while Mr. Gladstone could be at the head of affairs without the worry of the House of Commons. Besides, Mr. Morgan offered to resign his seat in the House of Commons in his favor. But Mr. Gladstone would not agree to any of these plans as far as they pertained to himself.

July 22, 1896, Mr. and Mrs. Gladstone returned to London to attend a great social function, the marriage of one of the daughters of the Prince and Princess of Wales to Prince Charles of Denmark. Mr. Gladstone evinced much interest in everything connected with the important event, and was himself the object of much attention.

September 23, 1896, Mr. Gladstone wrote a long letter to the

Paris Figaro in response to an appeal from its editor, M. Leudet, to Mr. Gladstone to arouse the French press in behalf of the Armenians. After expressing his diffidence in complying with the request, Mr. Gladstone declared his belief that the population of Great Britain were more united in sentiment and more thoroughly aroused by the present outrages in Turkey than they were by the atrocities in Bulgaria in 1876.

He said: "The question whether effect can be given to the national indignation is now in the balance, and will probably soon be decided. I have read in some Austrian newspapers an affected scruple against sole action by any one State in a European crisis, but there are two first-class Powers who will not make that scruple their own. One of these is Russia, who in 1878, earned lasting honors by liberating Bulgaria and, helping onward the freedom and security of other Balkan States. The other Power is France, who, in 1840, took up the cause of Egypt and pushed it single handed to the verge of a European war. She wisely forbore to bring about that horrible, transcendent calamity, but I gravely doubt whether she was not right and the combined Powers wrong in their policy of that period."

Mr. Gladstone denounced the Sultan as the "Great Assassin," and continued: "For more than a year he has triumphed over the diplomacy of the six Powers, they have been laid prostrate at his feet. There is no parallel in history to the humiliation they have patiently borne. He has therefore had every encouragement to continue a course that has been crowned with such success. The impending question seems to be, not whether, but when and where he will proceed to his next murderous exploits. The question for Europe and each Power is whether he shall be permitted to swell by more myriads the tremendous total of his victims.

"In other years when I possessed power I did my best to promote the concert of Europe, but I sorrowfully admit that all the good done in Turkey during the last twenty years was done, not by it, but more nearly despite it." The letter

Richard B. Cook

concludes by expressing the hope that the French people would pursue a policy worthy of their greatness, their fame and the high place they have held in European Christian history.

September 24, 1896, a meeting was called by the Reform Club, of Liverpool, to protest against the recent massacres of 2000 Armenians at Constantinople at the affair of the Ottoman Bank, and many more throughout the Turkish Empire. Mr. Gladstone was asked to address the meeting. When requested by the agent of the Associated Press for an advanced proof of his speech he declined, but wrote that he would "recommend giving the warmest support to the Queen's government, and would contend that England should act alone if necessary for the fulfillment of the covenants which have been so disgracefully broken."

Mr. and Mrs. Gladstone, with their son Herbert, arrived at noon at Liverpool, and were met at the railroad station by 2,000 enthusiastic people. The meeting was held in the vast auditorium of the Circus Building, which was filled. Thousands failed to obtain entrance.

Before the arrival of Mr. Gladstone there was a spontaneous outburst of applause, everybody present standing and singing "God save the Queen." When Mr. Gladstone entered, the prolonged roar of applause could be heard for miles, arising from thousands inside and outside the hall.

The Earl of Derby, Conservative, presided. He was accompanied by the Countess of Derby, who with many distinguished persons occupied the platform.

Mr. Gladstone stepped briskly to the front of the platform at 12.30 p.m. bowing repeatedly in response to the applause. He looked strong and well for a man of his age and labors, and was easily heard. After a few preliminary remarks, he moved the following resolution:

"That this meeting trusts that Her Majesty's ministers,

realizing to the fullest extent the terrible condition in which their fellow Christians are placed, will do everything possible to obtain for them full security and protection; and this meeting assures Her Majesty's ministers that they may rely upon the cordial support of the citizens of Liverpool in whatever steps they may feel it necessary to take for that purpose."

The resolution was received with great cheering.

Mr. Gladstone resumed: "We have a just title to threaten Turkey with coercion, but that does not in itself mean war; and I think that the first step should be the recall of our Ambassador, and it should be followed by the dismissal of the Turkish Ambassador from London. Such a course is frequent and would not give the right of complaint to anybody. When diplomatic relations are suspended, England should inform the Sultan that she should consider the means of enforcing her just and humane demands. I do not believe that Europe will make war to insure the continuance of massacres more terrible than ever recorded in the dismal, deplorable history of crime.

"Now, as in 1876, to the guilt of massacre is added the impudence of denial, which will continue just as long as Europe is content to listen. I doubt if it is an exaggeration to say that it was in the Sultan's palace, and there only, that the inspiration has been supplied, and the policy devised of the whole series of massacres. When the Sultan carries massacre into his own capital under the eyes of the Ambassadors, he appears to have gained the very acme of what it is possible for him to do. But the weakness of diplomacy, I trust, is about to be strengthened by the echo of this nation's voice."

Mr. Gladstone then referred to the supineness of the Ambassadors of the Powers at Constantinople, and continued: "The concert of Europe is an august and useful instrument, but it has not usually succeeded in dealing with the Eastern question, which has arrived at a period when it is necessary to strengthen the hands of the Government by an expression of national opinion. I believe that the continued presence of the Ambassadors at Constantinople has operated as a distinct countenance to the Sultan, who is thus their recognized ally.

"But, while urging the Government to act, it does not follow that, even for the sake of the great object in view, Great Britain should transplant Europe into a state of war. On the other hand, however, I deny that England must abandon her own right to independent judgment and allow herself to be domineered over by the other powers."

Mr. Gladstone expressed the opinion that the purpose of the meeting was defensive and prospective, saying that no one can hold out the hope that the massacres are ended, although he ventured to anticipate that the words spoken at the meeting would find their way to the palace at Constantinople. "The present movement," he said, "is based on broad grounds of humanity, and is not directed against the Mohammedans, but against the Turkish officials, evidence of whose barbarities rests in credible official reports." Mr. Gladstone declared his adhesion to the principles contained in the resolution, and said he came to the meeting not claiming any authority for sentiments expressed except that of a citizen of Liverpool.

"But," he remarked, "the national platform upon which the meeting is based gives greater authority for sentiments universally entertained throughout the length and breadth of the land, and I urge that in this matter party sympathy be renounced. I entertain the lively hope and strong belief that the present deplorable situation is not due to the act or default of the Government of this great country."

Mr. Gladstone spoke about twenty minutes and was repeatedly interrupted by applause. He was in good voice, and did not seem fatigued when he had finished.

The next day the Turkish Embassy at London telegraphed Mr. Gladstone's speech at Liverpool verbatim to the Sultan.

The London Times in an editorial said: "The spectacle of the veteran statesman quitting his retirement to plead the cause of the oppressed is well calculated to move the sympathy and admiration of the nation. The ardor of Mr. Gladstone's feelings on this subject is notorious. All the more striking and significant is the comparative restraint and moderation of the speech."

Other questions besides those mentioned were claiming the attention of English statesmen. In the Spring, prior to the great Liverpool meeting, the Venezuela boundary question was agitating the two great English speaking nations to the very verge of war. A large Peace Meeting was held in London, March 3, 1896, to favor arbitration. Mr. Gladstone wrote: "I am glad that the discussion of arbitration is to be separated from the Venezuela question, upon which I do not feel myself in final and full possession of the facts that I should wish. My views on arbitration in place of war were gathered from the part I took in the matter of the Alabama claims. I will only add that my conviction and sentiment on the subject grow in strength from year to year in proportion to the growth of that monstrous and barbarous militarism, in regard to which I consider England has to bear no small responsibility."

The meeting favored permanent international arbitration, and an Anglo-American treaty was finally signed by the representatives of the two nations, providing for the settlement of all questions between the two nations by arbitration instead of by war, but the Senate of the United States refused to ratify the treaty.

Mr. Gladstone deplored intensely the extraordinary misunderstanding which had prevailed on the subject of the Venezuela frontier. He seemed to think that nothing but a little common sense was needed to secure the pacific settlement of the question at any moment. A hundred square miles more or less on either side of the boundary of British Guiana was to him a matter of supreme indifference. He was extremely anxious to see justice done, and one of his last speeches in the House of

Commons was in favor of permanent arbitration between England and the United States.

Another one of the absorbing questions that came before the civilized world for consideration, and almost to the exclusion of the Armenian question, was the Cretan Question. Greece heroically sustained the insurrection of the Cretans against the Turkish rule. The scene of Turkish cruelty was now transferred to the isle of Crete. For the time the Armenian massacres were forgotten. The Greeks rushed to the rescue, while all Europe held aloof. Mr. Gladstone sent the following dispatch to the Chronicle: "I do not dare to stimulate Greece when I cannot help her, but I shall profoundly rejoice at her success. I hope the Powers will recollect that they have their own character to redeem." This was in February, 1897, Later he wrote that to expel the Greek troops from Crete and keep as police the butchers of Armenia, would further deepen the disgrace of the Powers of Europe.

In March, 1897, Mr. Gladstone addressed a letter, now justly celebrated, on the same subject to the Duke of Westminster in which he expressed his opinion more fully, and which was evidently the sentiment of the English speaking people of the world. The letter was in the form of a pamphlet of 16 pages, published, and entitled The Eastern Crisis.

In less than a week after this eloquent manifesto in behalf of the Cretans and of Greece was put forth, it was currently reported that the precise solution of the problem recommended by Mr. Gladstone was likely to be adopted. The Sultan himself, fearful of the effect of the appeal on public opinion in Europe, sought the settlement of the question in the manner suggested. The Greeks still clamored for war. In the war that followed between Greece and Turkey, Greece was defeated and crushed by the Turk. Only by the intervention of the Powers was Greece saved from becoming a part of the Sultan's Empire.

After peace had been concluded between Turkey and Greece,

Mr. Gladstone undertook to arouse public opinion by a trenchant review of the situation. Looking back over the past two years of England's Eastern policy, he inquires as to what have been the results, and then answers his own question. He thus enumerates:

1. The slaughter of 100,000 Armenian Christians, men, women and children, with no guarantee against a repetition of the crime.

2. The Turkish Umpire stronger than at any time since the Crimean war.

3. Christian Greece weaker than at any time since she became a kingdom.

These are facts, Mr. Gladstone claimed, for which the leading Christian nations and statesmen of Europe are responsible.

While Mr. Gladstone thus expresses himself, yet his vigorous protests had not been without effect. His voice penetrated into the very palace of the Sultan, and into every Cabinet of Europe, and was heard by every statesman and ruler throughout the world, and aroused the people everywhere. It was a mighty voice lifted for right and against oppression. The Sultan was afraid and was compelled to desist; not that he feared the protests and the warnings of the Christian Nations of Europe, but because that one voice was the expression of the popular feeling of all Christians throughout the world, and to defy such sentiment would be to court the overthrow of his throne, if not of the dominion of the Turk in Europe.

In June, 1894, an invitation was extended to Mr. Gladstone to visit the United States, signed by many representative men in public life. But Mr. Gladstone, while acknowledging the compliment, declined because of his age. It would, he thought, be a tremendous undertaking for him. The fatigue of the voyage and the strain of the receptions while in America, would prove greater than his physical condition could bear.

Later Mr. Gladstone was waited on at Hawarden by one hundred members of the Philadelphia Manufacturer's Club. He personally escorted them over the Castle grounds and narrated the history of the Castle to them. Greatly pleased with the warmth of their reception, they thanked Mr. Gladstone for his courtesy. They then gave him three cheers. This token of appreciation was very gratifying to Mr. Gladstone, who said that it was the first time he had ever heard American cheers.

Saturday afternoon, August 15, 1896, Li Hung Chang, the great Chinese Statesman and Embassador, visited Mr. Gladstone at Hawarden. Probably the three greatest living statesmen of the time were Gladstone, Bismarck and Li Hung Chang. The Embassador and his suite went to Chester in a special train, and were driven in three open carriages to Hawarden. Along the route as, well as at the station, the party was cheered by a large crowd. The Viceroy was sleeping when the train reached Chester and he was allowed to sleep until he awoke. Yet the party was ahead of time in reaching the Castle, but Mr. Gladstone hastened to receive them. The Chinese visitors were received at the door by Mr. Henry Gladstone. Li Hung Chang was escorted into the Library where he was introduced to Mr. and Mrs. Gladstone.

The intention of Mr. Gladstone was to have as escort a guard of honor to the Viceroy, the Hawarden corps of the Welsh Fusiliers, which reached the Castle, owing to the visitors being ahead of time, ten minutes after the arrival of the party.

The two aged statesmen sat near the window overlooking the terrace, and at once, with the aid of Lo Feug Luh, engaged in conversation, Li asked various questions concerning Mr. Gladstone's career, and was informed by Mr. Gladstone that he had been Prime Minister nearly thirteen years, and in the Cabinet nearly twenty-four years. When complimented upon the service he had rendered to his country, Mr. Gladstone replied that he had done what he could, but he should have done a great deal more. Li observed that British interests and British trade in China were greater than those of all other countries put together. The Viceroy also talked with Mr. Gladstone of free trade, of restrictions upon commerce, of the power of the British Navy, of the greatness of the British Revenues, of the vastness of the Colonial Empire, of the necessity of a railway system to commerce and upon a number of similar subjects. Refreshments were served which Li enjoyed, and then by request he wrote his autograph in three books, using Dorothy Drew's colors for the purpose. Mr. Gladstone and Li were photographed together sitting on chairs outside the porch. Mr. Gladstone presented Li with three books from his library, and then the Chinese visitors departed.

On Saturday evening October 10, 1896, the Right Hon. and Most Rev. Edward White Benson, D.D., Archbishop of Canterbury and Primate of all England, arrived at Hawarden with Mrs. Benson on a visit to his old friend Mr. Gladstone. Sunday morning Dr. Benson went with the Gladstone family to Hawarden Church and occupied the Gladstone pew. After the service had commenced a commotion was observed. It was caused by the fall of Dr. Benson In the pew while kneeling in prayer. Attendants removed Dr. Benson to the Rectory, and medical aid was summoned, but death came soon after from apoplexy. The Rev. Stephen Gladstone, rector, proceeded with the service until notified of the death of the Archbishop, when he dismissed the congregation. Mr. Gladstone, who had not attended church from indisposition, was deeply affected by the death of his guest and friend.

The morning papers of London, June 1, 1896, printed a long letter from Mr. Gladstone to Cardinal Rampolla for submission to the Pope Leo XIII, in favor of the unity of Christendom by means of a papal declaration in favor of the validity of Anglican orders. It created a great sensation. Shortly after this the Pope issued an Encyclical letter addressed to "all bishops in communion with the Holy See." The theme was the same as that of Mr. Gladstone's letter, to which it was regarded as an answer. The Pope invited all the English people "to return to the religion of the Roman Catholic Church." "This," remarks Mr. Justin McCarthy, "was exactly what any thoughtful person might have expected." While this letter and its answer did not satisfy the clergy of the established Church of England, who were favorably disposed towards Rome, on the other hand it aroused the dissenting Christians of England to reply that they were opposed to all state or established churches, whether Roman Catholic or English Episcopal.

On December 29, 1896, the eighty-seventh anniversary of Mr. Gladstone's birth was celebrated at Hawarden, surrounded by his family and friends. There were the usual demonstrations by the villagers, consisting in the ringing of bells and the appointments of deputations to wait upon the aged statesman at the Castle with congratulations. An enormous flow of telegrams and messages continued throughout the day from all parts of the kingdom, the United States and the Continent. Among those sending congratulations were the Prince and Princess of Wales, and Baroness de Rothschild. Mr. Gladstone was in good health, and in the afternoon went out for a walk.

May 10, 1897, the Prince and Princess of Wales, accompanied by the Princess Victoria, visited Mr. and Mrs. Gladstone at Hawarden. They were received by Mr. and Mrs. Gladstone in the porch erected in 1889 to commemorate their golden wedding. The mutual greetings were of the heartiest nature. The royal party inspected the ruins of the old castle, Mr. Gladstone acting as escort to the Princess of Wales. An interesting incident occurred on the lawn. The Princess took great interest in inspecting the favorite dogs of the Gladstone family. These were the black Pomeranians. Two puppies were carried in a basket, one of which the Princess accepted as a gift.

June 22, 1897, was celebrated with great pomp and rejoicing the Diamond Jubilee of Victoria, the Queen of England and Empress of India, when the Queen reached the 60th anniversary of her reign, which is the longest in English history. Victoria became queen at the age of 19 years, in 1837, and then the British Isles possessed a population of 26,000,000 and they had became 40,000,000. Her Empire has been extended until in India, South, Central and Western Africa,

Australia, New Zealand and North America, and including the British Isles, there were 360,000,000 people who owned her sway. And to this greatness and glory Mr. Gladstone had been one to contribute largely, while his influence has been felt more still by far in promoting the moral greatness of the people. Throughout all the Empire the event was celebrated, and the jubilee procession in London was swollen by representatives of all parts of the Queen's domain and all nations on earth which rendered it the greatest pageant ever beheld. Even the Turk was there, but Mr. Gladstone was not there, nor was his name even mentioned for a place in the march on jubilee day. Yet the period of Victoria's reign will often be spoken of in history as the Gladstonian Era.

"The public life of a leading statesman," says an eminent writer, "offers the boldest and stateliest outline to the public view. It may be that the most striking and memorable chapters in a future biography of Mr. Gladstone will contain the story of his private affairs and domestic life." His daily life at home was a model of simplicity and regularity, and the great secret of the vast amount of work he accomplished was owing to the fact that every odd five minutes were occupied. He had a deep sense of the preciousness of time and the responsibility which everyone incurs who uses or misuses it. "To such a length did he carry this that at a picnic to a favorite Welsh mountain he has been seen to fling himself on the heather and bury himself in some pamphlet upon a question of the day, until called to lighter things by those who were responsible for the provision basket."

Mr. Gladstone was ever a most severe economist of time, a habit acquired as long ago as 1839, when he awed his young wife by filling up all odd bits and scraps of time with study or work. Out of his pocket would come the little classic at every chance opportunity of leisure. This accounts for his ability to get through in one day more than most people do in a week. Then besides, he had the faculty of concentrating the whole power of his mind upon the one thing before him, whether small or great. He was unable to divide the machinery of his mind. Interruption was almost fatal to his train of thought, but he was generally oblivious to conversation buzzing around him. Hence it was some time before a questioner could get an answer—he did not seem to hear, but patience finally secured attention, after the train of absorbing thought was finished.

It was this power of concentrating all his faculties upon what he was doing, whether it was work or play, that made Mr. Gladstone one of the ablest as well as happiest of the century. He took the keenest delight in the scholarly and beautiful, and this accounts for his disregard of minor ills and evils. He was too absorbed to be fretful or impatient. But to be absorbed in great things did not mean, in his case, to be neglectful of little things. At one time his mind and time were so completely taken up with the Eastern question, that he could not be induced to spare a thought for Ireland, and afterward it was quite as difficult to get him to think of any political question except that of Ireland.

In the daily routine of private life none in the household were more punctual and regular than Mr. Gladstone. At 8 o'clock he was up and in his study. From 1842 he always found time, with all his manifold duties, to go to church regularly, rain or shine, every morning except when ill, at half-past 8 o'clock, He walked along the public road from the castle to Hawarden church. Writes an observer: "The old statesman, with his fine, hale, gentle face, is an interesting figure as he walks lightly and briskly along the country road, silently acknowledging the fervent salutations of his friends—the Hawarden villagers. He wears a long coat, well buttoned up, a long shawl wrapped closely around his neck, and a soft felt hat—a very different figure from that of the Prime Minister as he is known in London."

At the Castle prayers were read to the family and household soon after 9 o'clock daily. His customary breakfast was comprised of a hard-boiled egg, a slice of tongue, dry toast and tea. The whole morning whether at home or on a visit was devoted to business. Luncheon at Hawarden was without formality. "Lunch was on the hob," for several hours, to be partaken of when it suited the convenience of the various members of the family. Tea, of which Mr. Gladstone was particularly fond, and of which he could partake at any hour of the day, or night, was served in the afternoon at 5 o'clock, —after which he finished his correspondence.

In the afternoon, Mr. Gladstone was accustomed to a walk in the grounds, accompanied by his faithful little black Pomeranian dog, Petz, who was obtained on a trip abroad, and became and remained for many years, an important member of the household, and one of Mr. Gladstone's most devoted followers. Increasing years of over fourscore, prevented finally walks of fifty miles a day once indulged in, and the axes stood unused in their stands in the vestibule and library, but still Mr. Gladstone kept up his walks with his silent companion Petz. After walking for half an hour longer in his library after his return to the Castle, Mr. Gladstone would dress for dinner, which operation usually took him from three to five minutes. At 8 o'clock he joined the family, at dinner, which was a cheerful meal. Like Goethe he ate heartily and enjoyed his meals, but his diet was extremely simple, Mr. Gladstone eating only what was prescribed by his physician. At dinner he talked freely and brilliantly even when none but his family were present. When visitors were present he would enter upon whatever was the subject of conversation, taking his share with others, and pouring a flood of light upon any theme suggested, giving all the benefit of the fund of wisdom and anecdote collected through two generations of unparalleled political and social activity.

After dinner, when there were no visitors at Hawarden, Mr. Gladstone would quietly sit reading in his library, or conversing with his family. He never used tobacco. Shortly after 10 o'clock he retired to bed and to sleep. He never allowed himself to think and be sleepless. Mr. Bright had a habit of making his speeches after he had retired to bed, which Mr. Gladstone thought was detrimental to his health. Bight hours was the time Mr. Gladstone permitted himself to sleep.

His bed-room was on the second floor and reached by a fine staircase. Everything in the room was plain and homely.

On the walls of his bed-room and over the mantlepiece was a text emblazoned, on which at evening and morning he could look, which read: "Thou wilt keep him in perfect peace, whose mind is stayed on thee." This not only expresses Mr. Gladstone's trust in God, but doubtless accounts in a large degree for that tranquility of mind so notably his, even in those trying times that prostrated many and carried many more away from their bearings.

From the worry or weariness of business, Mr. Gladstone was ever ready to turn for rest to reading, which has thus proved of inestimable value to him. "His family cannot speak without emotion of that look of perfect happiness and peace that beamed from his eye on such occasions." When during the general elections of 1882, this was denied him, he turned with equal readiness to writing and thinking on other subjects. During the Midlothian Campaign and General Election, and through the Cabinet making that followed, he relieved the pressure on his over-burdened brain by writing an article on Home Rule, "written with all the force and freshness of a first shock of discovery;" he was also writing daily on the Psalms; he was preparing a paper for the Oriental Congress which was to startle the educated world by "its originality and ingenuity;" and he was composing with great and careful investigation his Oxford lecture on "The rise and progress of learning in the University of Oxford."

All during the morning hours he would sit in the silence of that corner-room on the ground floor reading. There were three writing-desks in the library, and one was chiefly reserved for correspondence of a political nature, and another for his literary work, while the third was used by Mrs. Gladstone. He spent his evenings when at Hawarden in a cosy corner of the library reading. He had a wonderfully constructed lamp so arranged for him for night reading, as to throw the utmost possible light on the pages of the book. It was generally a novel that employed his mind at night. Occasionally he gives Mrs. Drew about two hundred novels to divide the sheep from the goats among them. She divides them into three classes—novels worth keeping, novels to be given away, and novels to be destroyed.

Mr. Gladstone generally had three books in course of reading at the same time, changing from one to the other. These books were carefully selected with reference to their character and contents, and he was particular as to their order and variation. For instance at one time he was reading Dr. Laugen's Roman History, in German, in the morning, Virgil in the afternoon, and a novel at night. Scott was his preference among novelists. He read with pencil in hand, and he had an elaborate system of marking a book. Aristotle, St. Augustine, Dante and Bishop Butler were the authors who had the deepest influence upon him, so he himself said. His copy of the Odyssey of Homer he had rebound several times, as he preferred always to use the same copy.

Mrs. Drew says of her father: "There could not be a better illustration of his mind than his Temple of Peace—his study, with its extraordinarily methodical arrangement. Away from home he will write an exact description of the key or paper he requires, as: 'Open the left hand drawer of the writing table nearest the fireplace, and at the back of the drawer, in the right hand corner, you will find some keys. You will see three on one string; send me the one with such and such teeth.' His mind is arranged in the same way; he has only to open a particular compartment, labelled so and so, to find the information he requires. His memory in consequence is almost unfailing. It is commonly found that in old age the memory may be perfect as regards times long gone by, but inaccurate and defective as to more recent events. But with Mr. Gladstone the things of the present are as deeply stamped on his brain as the things of the past." Some one has said of Mr. Gladstone that his memory was "terrible." It is evident that he always kept abreast of the times—informing himself of everything new in literature, science and art, and when over

Richard B. Cook

eighty years of age was as ready to imbibe fresh ideas as when he was only eighteen, and far more discriminating.

Those who entered Mr. Gladstone's official room on a Sunday, during the busiest parliamentary session, could not fail to be struck by the atmosphere of repose, the signs and symbols of the day, the books lying open near the armchair, the deserted writing-table, the absence of papers and newspapers. On Sunday Mr. Gladstone put away all business of a secular nature, occupied his time in reading special books, suitable to the day, and generally attended church twice, never dined out, except he went on a mission of mercy, or to cheer some sorrowful friend. When the Queen invited him to Windsor Castle on Sunday for one night, as she did sometimes, he always arranged to stay in Windsor Saturday. In his dressing room he kept a large open bible in which he daily read. Physically, intellectually and spiritually Mr. Gladstone's Sundays were regarded by his family as a priceless blessing to him, and to have made him the man he was. Mr. Gladstone had strict notions of his duty to his church. Whenever he established himself in London, he always attended the nearest church, and became regular in his attendance, not only on the Sabbath, but daily. With an empire on his shoulders he found time for daily public devotion, and in church-going he was no "gadabout." When he resided at Carlton House Terrace he attended the church of St. Martin-in-the-Fields.

Mr. Gladstone's daily correspondence, when Prime Minister, was simply enormous. At first he felt it to be a conscientious duty to deal with the most of it himself, but finally came to trust the bulk of it to secretaries as other ministers did. Some letters came to him daily that he had to answer with his own hand; for example, from ministers or on confidental business, from the court, At the end of every Cabinet Council the Premier has to write a letter with his own hand to his sovereign, giving full information of the business transacted. The same kind of report is required daily from Parliament. Of course Mr. Gladstone, whenever he was Prime Minister, faithfully attended to this duty and dispatched the required letters written with his own hand to the Queen.

Mr. Gladstone was remarkable for the strength and endurance of his body as well as for the vigor of his intellect. "Don't talk to me of Mr. Gladstone's mind," said a contemporary; "it is his body which astonishes me." He never had any serious illness in his life, and up to quite recent years were vigorous exercise, sometimes walking when in Scotland 20 miles at a stretch over rough and mountainous country. The physical effort of speaking to twenty thousand people, and being heard in every part of the vast building by the audience, as was the case at Birmingham, in 1889, was remarkable. His power of endurance was wonderful. In 1882, he once sat up through an all-night sitting of the House of Commons, and going back to 10 Downing Street, at 8 o'clock in the morning, for half an hour's rest, again returned to the House and remained until the conclusion of the setting. Tree-cutting, which was with him a frequent recreation until he became a very old man, was chosen "as giving him the maximum of healthy exercise in the minimum of time." This favorite pastime of the great statesman was so closely associated with him that it was deemed the proper thing to do to place on exhibition in the Great Columbian Exposition at Chicago one of the axes of Mr. Gladstone.

The Psalmist says, "A man was famous according as he had lifted up axes upon the thick trees." These singular words were written long before Mr. Gladstone's day, but famous as he was for felling the great trees of the forest, the words have a deeper meaning and in more than one sense met their fulfilment in him. His swift and keen axe of reform brought down many hoary headed evils. Mr. Gladstone himself explained why he cultivated this habit of cutting down trees. He said: "I chop wood because I find that it is the only occupation in the world that drives all thought from my mind. When I walk or ride or play cricket, I am still debating important business problems, but when I chop wood I can think of nothing but making the chips fly."

The following story illustrates Mr. Gladstone's remarkable powers and the surprise he would spring upon those who met him. Two gentlemen who were invited guests at a table where Mr. Gladstone was expected, made a wager that they would start a conversation on a subject about which even Mr. Gladstone would know nothing. To accomplish this end they "read up" an "ancient" magazine article on some unfamiliar subject connected with Chinese manufactures. When the favorable opportunity came the topic was started, and the two conspirators watched with amusement the growing interest in the subject which Mr. Gladstone's face betrayed. Finally he joined in the conversation, and their amusement was turned into confusion, when Mr. Gladstone said, "Ah, gentlemen, I perceive you have been reading an article I wrote in the— Magazine some thirty or forty years ago."

CHAPTER XXI

CLOSING SCENES OF A LONG AND EVENTFUL LIFE

Mr. Gladstone died at Hawarden Castle, at 5 o'clock, Thursday Morning, May 19, 1898.

The first intimation of the rapidly approaching end of Mr. Gladstone was conveyed in a bulletin issued at 9 o'clock Tuesday morning, May 17. It read "Mr. Gladstone had a poor and broken sleep last night; he is somewhat exhausted, but suffers no discomfort." The report of the evening before was assuring as to any sudden change, so that the anxiety was increased. For hours no additional information was given, but there were indications outside the Castle of a crisis. Throughout the day could be heard expressions of deep regret among the working people, asking, "How is the old gentleman?" Despite the heavy rain the people collected in groups, and the hush and quiet that prevailed indicated the presence of death.

A bulletin at 5 p.m. said: "Mr. Gladstone has taken a serious turn for the worse. His death may be expected in twenty-four hours." All day the condition of the patient had been critical. The doctor doubted that his patient was fully conscious at any time, he answered, "Yes," and "No." He refused all medicine, exclaiming No! No! It was remarked that when addressed in English, Mr. Gladstone would answer in French, and sometimes was praying in French.

Later in the evening the servants of the household were

admitted to the sick room for a final farewell. They found Mr. Gladstone lying in a deep sleep; each in turn knelt down, kissed his hand and tearfully withdrew.

About 9 o'clock the patient rallied a little and fell into a peaceful sleep, which was thought to be his last.

The rain had continued to fall during the night, but the villagers had been coming singly and in groups to glance silently at the rain-beaten scrap of paper which was the latest bulletin, and then silently returning to the gate, and disappearing in the darkness only to return later.

About 4 o'clock in the morning Mr. Gladstone seemed to be sinking. The scene in the sick-room was painful. The Rev. Stephen Gladstone read prayers and hymns, including Mr. Gladstone's favorite, "Rock of Ages." When this was concluded, Mr. Gladstone murmured, "Our Father." As Mrs. Gladstone leaned over her husband, he turned his head and his lips moved slightly. Though extremely distressed, Mrs. Gladstone bore up with remarkable fortitude. But Mr. Gladstone rallied again, and Wednesday morning he was still living. By his almost superhuman vitality he had fought death away.

The morning was beautiful and clear and the sunshine came in at the open window of Mr. Gladstone's room. The aged sufferer was hovering between life and death, and only by the feeble beating of his pulse could it be told he was alive. He was sleeping himself away into eternal day. Mrs. Gladstone sat by the side of his bed, holding his hand, and never leaving except for needed rest. At times he seemed to recognize for a moment some of those with him. He surely knew his wife as she tenderly kissed his hand.

It soon became known abroad that Mr. Gladstone was dying. In the House of Commons it caused profound sorrow. Everything else was stopped while members discussed how best to honor him, even by taking steps without, precedent as that of adjourning, because the circumstances were unprecedented.

His former colleagues silently watched his last struggle with the relentless foe, to whom, true to himself, he was yielding slowly, inch by inch.

Telegrams of inquiry and sympathy came from all parts of the world to the Castle. The Queen wrote making inquiries and tendering assurances of profound sympathy. A long telegram from the Princess of Wales concluded: "I am praying for you." The Prince of Wales wrote: "My thoughts are with you at this trying time., God grant that your father does not suffer." The Duke of Devonshire before the British Empire League referred touchingly to the mournful scenes at Hawarden, when "the greatest of Englishmen was slowly passing away." And all over the land people of all conditions and at all kinds of gatherings, politicians, divines, reformers, and women joined in expressions of grief and sympathy. Many were the messages of regard and condolence that came from other lands.

Dr. Dobie furnishes the following picture of the dying man. "His grand face bears a most peaceful and beautiful look. A few days ago the deeply bitten wrinkles that so long marked it were almost gone; but now, strangely enough, they seem strong and deep as ever. He looks too in wonderfully good color."

At 2 o'clock in the morning, it was evident that the time had come, and the family gathered about the bed of the aged man, from that time none of them left the room until all was over. The only absentee was little Dorothy Drew, who tearfully complained that her grandfather did not know her. Behind the family circle stood the physicians and the nurses, and the old coachman, who had been unable to be present when the other servants took their farewell, and who was now sent for to witness the closing scene.

The end was most peaceful. There were no signs of bodily pain or of mental distress. The Rev. Stephen Gladstone read prayers and repeated hymns. The nurse continued to bathe with spirits the brow of the patient, who showed gratitude by murmuring,

"How nice!" While the son was engaged in praying, came the gentle, almost perceptible cessation of life, and the great man was no more. So quietly had he breathed his last, that the family did not know it until it was announced by the medical attendants. The weeping family then filed slowly from the room, Mrs. Gladstone was led into another room and induced to lie down. The only spoken evidence that Mr. Gladstone realized his surroundings in his last moments was when his son recited the litany. Then the dying man murmured, "Amen." This was the last word spoken by Mr. Gladstone and was uttered just before he died.

The death of Mr. Gladstone was announced to the people of Hawarden by the tolling of the church bell. The following bulletin was posted at 6 a.m.: "In the natural course of things the funeral will be at Hawarden. Mr. Gladstone expressed a strong wish to have no flowers at his funeral; and the family will be grateful if this desire is strictly respected."

There was something indescribably pathetic in the daily bulletins about Mr. Gladstone. All the world knew that he was afflicted with a fatal but slow disease, and all the world was struck with wondering admiration at his sustained fortitude, patience, and resignation. The tragedy of a life, devoted simply and purely to the public service, drawing to an end in so long an agony, was a spectacle that struck home to the heart of the most callous. These bulletins were posted on the front door of the Jubilee Porch, at Hawarden Castle, at 9 a.m., 5 p.m. and 10 o'clock at night daily, and published throughout the world.

When the sad event was announced that Mr. Gladstone had passed away, the action the House of Commons was prompt, decided and sympathetic. The House was crowded Thursday, May 19, when Speaker Gully called upon the government leader, Mr. A. J. Balfour, the First Lord of the Treasury, and all the members uncovering their heads, Mr. Balfour said:

"I think it will be felt in all parts of the House that we should do fitting honor to the great man whose long and splendid career closed to-day, by adjourning.

"This is not the occasion for uttering the thoughts which naturally suggest themselves. That occasion will present itself to-morrow, when it will be my duty to submit to the House an address to the Queen, praying her to grant the honor of a public funeral, if such honor is not inconsistent with the expressed wishes of himself or of those who have the right to speak in his behalf, and also praying the Queen to direct that a public monument be erected at Westminster with an inscription expressive of the public admiration, attachment and high estimate entertained by the House of Mr. Gladstone's rare and splendid gifts and devoted labors in Parliament and in high offices of State.

"Before actually moving the adjournment, I have to propose a formal resolution that the House to-morrow resolve itself into committee to draw up an address, the contents of which I have just indicated."

After a word of assent from Sir William Vernon-Harcourt, the Liberal leader, the resolution was adopted and the House adjourned.

The House of Commons was crowded again on Friday, and went into committee of the whole to consider the address to the Queen in regard to the interment of the remains of Mr. Gladstone in Westminster Abbey. Not since the introduction of the Home Rule Bill by Mr. Gladstone had there been such an assemblage in the House, members filled every seat, clustered on the steps of the speaker's dais, and occupied every space. The galleries were all filled. In the Peer's gallery were the foremost members of the House of Lords. United States Ambassador Hay and all his staff were present with other Ambassadors. The members of the House were in deep mourning, and all removed their hats, as if in the presence of the dead. An unusual hush overspread all. After the prayer by the chaplain, there was an impressive silence for a quarter of an hour, before Mr. Balfour rose to speak. The whole scene was profoundly affecting. The eulogies of Mr. Gladstone formed an historic episode. All, without respect to party, united in honoring their late illustrious countryman.

Mr. Balfour delivered a brilliant panegyric of the dead statesman, and his speech was eloquent and displayed great taste. He was so ill, however, from weakness of heart that he was barely able to totter to his place and to ask the indulgence of the speaker while he rested, before offering his oration. He was too sick for the sad duty imposed upon him, but he preferred to pay this last tribute to his friend. The circumstances were painful, but added a dramatic touch to the scene. His oration was lengthy and his eulogy spoken with evident emotion. He concluded by formally moving the presentation of the address to the Queen. The Liberal Leader, Sir William Vernon-Harcourt, the political as well as the personal friend of Mr. Gladstone, seconded the motion. He paid a heartfelt tribute to the memory of his eminent colleague, and spoke in a vein of lofty and glowing eloquence until overcome with emotion, so that he had to stop thrice to wipe his eyes; finally he completely broke down and was unable to proceed.

Mr. Dillon, the Irish leader, in a speech of five minutes duration, and in his most oratorical style, dwelt on Mr. Gladstone's fervid sympathy for the oppressed people of all races, and touched a chord which stirred the House. As Mr. Dillon had spoken for Ireland, so Mr. Abel Thomas followed as the representative of Wales.

The address to the Queen was unanimously adopted.

In the House of Lords there was also a full attendance of members. The Marquis of Salisbury, Prime Minister, spoke feelingly of Mr. Gladstone, who, he said, "was ever guided in all his efforts by a lofty moral idea". The deceased will be remembered, not so much for his political work as for the great example, hardly paralleled in history, of the great Christian Statesman.

The Earl of Kimberly, the liberal leader in the House of Lords, followed in a touching tribute, and the Duke of Devonshire expressed generous appreciation of Mr. Gladstone's services in behalf of the Liberal Unionists, saying their severance from Mr. Gladstone was a most painful incident. But, he added, he could "recall no word from Mr. Gladstone which added unnecessarily to the bitterness of the situation." The Earl of Rosebery delivered an eloquent panegyric. The honors of the occasion were unanimously accorded to him, whose eulogy of his predecessor in the leadership of the liberal party was a masterpiece of its kind. He spoke of the triumphs of life rather than the sorrows of death. Death was not all sadness. His life was full—-his memory remains. To all time he is an example for our race and mankind. He instanced as an illustration of the fine courtesy always observed by Mr. Gladstone towards his political opponents, that the last letter he had written with his own hand was a private note to Lady Salisbury, several weeks since, congratulating her and her husband on their providential escape from a carriage accident at Hatfield. Lord Salisbury was visibly touched by Lord Rosebery's reference to this circumstance.

The House of Lords then adopted the Resolution to the Queen.

The body of Mr. Gladstone, un-coffined, was laid on a couch in the Library of the Castle—the room called the Temple of Peace. He was dressed in a suit of black cloth, over which were the scarlet robes of the university, and by his side the cap was placed. His hands were folded on his breast. He rested on a most beautiful white satin cloth, with a rich border in Eastern embroidery. Above his head in letters of gold were the words sewn into the satin: "Requiescat in pace." There was the beauty of death—the terror was all gone. During Tuesday the body was viewed by the tenants on the estate, the neighbors and friends.

On Wednesday morning, May 25th, at 6 o'clock, the remains, having been enclosed in a plain panelled elm coffin, were removed to the village church, where they were lying in state during the day. The body was carried by half-a-dozen old retainers of the family to a bier on wheels, on which it was taken to the church, over the lawn, following the private path Mr. Gladstone used to tread on his way to church, and past the favorite nooks of the deceased in the park. The family— excepting Mrs. Gladstone, who came later, tenants, servants, friends, local officials and neighbors followed in procession, Thousands of people were arriving by public and private conveyances at Hawarden. At eleven o'clock the doors of the church were opened, when men, women and children, from all the surrounding country, and even tourists from abroad, entered to view the remains. All day long a constant stream of people poured into the church, while the streets were filled with people unable to gain admittance. Several ladies fainted from excess of emotion when passing the bier, and many men and women dropped on their knees and silently prayed.

At 6 o'clock in the evening the body was removed from Hawarden Church and carried to the station for the journey to London. The procession to bear the remains was composed of the family, representatives of organizations, friends and neighbors. Vast crowds lined the route, afoot and in every kind of vehicle. The cortege stopped at the entrance to the Park— Hawarden Lodge, and sang one of Mr. Gladstone's favorite hymns. Again, when the procession reached the Castle, it paused at the entrance and sang another hymn loved by the late resident of the house, and went on its way to Broughton Hall Station. Every step of the way, after leaving the park, was again lined with sympathetic spectators. While at the station the spectacle was remarkable for the surrounding crush of human beings. A special train was provided for the body and the family. As the body of Mr. Gladstone was placed upon the funeral car the sorrow of the people was manifest. The representatives of the Earl Marshall, of England, took possession of the funeral at this point. Henry and Herbert Gladstone accompanied the body to London and Mrs. Gladstone and family returned to the castle to follow later.

All along the route to London grief-stricken people were standing to view the funeral train as it passed at Chester, Crewe, Rugby, Stafford and Farnworth until the darkness and lateness of the night shut out the scene.

When the train reached London and passed to Westminster, it was early in the morning. A group of some thirty gentlemen, connected with the ceremonies, was at the station; among them the Duke of Norfolk, About two hundred people looked silently on while the body was removed from the train to the hearse, and the funeral cortege moved on to Westminster Hall at once and entered the Palace Yard just as "Big Ben" tolled the hour of one like a funeral knell.

The coffin was placed in position for lying in state in Westminster Hall, and at about 3 o'clock Canon Wilberforce conducted a special service in the presence of Henry and Herbert Gladstone and several members of the House of Commons.

The scenes that followed were remarkably impressive and unparalleled. The people began to arrive at Westminster at 2 o'clock in the morning. The line formed was continually augmented by all classes of people,—peers, peeresses, cabinet members, members of the House of Commons, military and naval officers, clergymen, costermongers, old and young, until 6 o'clock, when the doors were opened and the procession commenced to stream into the Hall, and passed the catafalque.

This long procession of mourners continued all day Thursday and Friday. Two hundred thousand people, at least, paid homage to the dead statesman. On Friday evening, after the crowd had departed, large delegations, representing Liberal organizations from all parts of the kingdom, visited the Hall, by special arrangement, and fifteen hundred of them paid respect to the memory of their late leader.

Saturday morning, May 28, thousands of people assembled in the square outside to witness the passage of the funeral cortege

Richard B. Cook

from Westminster Hall, where it was formed, to the Abbey, to find sepulchre in the tomb of kings. The procession passed through two lines of policemen. It was not a military parade, with all its pomp, but a ceremony made glorious by the homage of the people, among them the greatest of the nation. The funeral was in every respect impressive, dignified and lofty, in every way worthy the great civilian, and the nation that accorded him a public burial with its greatest dead. And the people were there. Every spot on which the eye rested swarmed with human beings. They looked from the windows of the hospital, and from the roofs of houses. Everybody was dressed in black.

The principal officials had assembled in Westminster Hall at 10 o'clock. The Bishop of London, the Right Rev. Mandell Creighton, D.D., read a brief prayer and at 10.30 o'clock the procession had formed and slowly passed through the crowds who with uncovered heads stood on either side of short pathway, a distance 300 yards, to the western entrance of the Abbey, between two ranks of the Eton Volunteers, the boys of the school where Mr. Gladstone received his early education, in their buff uniforms.

The pall-bearers who walked on each side of the coffin were perhaps the personages who attracted the most attention during the day. They were the Prince of Wales, the Duke of York, the Marquis of Salisbury, the Earl of Kimberly, A. J. Balfour, Sir William Vernon-Harcourt, the Duke of Rutland, Lord Rosebery, Baron Rendel and George Armitstead, the two latter being life-long friends of the deceased statesman.

When Mrs. Gladstone entered the Abbey the whole assembly rose and remained standing until she was seated. This honor was accorded only once beside—when the Princess of Wales, the Princess Mary and the Duchess of York appeared.

The Abbey was filled with people. Every gallery, balcony and niche high up among the rafters held a cluster of deeply interested spectators. Temporary galleries had been erected in long tiers around the open grave, which was in the floor of the Abbey. There were 2,500 persons assembled in the Abbey, all—both men and women—clothed in black, except a few officials whose regalia relieved this sombre background by its brilliancy. The two Houses of Parliament sat facing each other, seated on temporary seats on opposite sides of the grave. About them were the mayors of the principal cities, delegates from Liberal organizations, representatives of other civic and political societies, representatives of the Non-Conformists, while the long nave was crowded with thousands of men and women, among them being most of the celebrities in all branches of English life. In each gallery was a presiding officer with his official mace beside him, whose place was in the centre, and who was its most prominent figure. It was a distinguished assembly in a famous place. Beneath were the illustrious dead; around were the illustrious living.

The members of the bereaved family sat in the stall nearest the bier—Mrs. Gladstone, her sons Henry, Herbert and Stephen; with other members of the family, children and grand-children, including little Dorothy Drew, Mr. Gladstone's favorite grand-child, in her new mourning.

The Princess of Wales and the Duchess of York occupied the Dean's pew opposite. Other royalties were present in person or by their representatives.

Within the chancel stood the Dean of Westminster, and behind him were gathered the cathedral clergy, the Archbishop of Canterbury, and the scarlet and white surpliced choir, filling the chapel.

It was the wish of the deceased for simplicity, but he was buried with a nation's homage in the tomb of kings. In the northern transept, known as the "Statesmen's Corner", of Westminster Abbey, where England's greatest dead rests, the body of Mr. Gladstone was entombed. His grave is near the graves of Pitt, Palmerston, Canning and Peel, beside that of his life-long political adversary, Lord Beaconsfield (Benjamin

Disraeli), whose marble effigy looks down upon it, decked with the regalia Mr. Gladstone had so often refused. Two possible future kings of Great Britain walked besides the great commoner's coffin and stood beside his grave, and all the nobility and learning of the nation surrounded his bier. This state funeral, the first since that of Lord Palmerston, was rendered more imposing by the magnificence of the edifice in which it was solemnized. The coffin rested on an elevated bier before the altar, its plainness hidden beneath a pall of white-and gold embroidered cloth.

A choir of one hundred male singers, which had awaited the coffin at the entrance to the Abbey, preceded it along the nave, chanting, "I am the Resurrection and the Life." When the coffin was laid on the bier, Purcell's funeral chant, "Lord, Thou Hast Been Our Refuge," was sung, and Dean Bradley and the whole assemblage sang, "Rock of Ages," and then while the coffin was being borne along the aisle to the grave, sang Mr. Gladstone's favorite hymn, "Praise to the Holiest in the Height."

The choir of Westminster Abbey is said to be fine at any time, but for this great occasion special arrangements had been made, and there was a recruiting of the best voices from several of the choirs of London, and many musical instruments beside. The result was to win general praise for the beauty, harmony and perfection of the music. The weird, dismal strains of a quartette of trombones, in a recess far above the heads of the congregation, playing the three splendid "Equali," Beethoven's funeral hymn, swept through the vaulted roof of the Abbey, in pure tones never to be forgotten. When these ceased and finally died away, the great organ and a band of brass instruments took up Schubert's funeral march, booming sonorously; and changed to Beethoven's funeral march with a clash of cymbals in the orchestral accompaniment. A third march being required, owing to the time needed by the procession to reach the Abbey, "Marche Solennelle" was played.

The choir, and a large number of bishops and other clergy, joined the procession at the west door and together they all proceeded to the grave.

There was no sermon. The service was simple and solemn. The final paean of victory over death and the grave from Paul's great epistle was read, and the last hymn sung was, "Oh God! Our Help in Ages Past." The dean read the appointed appropriate service, committing the body to the earth, and then the Archbishop of Canterbury, in a loud voice, pronounced the benediction. The family and others near the grave kneeled during the concluding ceremonies, and then Mrs. Gladstone was helped from her knees to her unoccupied chair at the head of the grave.

After the benediction came one of the saddest moments of the day. Mrs. Gladstone stood, with great courage and composure, throughout the service, supported on the arms of her two sons, Herbert and Stephen, and with other members of her family near the grave. Her face was lifted upward, and her lips were moving as though repeating the lines of the service. She also kept standing during the one official feature of the service; "The Proclamation by Garter, by Norroy, King of Arms, of the Style of the Deceased," as the official programme had it, and in which the various offices which Mr. Gladstone had held in his lifetime, were enumerated. Then, when the final word was spoken, the widow, still supported by her sons, approached the edge of the grave and there took a last, long look and was conducted away. Other relatives followed, and then most of the members of Parliament. Finally the Prince of Wales, the Duke of York and other pall-bearers defiled past the grave, took a last view of the coffin in the deep grave, and when they had been escorted down the nave to entrance, the people slowly departed.

The "Dead March" from "Saul" and the "Marche Solennelle" of Schubert was played as the congregation slowly wended its way out of the sacred edifice.

Perhaps the most solemn function of all, witnessed by none but the Gladstone family and the officials, was when the casket was opened shortly after midnight on Thursday to allow the Earl Marshal to verify with his own eyes that it really contained the remains of the dead statesman. It was said that the old man's face, seen for the last time by the Duke of Norfolk, who is responsible to England for his sacred charge, was more peaceful and younger looking than it had seemed for years. At the very last moment a small gold Armenian cross, a memento of that nation for which the great statesman worked so zealously, was placed by his side. Then all was sealed.

As the deceased statesman was undoubtedly the greatest parliamentarian of our time, the following concise expressions with regard to his character and influence have been collected from a number of representative members of different political parties in both Houses of Parliament:

The Marquis of Londonderry said: "What impressed me about Mr. Gladstone was his extraordinary moral influence."

Lord George Hamilton: "I doubt whether we ever had a parliamentarian who equalled Mr. Gladstone."

The Marquis of Lorne: "I share the universal regret at Mr. Gladstone's death as a personal loss."

Sir John Gorst: "One feature, which greatly distinguished Mr. Gladstone, was his remarkable candour in debate. He never affected to misunderstand his opponents' arguments, and spared no pains in trying to make his own meaning understood."

Sir Charles Dilke: "I think Mr. Gladstone's leading personal characteristic was his old-fashioned courtesy. Whilst a statesman, his absolute mastery of finance, both in its principles and details, was incomparably superior to that of any of his contemporaries."

Mr. Thomas Ellis, the chief Liberal Whip, confessed that the greatest interest of his life in Parliament was to watch Mr. Gladstone's face. "It was like the sea in the fascination of its infinite variety, and of its incalculable reserve and strength. Every motion in his great soul was reflected in his face and form. To have had opportunities of watching that face, and of witnessing one triumph after another, is a precious privilege, for some of the charms of his face, as of his oratory and character, were incommunicable. He more than any man helped to build up and shape the present commercial and political fabric of Britain, but to struggling nations his words and deeds were as the breath of life."

Sir Joseph Pease: "His memory will be kept green by a grateful country. Death soon buries the battle-axe of party, and he who devoted a long life and immense intellectual power, coupled with strong convictions on moral and Christian ethics, to the well being of his country and the world, will never be forgotten by the English people."

Mr. James Bryce, author of "The American Commonwealth": "This sad event is the most noble and pathetic closing of a great life which we have seen in England in historical memory. I cannot recall any other case in which the whole nation has followed the setting of the sun of life with such sympathy, such regret, and such admiration."

Lord Kinnaird: "Few men in public life have been able to draw out such personal love and devotion from his followers and friends. In the midst of an ever-busy life he was always ready to take his part in the conflict of right against wrong, of truth against error, and he earned the gratitude of all patriots, for he was never ashamed of contending that no true progress could be made which left out of sight the moral well-being of the people."

Mr. Labouchere: "What impressed me most in Mr. Gladstone was his power of concentrated effort. Once he had decided on a course, action at once followed. Every thought was bent to attain the end, no labour was deemed to arduous. He alone knew how to deal with supporters and opponents. The former he inspired with his own fierce energy."

Mr. John Redmond, leader of the Parnellite group of the Irish Nationalists: "The loss to England is absolutely incalculable. I regard Mr. Gladstone as having been the greatest parliamentarian of the age, and the greatest parliamentary orator. Englishmen of all parties ought to be grateful to him for his services in promoting the greatness and prosperity of their empire."

John Dillon: "The greatest and most patriotic of Englishmen. If I were asked to say what I think most characteristic of Gladstone, I should say his abiding love for the common people and his faith in the government founded upon them, so that, while he remained the most patriotic of Englishmen, he is to-day mourned with equal intensity throughout the civilized world."

Justin McCarthy, M. P.: "The death of Mr. Gladstone closes a career which may be described as absolutely unique in English political history. It was the career of a great statesman, whose statesmanship was first and last inspired, informed and guided by conscience, by principle, and by love of justice. There were great English statesmen before Mr. Gladstone's time and during Mr. Gladstone's time, but we shall look in vain for an example of any statesman in office, who made genius and eloquence, as Mr. Gladstone did, the mere servants of righteousness and conscientious purpose. Into the mind of Gladstone no thought of personal ambition or personal advancement ever entered. He was as conscientious as Burke. In the brilliancy of his gifts he was at least the equal of Bolingbroke. He was as great an orator as either Pitt, and he has left the imprint of his intellect on beneficent political and social legislation. In eloquence he far surpassed Cobden and was the peer of Bright, while his position as Parliamentary leader enabled him to initiate and carry out measures of reform which Bright and Cobden could only support. He was, in short, the greatest and the best Prime Minister known to English history."

Michael Davitt: "One can only join with the whole world in admiration of the almost boundless talents of Mr. Gladstone, which were devoted with unparalleled power of charm to the service of his fellow-men. He was probably the greatest British statesman and leaves behind a record of a career unequalled in the annals of English politics. For the magnitude of his national labors and integrity of his personal character, Irishmen will remember him gratefully."

The *Daily Chronicle* heads its editorial with a quotation from Wordsworth:

> "This is the happy warrior: this is he:
> That every man in arms should wish to be."

The editorial says: "A glorious light has been extinguished in the land; all his life lies in the past, a memory to us and our children; an inspiration and possession forever. The end has come as to a soldier at his post. It found him calm, expectant, faithful, unshaken. Death has come robed in the terrors of mortal pain; but what better can be said than that as he taught his fellows how to live, so he has taught them how to die?

"It is impossible at this hour to survey the mighty range of this splendid life. We would assign to him the title. 'The Great Nationalist of the Nineteenth Century;' the greatest of the master-builders of modern England. Timidity had no place in Mr. Gladstone's soul. Ho was a lion among men, endowed with a granite strength of will and purpose, rare indeed in our age of feeble convictions."

The *Daily News* says: "One of his most characteristics qualities was his personal humility. This cannot be explained without the key, for Mr. Gladstone did not in the ordinary meaning of the word, underrate himself. He was not easy to persuade. He paid little attention to other people's opinions when his mind was made up. He was quite aware of his own ascendency in counsel and his supremacy in debate. The secret of his humility was an abiding sense that these things were of no importance compared with the relations between God's creatures and their Creator, Mr. Gladstone once said with characteristic candour that he had a vulnerable temper. He was quickly moved to indignation by whatever he thought injurious either to himself or to others, and was incapable of concealing his emotions, for, if he said nothing, his countenance showed what he felt. More expressive features were never given to man.

"Mr. Gladstone's exquisite courtesy, which in and out of Parliament was the model for all, proceeded from the same source. It was essentially Christian. Moreover, nobody laughed more heartily over an anecdote that was really good. He was many men in one; but he impressed all alike with the essential greatness of his character.

"He was built mentally and morally on a large scale. Of course it cannot be denied that such a face, such a voice, such natural dignity, and such perfect gesture produced in themselves an immense effect. There was nothing common-place about him. Mr. Gladstone was absolutely simple; and his simplicity was not the least attractive element of his fascinating personality.

"His life presented aspects of charm to all minds. His learning captivated the scholar, his eloquence and statesmanship the politician, his financial genius the business man; while his domestic relations and simple human graciousness appealed to all hearts.

"There is a prince and a great man fallen this day in Israel."

Public Ledger, Philadelphia: "To write Gladstone's career is to write the history of the Victorian era and that of the closing years of the reign of William IV, for Gladstone took his seat in Parliament for the first time in 1832, two years after he was out of college, and Victoria's accession took place in 1837.

Since that remote day Gladstone has been four times Premier; has delivered numberless speeches of the highest order of excellence; has published a multitude of pamphlets and volumes which attest consummate intellectual gifts, and has been a great force in English statesmanship and scholarship through an exceptionally long life and almost to the very close of it. It has been given to exceedingly few men to play so great, so transcendent a role in any country or at any time."

Richard B. Cook

Choose from Thousands of 1stWorldLibrary Classics By

A. M. Barnard
Ada Leverson
Adolphus William Ward
Aesop
Agatha Christie
Alexander Aaronsohn
Alexander Kielland
Alexandre Dumas
Alfred Gatty
Alfred Ollivant
Alice Duer Miller
Alice Turner Curtis
Alice Dunbar
Allen Chapman
Alleyne Ireland
Ambrose Bierce
Amelia E. Barr
Amory H. Bradford
Andrew Lang
Andrew McFarland Davis
Andy Adams
Angela Brazil
Anna Alice Chapin
Anna Sewell
Annie Besant
Annie Hamilton Donnell
Annie Payson Call
Annie Roe Carr
Annonaymous
Anton Chekhov
Archibald Lee Fletcher
Arnold Bennett
Arthur C. Benson
Arthur Conan Doyle
Arthur M. Winfield
Arthur Ransome
Arthur Schnitzler
Arthur Train
Atticus
B.H. Baden-Powell
B. M. Bower
B. C. Chatterjee
Baroness Emmuska Orczy
Baroness Orczy
Basil King
Bayard Taylor
Ben Macomber
Bertha Muzzy Bower
Bjornstjerne Bjornson

Booth Tarkington
Boyd Cable
Bram Stoker
C. Collodi
C. E. Orr
C. M. Ingleby
Carolyn Wells
Catherine Parr Traill
Charles A. Eastman
Charles Amory Beach
Charles Dickens
Charles Dudley Warner
Charles Farrar Browne
Charles Ives
Charles Kingsley
Charles Klein
Charles Hanson Towne
Charles Lathrop Pack
Charles Romyn Dake
Charles Whibley
Charles Willing Beale
Charlotte M. Braeme
Charlotte M. Yonge
Charlotte Perkins Stetson
Clair W. Hayes
Clarence Day Jr.
Clarence E. Mulford
Clemence Housman
Confucius
Coningsby Dawson
Cornelis DeWitt Wilcox
Cyril Burleigh
D. H. Lawrence
Daniel Defoe
David Garnett
Dinah Craik
Don Carlos Janes
Donald Keyhoe
Dorothy Kilner
Dougan Clark
Douglas Fairbanks
E. Nesbit
E. P. Roe
E. Phillips Oppenheim
E. S. Brooks
Earl Barnes
Edgar Rice Burroughs
Edith Van Dyne
Edith Wharton

Edward Everett Hale
Edward J. O'Biren
Edward S. Ellis
Edwin L. Arnold
Eleanor Atkins
Eleanor Hallowell Abbott
Eliot Gregory
Elizabeth Gaskell
Elizabeth McCracken
Elizabeth Von Arnim
Ellem Key
Emerson Hough
Emilie F. Carlen
Emily Bronte
Emily Dickinson
Enid Bagnold
Enilor Macartney Lane
Erasmus W. Jones
Ernie Howard Pie
Ethel May Dell
Ethel Turner
Ethel Watts Mumford
Eugene Sue
Eugenie Foa
Eugene Wood
Eustace Hale Ball
Evelyn Everett-green
Everard Cotes
F. H. Cheley
F. J. Cross
F. Marion Crawford
Fannie E. Newberry
Federick Austin Ogg
Ferdinand Ossendowski
Fergus Hume
Florence A. Kilpatrick
Fremont B. Deering
Francis Bacon
Francis Darwin
Frances Hodgson Burnett
Frances Parkinson Keyes
Frank Gee Patchin
Frank Harris
Frank Jewett Mather
Frank L. Packard
Frank V. Webster
Frederic Stewart Isham
Frederick Trevor Hill
Frederick Winslow Taylor

Friedrich Kerst
Friedrich Nietzsche
Fyodor Dostoyevsky
G.A. Henty
G.K. Chesterton
Gabrielle E. Jackson
Garrett P. Serviss
Gaston Leroux
George A. Warren
George Ade
Geroge Bernard Shaw
George Cary Eggleston
George Durston
George Ebers
George Eliot
George Gissing
George MacDonald
George Meredith
George Orwell
George Sylvester Viereck
George Tucker
George W. Cable
George Wharton James
Gertrude Atherton
Gordon Casserly
Grace E. King
Grace Gallatin
Grace Greenwood
Grant Allen
Guillermo A. Sherwell
Gulielma Zollinger
Gustav Flaubert
H. A. Cody
H. B. Irving
H.C. Bailey
H. G. Wells
H. H. Munro
H. Irving Hancock
H. R. Naylor
H. Rider Haggard
H. W. C. Davis
Haldeman Julius
Hall Caine
Hamilton Wright Mabie
Hans Christian Andersen
Harold Avery
Harold McGrath
Harriet Beecher Stowe
Harry Castlemon
Harry Coghill
Harry Houidini

Hayden Carruth
Helent Hunt Jackson
Helen Nicolay
Hendrik Conscience
Hendy David Thoreau
Henri Barbusse
Henrik Ibsen
Henry Adams
Henry Ford
Henry Frost
Henry James
Henry Jones Ford
Henry Seton Merriman
Henry W Longfellow
Herbert A. Giles
Herbert Carter
Herbert N. Casson
Herman Hesse
Hildegard G. Frey
Homer
Honore De Balzac
Horace B. Day
Horace Walpole
Horatio Alger Jr.
Howard Pyle
Howard R. Garis
Hugh Lofting
Hugh Walpole
Humphry Ward
Ian Maclaren
Inez Haynes Gillmore
Irving Bacheller
Isabel Cecilia Williams
Isabel Hornibrook
Israel Abrahams
Ivan Turgenev
J.G.Austin
J. Henri Fabre
J. M. Barrie
J. M. Walsh
J. Macdonald Oxley
J. R. Miller
J. S. Fletcher
J. S. Knowles
J. Storer Clouston
J. W. Duffield
Jack London
Jacob Abbott
James Allen
James Andrews
James Baldwin

James Branch Cabell
James DeMille
James Joyce
James Lane Allen
James Lane Allen
James Oliver Curwood
James Oppenheim
James Otis
James R. Driscoll
Jane Abbott
Jane Austen
Jane L. Stewart
Janet Aldridge
Jens Peter Jacobsen
Jerome K. Jerome
Jessie Graham Flower
John Buchan
John Burroughs
John Cournos
John F. Kennedy
John Gay
John Glasworthy
John Habberton
John Joy Bell
John Kendrick Bangs
John Milton
John Philip Sousa
John Taintor Foote
Jonas Lauritz Idemil Lie
Jonathan Swift
Joseph A. Altsheler
Joseph Carey
Joseph Conrad
Joseph E. Badger Jr
Joseph Hergesheimer
Joseph Jacobs
Jules Vernes
Julian Hawthrone
Julie A Lippmann
Justin Huntly McCarthy
Kakuzo Okakura
Karle Wilson Baker
Kate Chopin
Kenneth Grahame
Kenneth McGaffey
Kate Langley Bosher
Kate Langley Bosher
Katherine Cecil Thurston
Katherine Stokes
L. A. Abbott
L. T. Meade

L. Frank Baum
Latta Griswold
Laura Dent Crane
Laura Lee Hope
Laurence Housman
Lawrence Beasley
Leo Tolstoy
Leonid Andreyev
Lewis Carroll
Lewis Sperry Chafer
Lilian Bell
Lloyd Osbourne
Louis Hughes
Louis Joseph Vance
Louis Tracy
Louisa May Alcott
Lucy Fitch Perkins
Lucy Maud Montgomery
Luther Benson
Lydia Miller Middleton
Lyndon Orr
M. Corvus
M. H. Adams
Margaret E. Sangster
Margret Howth
Margaret Vandercook
Margaret W. Hungerford
Margret Penrose
Maria Edgeworth
Maria Thompson Daviess
Mariano Azuela
Marion Polk Angellotti
Mark Overton
Mark Twain
Mary Austin
Mary Catherine Crowley
Mary Cole
Mary Hastings Bradley
Mary Roberts Rinehart
Mary Rowlandson
M. Wollstonecraft Shelley
Maud Lindsay
Max Beerbohm
Myra Kelly
Nathaniel Hawthrone
Nicolo Machiavelli
O. F. Walton
Oscar Wilde

Owen Johnson
P.G. Wodehouse
Paul and Mabel Thorne
Paul G. Tomlinson
Paul Severing
Percy Brebner
Percy Keese Fitzhugh
Peter B. Kyne
Plato
Quincy Allen
R. Derby Holmes
R. L. Stevenson
R. S. Ball
Rabindranath Tagore
Rahul Alvares
Ralph Bonehill
Ralph Henry Barbour
Ralph Victor
Ralph Waldo Emmerson
Rene Descartes
Ray Cummings
Rex Beach
Rex E. Beach
Richard Harding Davis
Richard Jefferies
Richard Le Gallienne
Robert Barr
Robert Frost
Robert Gordon Anderson
Robert L. Drake
Robert Lansing
Robert Lynd
Robert Michael Ballantyne
Robert W. Chambers
Rosa Nouchette Carey
Rudyard Kipling
Saint Augustine
Samuel B. Allison
Samuel Hopkins Adams
Sarah Bernhardt
Sarah C. Hallowell
Selma Lagerlof
Sherwood Anderson
Sigmund Freud
Standish O'Grady
Stanley Weyman
Stella Benson
Stella M. Francis

Stephen Crane
Stewart Edward White
Stijn Streuvels
Swami Abhedananda
Swami Parmananda
T. S. Ackland
T. S. Arthur
The Princess Der Ling
Thomas A. Janvier
Thomas A Kempis
Thomas Anderton
Thomas Bailey Aldrich
Thomas Bulfinch
Thomas De Quincey
Thomas Dixon
Thomas H. Huxley
Thomas Hardy
Thomas More
Thornton W. Burgess
U. S. Grant
Upton Sinclair
Valentine Williams
Various Authors
Vaughan Kester
Victor Appleton
Victor G. Durham
Victoria Cross
Virginia Woolf
Wadsworth Camp
Walter Camp
Walter Scott
Washington Irving
Wilbur Lawton
Wilkie Collins
Willa Cather
Willard F. Baker
William Dean Howells
William le Queux
W. Makepeace Thackeray
William W. Walter
William Shakespeare
Winston Churchill
Yei Theodora Ozaki
Yogi Ramacharaka
Young E. Allison
Zane Grey